Praise for *House of Pretend*

"With unflinching honesty and unexpected wit, Joanne Redding has written a brave story about the cost of silence, the complexity of forgiving those who've hurt us, and the harder task of forgiving ourselves. She writes with the heart of someone who refuses to hide anymore—not just from the world but from the truth."

—Michael Hainey, author of *After Visiting Friends*

"*House of Pretend* is raw, unsentimental, and deeply human—an unmasking of survival, resilience, and self-worth. Joanne's story lingers long after the final page, a testament to the power of choosing oneself and telling the truth out loud."

—Laura Munson, *New York Times* best-selling author and founder of the Haven Writing Retreats

"Joanne Redding's immensely satisfying and resonant memoir should be a classic for years to come. Touching on questions that are universal in the examination of her life, it's everything you want in a good read—rich, unexpected, funny, heartbreaking, and, ultimately, full of grace and wisdom."

—David Kirkpatrick, former president of Paramount Pictures and former production chief of Walt Disney Studios

House of Pretend

House of Pretend

A Memoir

Joanne Redding

SHE WRITES PRESS

Published in 2026 by
She Writes Press, an imprint of The Stable Book Group

1569 Solano Ave #546
Berkeley, CA 94707
https://shewritespress.com
Library of Congress Control Number: 2026904251
ISBN: 979-8-89636-308-8
eISBN: 979-8-89636-309-5

Interior Designer: Kiran Spees

Printed in the United States
Names and identifying characteristics have been changed to protect the privacy of certain individuals.

For Hannah and Cole—

You are the reason I found the strength to face the past,

and the courage to write it down.

Because of you, I became the mother I never had.

I hope you always know how deeply, fiercely, endlessly you are loved.

Author's Note

This memoir is a personal account based on the author's memories, interpretations, and experiences. Some names, locations, and identifying details have been changed to protect the privacy of individuals. While every effort has been made to present events truthfully, memory is subjective, and others may remember events differently.

The author does not intend to defame, harm, or malign any individual or group. The views expressed are solely those of the author and do not reflect the opinions of any organizations or institutions with which the author may be affiliated.

The sweet white paper of life. Traces of what remained, shadows of ghosts.

What happened was not our fault. We were simply collateral damage.

Chapter 1

New York, New York, 1988

Like most stories on Wall Street, it began with cocktails. It was an early summer evening when a bunch of us from the bond trading desk, already buzzed from drinks at the bar downstairs, took a private car, provided by our brokers, to Tribeca for dinner and more drinks. In the 1980s Tribeca was a place where hot restaurants and bars with no signs sat beside meatpacking plants with carcasses hanging from hooks. It was gritty yet glitzy, a good place to hang out to de-stress after a day of losses or to celebrate our wins. It was usually a dozen or so guys and me, just like the trading floor.

I spent my whole life searching for father figures. I just never imagined one would offer me a million dollars to have a baby with him.

I was twenty-nine, standing in the glass and steel offices of Chicago Research and Trading—a place that didn't just smell of money but reeked of it. Hanover Square pulsed beneath my heels, the heart of Wall Street just outside. I was exactly where I wanted to be. A bond trader in the big leagues, playing with fire in heels and designer suits.

Blonde, petite, with hair to my waist, I stood five foot four but felt six feet tall—invincible—seeing my reflection shine back at me from the vast panes of gleaming glass that surrounded me. Chicago Research and Trading (CRT) had it all. A private chef. A corporate tab at the downstairs bar. Power in excess.

Running it all was my boss, Jim Harrison, handpicked to lead the office by owners of the firm, a group of extremely successful options traders based in Chicago.

Why was Harrison the chosen one? I had no idea. He was a hulking, pale, obese, balding man who looked decades older than his age. He was a sycophant, stroking the talented traders who worked for him to sustain his inflated ego and elevated lifestyle.

And I was easy prey.

Our crowd had thinned a few hours later when I stood outside the Odeon, waiting for my ride home. Jim, my boss, pushed open the door of the restaurant and called my name. "Joanne?" My body tensed instinctively. A knot twisted hard in my gut. My eyes looked up, scanning the stars, hoping for divine intervention.

Harrison oozed creepiness, making me want to cross my arms over my full chest whenever his gaze fell upon me. His belly jiggled like a bowl of Jell-O when he laughed, his slick smile exposing teeth reminiscent of a ravenous hyena. I fought the urge to wipe my mouth, fearing that the small globs of spit I pictured spewing from his lips might have landed on mine.

I glanced up West Broadway, hoping desperately for one of the sleek black cars that the brokers routinely provided for us traders to appear. I was living a good life and wanted it to continue, but feeling Jim's eyes on me that night gave me pause.

"Hey. I've been thinking a lot about you," he said slowly, as if drawing a dagger out of its sheath.

Ewww. I cringed internally but tried to keep my face neutral, a skill I had learned. As a trader I knew to never let anyone know what my position was, like playing poker. A zero-sum game. My win was someone else's loss.

"What's up?" I asked, racking my brain as to what he could

possibly mean. Was he thinking about a promotion? Was I getting fired? You never knew in this business.

"Well, I've been thinking about this for a while now and I wanted to talk to you. I've got a proposal for you. A really good one."

Oh fuck. I knew this would be bad. Really bad.

He continued. "It's very important to me and I've given this a lot of thought."

I scanned Broadway, praying for an angel. *Please, town car, show up now.*

Harrison ran his tongue over his bottom lip and stepped closer to me.

"I'd love for you to have my baby. I know it sounds crazy, but I think it would be perfect. I'll pay you a million dollars in cash to do it. Please. This is really important to me. It would mean a lot."

I stood there, staring at him, feeling my jaw tighten. He was married to a lovely woman who was battling breast cancer in a fight she ultimately lost, living at their Southampton home without him. Big and round, he loomed over me, awaiting my answer. *What the fuck?* my mind screamed. I was recently out of a marriage, currently entangled in a secret relationship with a trader on the desk, and now the big boss was proposing that *I have his baby.* Holy shit.

Just then, the town car driver tapped his horn to let me know he had pulled up.

"Wow. Okay. Hey. Thanks. We'll talk. Gotta go," I sputtered, summoning all the strength I had to keep my face and voice neutral, knowing I'd have to deal with this in the morning. I lurched for the handle of the passenger door, slid in, and took off, avoiding any further response, at least for the moment while the question roared in my head.

Did I want to have my boss's baby for a million dollars cash?

Chapter 2

New York, New York, 1988

On the drive back to my apartment in Battery Park City, my boss's "proposal" got me thinking about my own father. What would he have said to this outrageous proposition? A million dollars cash was a lot of money. Money didn't come easily, and as a kid there wasn't much to go around when my mother raised me and my two siblings. My father probably would have told me to tell him to go to hell. My mother, on the other hand, would have wondered if I was nuts. *You walked away from a million bucks?*

Ma was different from most mothers. I remember one afternoon, when I was little, bolting out of kindergarten after the bell rang. I scanned the crowd of mothers, searching for my mother's faded floral kerchief that always covered her hair, knotted neatly under her chin—a fashion accessory in the 1950s that my mother never shed. My stomach growled, low and insistent, as if it had a mind of its own. I could almost taste the liverwurst on white, topped with relish, she'd make for me when I got home.

But today, I didn't see her. Instead, I saw something much better—my dad.

"Da!" I shouted, flailing my arms as I waved. His fedora bobbed above the group of moms clustered on the corner. He stood tall in his overcoat, looking a bit out of place.

I didn't wait for him to come to me. My legs were pogo sticks, bouncing up and down, my skirt flaring behind me like a parachute. He bent down and scooped me up in his arms, spinning me so fast the world turned into streaks of color. I laughed and laughed until my breath caught in my throat. Da was here and I would not be eating liverwurst.

He set me down as we rounded the corner, heading toward the diner. The door jingled as we stepped inside, the clang of the bell familiar and comforting. We settled into a booth near the back, the vinyl banquette sticking to my legs as I scooted in.

"A hamburger and fries and an egg cream, please," I told the waitress as she took her pencil from behind her ear. My dad had told me there were no eggs or cream in egg creams, but that's what we called them in Brooklyn. They were made with Fox's U-Bet chocolate syrup, ice-cold milk, and seltzer from one of those old-fashioned green bottles with the siphon on top. The sweet chocolate frothed up against the sharp fizz of the soda as I sipped it through a straw.

I loved the food, but the best part of lunch was Da. He listened to me like he had nothing else in the world to do. Like what I had to say mattered. He was a journalist and not only a trained observer but a good listener. I told him about Mrs. Kennedy, our teacher, who would turn as red as a tomato when she got mad.

"I made the whole class color outside the lines on purpose just to see her face," I bragged. "She was so mad, her ears turned purple."

Da let out a laugh, deep and warm, like it came from his belly. "You little troublemaker," he said, his voice rumbling. I could tell he was proud of me.

I wasn't sure if my mother would have laughed at all. She didn't always listen the way Da did. She'd nod along, but her eyes would be distant, like her mind was elsewhere. Maybe it wasn't that she didn't care; she just didn't seem to have time to really *see* me sometimes.

After lunch, Da stood up, grinning. "Race you home!" he said, and before I could even nod, he was off, darting out the door, his coat flying behind him. I chased him all the way down the street, but when we reached the stoop of our building, he was already there, waiting, hands on his hips like a champion.

"Well," he said, feigning disappointment, "I guess I'll have to give you another chance next week! We have a date."

My dates with Da are some of the best memories I have of him, and some of the last. He worked the night shift as city editor for the *New York World Telegram and Sun*, so he'd be heading off to work later that afternoon. But for right now, my belly was full of egg cream and I had him all to myself, and that felt like winning the lottery.

Chapter 3

Greenwood Lake, New York, 1964

A few months later, summer vacation spread out before us like a banquet piled high with fun and games. I shot out of bed like a rocket that Monday morning, anticipating our trip to the lake. My mother had been helping me count the days on the calendar taped on the refrigerator. Today was the day.

"Everybody up and at 'em," my father shouted.

I shoved my skinny legs into my shorts as my brother yanked a T-shirt over his head. My sister raced out of her room already dressed, beating us to the door of the apartment. My father led, my mother brought up the rear, and we were corralled out the door, slamming it shut behind us.

Wisps of heat shimmered off the black asphalt, tiny ghosts reaching up to join the clouds, and the faint bitter scent of tar drifted up our freckled nostrils. As August broke in all its sweaty glory, we piled in the car, ready to hit the road. The sun burned hot, but it didn't bother us. We were going to the cabin up north, and that was all that mattered.

The night before, my father had topped off the gas tank of our VW Beetle, the smell of gasoline still lingering as we left Brooklyn. My mother loaded a cooler, the one we took on the subway to Coney Island, with everything from the fridge: eggs, butter, mayonnaise, cold cuts. She plopped it on my lap, and I sat there in the back seat, legs sprawled across the sacks wedged behind the front seats, the bags bunched up under my knees. My brother got the left window, my sister the right, and I was on the hump in the middle.

We left Brooklyn behind, the concrete giving way to something that felt like freedom. As we passed the Red Apple Restaurant, my heart beat a little faster. That huge red apple atop the diner confirmed it—this was real, this was happening. We were going to Greenwood Lake. We would be free for a whole week. A week of grass between our toes, of trees to climb, of rolling down hills, and jumping into the cool water of the lake.

I couldn't wait. *We'd be gone a whole week. Yay!*

When we arrived at the cabin, Da unlatched the screen door with a squeak, and shoved the wooden one open with his shoulder. Thomas, Peggy, and I elbowed each other, following him into the cabin. Being the youngest I came up last. The scent of mildew assaulted us, but I didn't mind it. For me it was the sweet smell of summer. The walls of the cabin were soaked with hope and whitewash. The spindle-legged chairs and crocheted afghans piled on the side table bore witness to summers full of memories.

To the left was a tiny cooking area, its floors covered with bottle-green linoleum, sticky with years of oil splatter, peeling at the edges. The kitchen didn't matter much as my father would cook on the Weber barbecue every night, gripping the spatula in one hand, a cold can of Pabst in the other. He turned the dial on the turquoise Bakelite transistor radio to Frank Sinatra, set down the spatula, held out his hand, and we danced, Peggy, Thomas, and I, laughing in a circle, twirling to the music. Then he reached for my mother who swayed and sang low, in a voice I didn't recognize.

Like a Slinky, my mother tentatively coiled around Da, letting her shoulders lower and her breath slow down. Holding her hand, he managed to coax her face to soften a bit. She didn't pull away as she always did with me and my siblings.

The week away from Brooklyn felt like a huge exhale. Our bodies softened, our muscles relaxed, all our worries were left behind baked in the concrete.

Late in the afternoon, when the sun was soft and butter yellow, Da enticed us off the grass and out of the trees to the long wooden dock jutting out into the lake. Next to him was a box, like the toolbox back at our apartment with its screwdrivers and nails, this one filled with fishhooks and nylon string. Alongside it lay a few fishing rods and some bread slices, torn to pieces and piled into a rinsed-out potato salad tub brought from home.

After a little while, Peggy and Thomas tired of sitting on the edge of the dock watching their lines drift lazily in the water without a nibble. I stayed, absorbing the warmth of the sun deep inside my bones. Da was so close I could lean over and feel my cheek rub against his days-old whiskers.

My eyes slowly checked out the scenery around the lake. The stands of white pine and scruffy cedar were drawn around the blue-green waters of the lake like a shower curtain around a tub. Slatted wooden docks poked through the ring at irregular intervals, some equipped with small metal ladders, dangling in the warm waters. It was peaceful, the quiet broken only by the sound of the water lapping against the pylons.

A tug on my rod yanked me out of my daydream, and I leaped to my feet. "Da!" I screamed, my voice high with excitement. He wrapped his arms around my tiny body and helped hold the rod steady. "Hold it tight, sweetie," he said, guiding me to turn the handle on the black plastic reel, pulling the fish closer to the dock. "You have to do it yourself, so it counts as your catch."

I braced my sneakered feet against the dock, leaning back, prepared for a battle, like I was a knight wielding a sword. I grasped the plastic knob with my right fist and started turning as fast as I could. The rod jerked a bit, as I was left-handed, so the motion was awkward. It felt bouncy but I kept at it, willing the fish to come closer. Finally, its metallic green scales broke the water's surface, glinting in the sunlight.

"A sixteen-inch pickerel!" Da shouted, his voice booming across the water. He measured it with the frayed yellow tape measure he had stashed in his pocket, holding it up for all to see. "Joanne caught a sixteen-inch pickerel all by herself!" he cheered, and everyone around us clapped and cheered with him. My heart pounded in my chest as I grinned, feeling proud and a bit invincible.

That night we feasted. Da cooked the fish on the grill, basted with butter and drizzled with herbs. Afterward we trapped fireflies in jelly jars, hoping we could take home our own stars captured from the sky.

Chapter 4

Queens, New York, 1964

Later that summer, the World's Fair took over Flushing Meadows, Queens. The air hummed with excitement, the grounds of the site filled with promises of the future: flying cars, lunar colonies, robots that could cook dinner. We arrived breathless and wide-eyed, the sounds of laughter and chatter mixing with the faint hum of machinery. The air was hot and sticky—summer in New York—but none of us cared.

My family had tickets to the future, and we handed them to the attendant, who smiled and directed us through the turnstiles. The huge venue was a maze of dazzling pavilions, and above them the Swiss Skyride Cable Cars beckoned us. As we climbed into the small seats, I pressed my nose to the wire mesh, peering down at the sprawling sea of people below. We soared high above the fairgrounds, the buildings shrinking beneath us. It felt like we were flying. Peggy and Thomas opened up the map we were given and spread it out on the seat, pointing out places they wanted to see. I didn't need to know where we were going next. I was so happy. The whole world felt like an adventure.

We hurried to Futurama II, a sense of wonder overtaking us as we shuttled from a lunar base to the depths of the ocean, then streaked past sparkling skyscrapers. I was so awestruck my mouth hung open.

But the best was yet to come. I was buzzing with anticipation to see Dinoland, where gigantic dinosaurs—bright orange and purple—loomed high above us. Their curved claws stretched skyward, their sharp teeth gleaming like knives. I felt so tiny next to them. Suddenly I realized one of the dinosaurs was moving. Its tail was swaying, and its massive jaws were opening. It was alive.

I screamed, "Da, Da!"—the words bursting out of my chest. I grabbed my father's hand, my heart thudding in my ears. His arms wrapped around me, tight and steady. His smile was big and warm, the kind that made me feel safe again. "Don't worry," he comforted me. "I'll always protect you." His hand squeezed mine.

Peggy was already far ahead of us, her long legs sprinting toward the Belgian Village, testing her boundaries as usual. She was feeling pretty grown-up at eleven years old. My mother followed at a slower pace, holding Thomas's hand, his small body trailing behind. Thomas was quieter than me and Peggy, as if there were too many thoughts in his head. It seemed like he was trying to figure out how to be noticed but was unsure how to make that happen.

Just the day before, a blanket of humidity forcing us to slow down, my best friend Jane and I sat giggling on the steps outside our apartment building. Off to the side, Thomas stood scuffing his sneakers on the sidewalk, eyes fixed somewhere in the distance. Every so often he'd shift his weight and glance over as if trying to decide whether to join us.

"Hey, Thomas! Come over here," Jane called, trying to draw him out of his bubble.

Thomas hesitated. I could see his hands tense and unclench, as if unsure how to relax. Finally, he took a few steps toward us, searching for words to say. His voice, when he spoke, was quiet and unsure. "What are you two talking about?"

"We're just being goofy. Come sit with us."

He seemed to be debating whether he had anything worth saying. Simply joining us was a big step for him. He was stepping out of the shadows of his own thoughts.

At the World's Fair, the Belgian Village tempted us all. The sun warmed our shoulders as we followed the sweet, sugary smell to the waffle stand. These Belgian waffles weren't like the Bisquick ones that my mother made on special Saturday mornings. They were thick and crispy on the outside with deep pockets, perfect to catch the fresh strawberries and powdered sugar piled on top. They were as big as dinner plates, soft and fluffy on the inside.

I thought nothing could top this until we stumbled upon something even more magical: the chick hatchery. It was a gigantic dome with a heat lamp that kept the chicks warm. We were delighted to see dozens of tiny yellow chicks, their feathers soft and downy, chirping a chorus of happiness. They were so small—barely bigger than the marshmallow Peeps I loved so much at Easter. They fluttered around, their little legs wobbling as they ran back and forth. My feet were glued to the spot as I watched in awe. "Wow!" was all I could muster.

Da stayed with me, patient, knowing I didn't want to leave.

"Dorothy, I'll stay here with Joanne a bit," he said, touching my mother's cheek. "We'll catch up to you soon."

I crouched down, my face inches from the chicks, little balls of fluff bouncing around. They came close to me, pecking at the ground, as if they liked me. I named each one. "Chirpy, Biscuit, Goldilocks,"

I whispered. Da suggested “Fluffy, Spots, Marvin!” when I ran out of names for the others. He was always being goofy, making me laugh.

After we christened the chicks with names, we met up with the rest of the family to explore the other wonders of the world. It was a perfect day. We were all together, the world was full of magic, and the future was full of hope.

Chapter 5

New York, New York, 1964

I was excited to begin first grade, filled with new thoughts about the world and my place in it. Peggy and Thomas were not happy about going back to school, and to assuage the pain of our summer ending, Da surprised all of us with tickets to *The Ed Sullivan Show.*

We were pinching ourselves with excitement. *Ed Sullivan? Really?* None of us had ever been to see a live TV show, let alone been invited to see a live program that millions of others would be watching at home. Da scored the tickets through his work at the paper, and Peggy and Thomas and I could barely sit still; we were so excited to go.

The late September air was crisp, and yellow ginkgo leaves, miniature fans, fluttered in the cool breeze. The theater was majestic, outfitted with red velvet seats and shimmering stage lights. I sat on the edge of my chair, swinging my feet in my frilly socks, barely tall enough for my patent leather shoes to tap the seat's metal frame. The world hummed with excitement and hushed, reverent voices. Ed Sullivan was a god.

We were seated in the front row, stage right. My mother's gloved hands rested on Peggy and Thomas's knees, keeping them in place as her eyes darted around the packed theater. We were all dressed in our best clothes, like we were going to church. I sat on the end of the aisle, next to Da. Here we were—the place where all the famous people came, where the whole world tuned in from their living rooms on Sunday nights.

My heart thumped like a drum in a marching band when I caught sight of Ed Sullivan backstage. He was tall and commanding, his suit crisply tailored, his smile faint but warm. His presence sent a ripple through the audience as he strode out on stage.

He delivered his opening pitch in that familiar, deliberate voice, and then introduced Topo Gigio, the little Italian mouse I loved so much. The puppet's floppy ears and goofy smile captivated everyone. He then asked for a volunteer to come on stage. His eyes scanned the audience, and his gaze landed on me. "How about you, little lady," he said, stopping right in front of me. "How would you like to come up on stage with me?"

Everything slowed down. My heart pounded with joy. The spotlight hit me like a bucket of sunshine. My father gave me a gentle nudge, his eyes sparkling with encouragement. My brother and sister stared in awe, mouths open. But my five-year-old self was terrified. I shook my head, lips pressed into a stubborn line.

"Come on, it'll be fun," coaxed Ed Sullivan, crouching slightly to meet my gaze. "We've got someone special waiting for you—Topo Gigio." The audience murmured in delight.

But I was unmoved. "No, thank you," I said with a polite firmness beyond my years. The crowd chuckled, amused by my tiny defiance.

Ed Sullivan straightened up, looking impressed.

"Well, folks, you heard her," he said with a wry grin, turning back to the stage. "She knows her mind, this one." I smiled shyly, content in my seat.

Maybe I didn't need the spotlight. My father's attention was enough.

Chapter 6

Brooklyn, New York, 1964

The next morning, I woke up with a grin, smelling toast and coffee coming from the kitchen, feeling warm and safe. I wandered out for breakfast with a box of crayons and paper and sat at the table, determined to capture my father's handsome, kind face. His deep-set blue eyes sparkled like stars, made more startling by the contrast of his jet-black hair. I chose the cerulean, black, and apricot crayons after glancing back and forth from his face to the open Crayola box to try to match the shades of color I saw in him. My box only had twenty-four crayons in it. I was going to ask Santa for the sixty-four-crayon box at Christmas.

Da's jaw and cheekbones were strong and sharp, as if chiseled from stone. I gripped the apricot crayon tightly as I tried to translate his face into lines on the paper. As far as I was concerned, he was more of a god than Ed Sullivan. I studied him carefully while he stood by the sink, washing dishes, humming a song with no words. His sleeves were rolled up past his elbows, showing strands of dark hair on his forearms.

I tried to render his features with my crayons, but the paper was wrinkled, and my drawing looked a little wobbly. Ma sat across from me, quiet like she got sometimes. Her fingers circled the edge of her mug, round and round, like she was tracing something invisible. Her eyes flicked from Da to the window that overlooked the back alley behind our Brooklyn apartment, where crisscrossing clotheslines formed a geometric pattern reminiscent of an Escher drawing. The squeaks of the pulleys, yanked by women wrestling their laundry on and off the thick twine, filled the early morning air.

"You're going to be late," she said, sharp but not loud.

Da looked at the clock and smiled. "Got time."

He dried his hands on the dish towel and leaned against the counter.

"Can't leave without kisses from my girls."

He kissed me on the top of my head. Ma's mouth pressed into a tight line. She looked down at her mug, swirling the tea inside.

"You don't have to wait for me," she said, her voice scratchy.

Da walked over to her slowly, as though he were approaching a spooked animal. He crouched beside her chair, resting one hand on hers. I watched her fingers go stiff, but she didn't pull away.

"Dorothy, hey," he said gently, his voice warm like a blanket. "I'm not going anywhere without it."

Ma blinked fast, like she had something in her eye. Her hand twitched beneath his, like it was trying to decide what to do, but then she laced her fingers with his, tight but shaky, like when I tried to hold onto the monkey bars.

"I don't know why it's so hard," she whispered, but I heard it anyway.

"It's okay," Da said softly. "I know you love me. I feel it, even when you can't say it."

Ma's face changed, like the wall between them was becoming porous. She leaned forward and gave him a quick, awkward kiss on the cheek.

"There," she said, her voice rough. "Happy now?"

"Over the moon," Da agreed, grinning as he stood up. He kissed the top of her head, slow and gentle, as though he didn't want to rush it.

Da grabbed his coat and headed for the door. Ma's eyes followed him, soft but shiny, like she had secret tears. "Drive safe," she called after him, steadier now.

"Always," Da said with a wink. The door closed, but the warmth he left stayed in the room with us. I drew faster, trying to catch his smile in my wrinkled drawing.

Chapter 7

Brooklyn, New York, 1964

I loved first grade and felt like a big shot with a few months of it under my belt. I could read, write, and do arithmetic, and that was pretty exciting. So when my parents suggested we visit Aunt Honor, Da's sister, I couldn't wait to show her what I had learned, hoping she might let me touch her piano. Usually, our visits were fairly boring, but I was eager for her to see how grown-up I was now.

That fall day, with the air crisp and the sun bright, I put on my best dress for the visit, the powder-blue one with a frill around the neck. Our routine quarterly visits felt almost like a religious event. Everything in Aunt Honor's apartment, tucked away in Park Slope with high ceilings and crown molding, was precious and serene, the walls lined with bookshelves and interesting artifacts, but it was her piano that filled me with the most reverence.

My heart raced when we opened the front door and I saw Aunt Honor standing in her living room, the baby grand piano behind her. She was shaped like an avocado, with skin as smooth as porcelain. I thought she looked like a nun wearing a floral muumuu. Her voice was soft, her mannerisms delicate. Her hands fascinated me; her fingers, long and thin, skittered like flamingo legs when she gestured. Maybe it came from her piano playing.

She was Da's only relative. She had never married.

"Jack, how are you? How are things at the paper?" she asked, giving my father a warm embrace.

"And Dorothy. You look lovely. It's good to see you," she said as she gently touched my mother's arm, knowing my mother did not like much physical contact. Ma gave her a small smile in return. Peggy and Thomas darted to their respective places on the couch and the floor to pass the time.

I reached up and hugged her waist, inhaling the scent of baby powder. "Hi, Aunt Honor. I'm a big girl now. I'm in first grade and can read, and write, and do all the things that Peggy and Thomas can do," I let out in a rush before the adults retreated to the dining room.

"Hey, want to play soldiers with me?" Thomas called out to me, his voice eager.

"Nah. I'm just gonna sit here for a while," I said, my gaze already settling on the gleaming black piano.

"Why do you like the piano so much?" Thomas muttered. "I think it's dumb. We can't even touch it."

He shook his head, dumping his toys on the soft Persian carpet, and began to set up his battlefield. But I couldn't take my eye off the piano, that magnificent shiny black monument in the center of the room. Just the idea of it took my breath away. I saw myself in its polished surface, the light throwing reflections like tiny diamonds across the room.

This was the only piano I had ever seen up close, in person. I was awestruck. Everything about it—owning one, playing one, hearing one played—felt like a privilege that belonged to someone else.

I wanted to touch it so badly. I had never asked to touch it. Nobody did.

Sitting there, yearning to touch it, broke my heart.

Just then my Aunt Honor returned with a plate of cookies for us.

"Joanne, honey, would you like some?" she paused, offering me a chocolate chip.

I shook my head. "No, thank you," I said. I took a big swallow, then craned my neck to look in her eyes and asked, "Aunt Honor, may I touch the piano keys?"

Time came to a halt, and the only sound was my brother's gasp.

No one had ever dared to ask about the piano before.

Aunt Honor bent down slowly, and for a second, I was worried she was going to smack me. Instead, she placed her cool hand gently on my cheek, and then took my hand in hers. She walked me to the baby grand and helped me onto the bench. Ma and Da had followed her into the living room.

"Play, my dear," she whispered, almost like a secret.

My fingers hovered over the keys. I could hardly breathe. She gently placed her fingers over mine, guiding me through "Chopsticks."

As the final C note hung in the air, a sense of peace washed over me. A peace I had never known before. I glanced over at Da and caught the gleam in his eyes that said it all. He saw me, truly saw me, just as I had seen the piano—beautiful and magnificent.

That moment stuck with me forever. Even when the world moved on, when the music faded, that sense of being seen by my father lingered. Like a sweet song playing in my head.

Chapter 8

Bear Mountain, New York, 1964

Soon Christmas carols replaced "Chopsticks," but the validation I had from Da remained the same. It was still there, humming in the back of my head as we headed toward the holidays. Everything felt like it was building to something grand. Christmas vacation. It was my favorite time of the year. The snowflakes were desperate to fall from the sky, but the clouds weren't letting them go. Not yet.

I remember jumping out of bed that morning before Ma even yelled for us kids. It was so strange to me how much easier it was to wake up when there was no school. I shook my brother. "Thomas, Thomas," I shouted, right in his ear.

"What? What?" he sputtered, turning over in his bed, confused. I ducked as his arm swung out.

"We're going to Bear Mountain today. Remember?" I poked him. "Get up so we can get going early!"

Sliding the box with our snow stuff out from under the cot where I slept, I took out the thick mittens, scarves, and hats. I threw Thomas's things across the room to him.

"Ma? What do we need to bring?" I bellowed, hoping to get her moving.

She stuck her head out of the kitchen where she'd been packing up a cooler.

"Show me what you pulled out," she responded, her voice a bit lighter than usual.

I held the clothes above my head.

"Looks good," she said, nodding approvingly. "Come have some breakfast so we can get going. Your da's gassing up the car."

With bellies full and our bodies muffled in wool, we picked up my grandmother and my mother's sister, Aunt Joan, at the house where Ma grew up and headed to Bear Mountain State Park, north of Brooklyn. The car was a tangle of elbows and knees with everyone trying to fit into their assigned seats like puzzle pieces that didn't quite match. My mother scooted to the back seat, Grandma settled in next to Da, and the rest of us piled into the rear. Peggy climbed onto Joan's lap, Thomas plopped on Ma's, and I squished in between them all, sitting on the hump in the middle.

"Patty-cake, patty-cake, baker's man," we sang, our voices bouncing off the windows, tapping our feet in rhythm. The excitement was almost unbearable. We took turns begging for songs. "These Are a Few of My Favorite Things," I shouted above the noise. It was my favorite song. When our voices tired, Joan led us three kids in endless rounds of I Spy. She occasionally whispered a clue to me to help me keep up with Peggy and Thomas. Joan was really fun to be around. Her enthusiasm made up for the disinterest I sensed from Ma and Grandma.

Two hours later, Da pulled the Volkswagen into the gravel parking lot in front of Bear Mountain Lodge, which rose up from the ground like a giant log cabin with a massive stone base. I could hardly breathe from the thrill of it all. Spruce and pine trees encircled it; they seemed to bow in reverence.

"Look at that, Thomas! Look!" I shouted, pointing at the huge structure, thinking it looked as if it had been plucked straight from the pages of a picture book. *Wow!* It looked sort of like the Lincoln Log cabins my brother and I built in our living room, only much, much bigger.

My sister, who was ready to burst, tugged at Joan's hand and dragged her to the ice-skating rink. "Let's go!" she shouted, as Joan laughed and ran to keep up, her long, dark coat swirling around her. Joan was my mother's sister—younger by eight years, with a face that could turn on the charm. She was different from my mother in most ways. While Ma seemed always to hold back, a little fearful of joy, Joan leaped into life, seeking new adventures, always ready to have fun.

I adored Joan, with her knack for glamour that existed in stark contrast to my mother's dour, practical style. Joan dressed like the women I saw on magazine covers at the newspaper stand on the corner—Jackie Kennedy or Twiggy. Her clothes were always well-tailored, always bright, always fun-looking. She wore chunky earrings that clinked when she moved, neon-colored bracelets that jingled on her wrists, and tight sweaters that accentuated her figure. She used enough hair spray to make her hair stiff like a helmet and painted her lips redder than Santa's suit.

Ma, on the other hand, was as predictable as Joan was spontaneous. She hid her hair under the ever-present kerchief, applied a few patches of caked powder on her cheeks and nose, and finished with a dab of lipstick from a stub dug out of the bottom of her pocketbook, which she always draped on her forearm as if she were Queen Elizabeth.

For two women who grew up in the same house, they couldn't have been less alike in every way. Joan didn't know how cool I thought she was. Every time I tried to get close, Peggy was already there, hogging her. It wasn't Joan's fault; Peggy stuck to her like glue. And it wasn't even Peggy's fault; I would've done the same.

The cold bit at my cheeks as Ma helped tighten the laces on my skates, my hands already frozen. Around me, the air smelled like ice and snow, crisp and sharp. Grandma had already settled into a chair near the rink, draping a knitted blanket across her lap, the cooler packed with sandwiches and a thermos of hot coffee beside her. We weren't close at all; I could never get her to talk with me no matter how hard I tried. She wasn't the warm and fuzzy kind of grandma. There she sat in her chair, a quiet sentinel, as we whizzed around the ice, the sound of blades cutting the frozen surface punctuated by peals of laughter. When we circled past her, looping around the rink, her hand rose in a small wave, her smile tight.

I tilted my skate, the blade carving sharply into the ice, copying the older kids as they zipped around the rink. Joan was just ahead—close enough that I could almost reach her. My heart raced. There was something about her; she seemed free and light. I found her fascinating. Not just her makeup and clothes, but her attitude. She was the polar opposite of Ma, and I couldn't take my eyes off her.

But Peggy was watching. She saw me inching closer, her gaze flicking over her shoulder.

"Joan! Peggy! Wait for me!" My pleas were tossed aside in the wind.

Without missing a beat, my sister shook her head—sharp, almost a warning. It seemed like Peggy had claimed Joan long before I even existed. They were inseparable. With a twist of her skates, Peggy pulled Joan into a spin, her grip tightening as they glided away from me.

I pushed off, cruising past Grandma, and felt the rush of wind against my face. I reached for Da's outstretched hand as he skated by and threw up my other arm, reaching for the sky. It wasn't such a big deal I couldn't catch up with Joan. I had Da.

Hours slipped by, and my toes went numb. With red noses

and a few bruises, we headed inside to warm up. The lodge at Bear Mountain was a Christmas card come to life. Moose heads mounted on the walls peered down at a massive tree that dominated the entryway. Its branches were weighed down with sparkling tinsel, strings of fat lights of every color, and ornaments that glistened. Christmas carols hummed softly in the background, and the air held the woodsy scent of birch and pine.

I sneezed and Da said "Gesundheit," echoing the alpine feel of the lodge. Grandma looked over at us in surprise.

I turned to Da, wide-eyed. "Da, do the Von Trapps live here?" I wondered, only half joking.

He chuckled. "No, honey, but it sure feels like they could."

I felt hot steam wafting through the air and smelled something sweet—and suddenly realized how hungry I was. Ma found us a spot by the hearth and unpacked the cooler, spreading food all over the thick wooden coffee table. She poured the coffee into mismatched mugs, the chipped ones that felt like home. The sandwiches were simple—bologna and mayo—but tasted incredible. We stretched our legs, leaning back on the cozy couches, feeling content.

Da popped up and grabbed Thomas's hand. "Come help me," he said, surprising my brother. They scurried away, returning with three hot chocolates topped with tiny marshmallows and mounds of whipped cream and a chocolate brownie for us to share.

Stuffed to the brim, we twisted like pretzels to fit ourselves back into the car. The sun slipped behind the mountain, casting a warm glow across the sky as we drove south, our bellies full, our hearts content. For a brief moment, it felt like time had slowed. The fading light clung to us a little longer, reminding us of the magic in the air. I squeezed my eyes tight, wishing that feeling would last forever as we headed into Christmas.

Chapter 9

Brooklyn, New York, 1964

Sitting on the hump in the back of the VW, I was afraid I was going to pee myself, Da had us laughing so hard.

"As the Grinch said, 'And they'll feast, feast, feast, feast. They'll eat their Who-Pudding and rare Who-Roast Beast. But that's something I just cannot stand in the least. Oh, no. I'M SPEAKING IN RHYME!'" Da grunted, keeping his voice gravelly like the Grinch.

Even Ma was snorting as he spoke in a silly low-pitched voice, pretending to be the Grinch. I didn't want to ruin the velvety red pants I had on, hand-me-downs from Peggy that finally fit me. I rubbed my hands up and down my legs and squeezed them together. Nothing was going to ruin this night. We were on our way to Grandma's for Christmas Eve, but we were also going to celebrate my sixth birthday. There would be cake and candles—and extra gifts for me.

The wind outside was a soft whisper against the window in the hallway as Peggy, Thomas, and I yanked off our boots and raced up the stairs, two at a time, competing to reach the top first.

Visiting Grandma's when Joan was home was always fun. When she was away the house felt different—cold, a little too quiet, the scent of mothballs and old wood in the air. The rooms felt like they were holding their breath, waiting for something to happen, but nothing ever did. Grandma reminded me of Ma—always seeming like she was on the edge of feeling something, like there was something underneath that I could never dig out.

But Christmas Eve at Grandma and Joan's was the one night of the year that felt like its magic was made just for us. Their home was a beautiful brownstone bought by Ma's grandma and grandpa when they moved here from Germany. Ma and Joan grew up there, with their two older brothers, Charlie and John. I never met Charlie but loved to hear stories about him. He died in World War II. John came to Brooklyn to visit once in a while.

We burst into the living room, where the air was thick with the fragrance of fir, cinnamon, and dinner roasting in the oven. "Merry Christmas!" everyone shouted at once, drowning out the sound of carols playing on the radio. Joan had outdone herself. The tree, a towering Douglas fir that brushed the ceiling, was the centerpiece, but the entire room seemed to glow. The branches twinkled, bursting with delicate glass ornaments brought over from Germany by Grandma's parents, each a symbol of holiday wonder. Boughs dripped with tinsel and dipped with strands of chunky, colored lights. The tree reflected my aunt's flair for beauty, which gave it the gift of enchantment.

Underneath it, presents were piled high like a mountain of promises. Thick, patterned paper wrapped each gift, and pine cones sat nestled on top. Cut-out snowflakes, painstakingly folded and snipped by Joan, dangled like snow in the corners of the room, casting patterns that danced on the walls. The radiator hummed, its warmth pushing the glorious scents throughout the room. Peggy and Thomas were poking around the gifts, but I was momentarily frozen by the sheer magic of it all. This wasn't at all like the tree in our apartment, the one that we folded up and put back in the box after Christmas. This was something special.

Like a tornado, Snoopy, Joan's spunky wire-haired terrier, raced out of her bedroom. He had been napping, preparing for the excitement. The dog was a December baby, just like me, and we celebrated our birthday together on Christmas Eve. We shared a birthday cake—yellow with chocolate buttercream frosting. Snoopy, clearly the favorite, got top billing on the cake, but I'll admit I got a bigger slice.

"Snoopy!" I shouted, snuggling my face into his belly as he rolled over to be petted. He smelled like lavender from the baths Joan loved to give him. "Happy birthday, Snoopy!" He licked my nose in response.

We darted around the gifts like bees inspecting a hive. "Santa's rule is," Da reminded, wagging a finger, "you can sniff and shake, but no opening till after dinner!"

I huffed. My fingers itched to rip through the paper, but my focus wasn't on the Christmas gifts. It was on something else. My birthday present. My heart thudded as I scanned the mess under the tree for a package wrapped in non-Christmas paper, the special touch Joan never forgot. But there was nothing.

Panic tightened my throat. *They forgot my birthday,* I thought, my chest squeezing. A hot tear slid down my cheek, and I clutched Snoopy tighter. I looked for Da, but his usual reassuring presence was nowhere to be found.

Suddenly, his voice cut through the chatter. "Hey, look what I found!"

We all whipped around. Da rolled a gleaming pink-and-white bicycle into the room, the handlebars glinting under the twinkling lights. "It's got Joanne's name on it," he said with a huge grin. "Happy, happy birthday, my big girl!"

Peggy, Thomas, and I gasped. "Wow!" Peggy's eyes were wide as saucers. "That's cool!" We circled the bike like it was a treasure unearthed, fingers tracing the smooth vinyl seat and tugging at the shiny streamers that hung from the handlebars.

My sadness vanished, replaced by sheer wonder. I wanted to hop on right then and pedal through the snow-covered streets, but even I knew it was still sledding season. I grinned, plotting. "Guess I'll practice my steering on the sled till spring," I declared.

Da chuckled, ruffling my hair. "That's my girl."

The world outside was cold and dark, but in that moment surrounded by the warmth of family, the glow of the tree, and the magic of Christmas, everything felt perfect. It was my sixth birthday and Da had just surprised me with my first bike.

What more could I have ever wanted?

Right then, I had everything.

Everything.

Chapter 10

Brooklyn, New York, 1965

The last days of winter crept by as slowly as maple syrup dripping from the bottle. It was late in the afternoon; Da had already left for work and Peggy was still at school preparing for an upcoming science fair. Faint sunlight pressed against the front windows trying to get in, but the living room stayed dim. Ma turned on the light in the corner as Thomas leaned on the coffee table drawing intently with his colored pencils. I kneeled next to him, hunched over, trying to decide which crayon would be the best color for my princess's gown.

Ma sat in the recliner, gazing blankly toward the window, legs crossed, a mug of tea cooling in her hand.

"Look, Ma! I made Cinderella's gown pink, like cotton candy, instead of blue like it is in the movie!" I scrambled up off my knees to show it to her. She glanced at the coloring book in my hand.

"Hmm. That's nice," she said in a voice that was flat but not unkind. She smiled faintly, a hollow curve of the lips, turning back toward the window.

I frowned slightly, feeling disappointed, and plopped back on the floor.

"Ma, do you like cats or dogs better?" my brother asked. My mother, lost in her thoughts, didn't answer Thomas.

"She's probably just thinking," I whispered to him. He turned to me, sadness in his eyes. It was quiet, save for the ticking of the clock.

I'd heard Ma and Da talking late the night before, their voices soft like they were telling secrets. Normally, I'd hear a few belly laughs from Da, and Ma saying, "Oh, Jack," in a softer voice than she used during the day. But lately their voices were different. They weren't laughing so much. They sounded quiet, their voices low, like they didn't want anyone to hear. Even the air felt thicker, but I couldn't figure it out.

"Cats, I think. They're beautiful, but they'll scratch you if you're not careful," she finally responded.

"But their fur is really fluffy, isn't it?" I asked.

Ma exhaled softly and said, "Yes, I guess it is."

And for that brief moment, I felt seen by her, like the winter light had finally made it inside, warming the spaces that always felt too cold.

Chapter 11

Brooklyn, New York, 1965

A few months later, the first day of spring broke through the cold gray sky like a promise—fresh, alive, and full of possibility. The sun stretched long across the sidewalk, throwing gold on everything it touched. My legs bounced up and down in anticipation. My heart raced with excitement. It felt like the world had decided it was time for something new, something exciting. Something warmer than the weak light of winter.

I was ready to do more. Explore more. Grow more. Being the youngest wasn't fun. I spent a lot of time seeing Peggy and Thomas do things I wasn't allowed to do yet. I was always watching and waiting. Every Tuesday afternoon at the Ninth Street YMCA, I had to sit on a bench with my mother, inhaling chlorine, watching them glide through the water, their strokes getting stronger and smoother from swim lessons. I couldn't wait for my turn, and soon I was given my moment to shine.

Da stood next to me, one hand gripping the handlebars of the bike I got for my birthday. I held his other hand as we walked it down the street, tires bumping over the pavement cracks. I heard the rapid-fire *click-click-click* of the old baseball card that Thomas had clipped to the spoke of my tire. It gave it a cool sound that made me smile.

The wide sidewalks of Fourth Avenue were the perfect place to practice turning. The sidewalk was empty; it was just the two of us, the Schwinn—and my courage.

Da crouched down and, with a few quick turns of a wrench, raised the training wheels. I felt like I wasn't just learning to ride a bike. It was bigger than that. I was stepping into a new world. The world of the big kids.

"Ready, big girl?" Da's voice was steady, comforting.

I nodded, swallowing the nerves that tickled my stomach.

My father held the bike with his hand on the back of the squishy seat, and my feet pushed against the pedals, gaining certainty with each minute. His voice low, encouraging me, he said, "Just keep your eyes up. Don't look at your feet." He gave my shoulder a firm pat. "You got this." And I was off. He let me fly. My body swayed a bit, left and right, wobbling, but I could sense Da close behind. Ready to catch me if I fell.

But I didn't fall.

Then I heard it. Da's voice rang out from afar, full of joy. "Hey, look at you go! What a speed racer! Woo-hoo!"

The rush of wind kissed my cheeks, and suddenly I wasn't thinking about balance or the training wheels I'd left behind. I was flying, my Schwinn slicing through the world like a comet. I tightened my grip on the pink handlebars, the streamers fluttering in the breeze. The training wheels that had clattered beside me for weeks were gone now, and their absence left an exhilarating thrill—and a lump of fear in my throat.

It hit me. I was riding on my own. The world was mine to conquer. When I reached the end of the block, I hopped off the bike, my legs still wobbly but my heart strong. Da ran to me, arms open, and I jumped into them without a second thought. His whiskers rubbed against my cheek as he held me close, and I breathed him in. The familiar smell of Barbasol aftershave, cigars, and that hint of stale beer. It was a smell I'd known all my life, the one that meant safety, protection, love.

"I did it, Da," I whispered, my voice surging with joy.

"You sure did, sweetheart," he said, his voice warm and deep, like the hug he gave me. He smiled, and I knew, right then, that there was nothing I couldn't do with him by my side.

Chapter 12

Brooklyn, New York, 1965

The streetlights threw thin slats of light that stretched across the floor as I lay awake in my bed. Summer was slipping in, and sleep seemed further away with each passing night. All I wanted to do was ride my new bike. It was the best part of my day, riding around with Peggy and Thomas, feeling like a big kid. Da would be with us, laughing as we raced, and Ma would sit on the stoop, her voice cheering us on.

But lately, Da had seemed different. Distracted. His voice was a touch quieter, slower, and it made my stomach twist. The past few nights I'd heard him and Ma talking in the living room again, snippets of their conversations mixing with voices from the television.

"Jack, we'll go see Dr. Caraff again. Let's have him take another look, see what else can be done." Ma's voice, soft, unfamiliar. "Maybe there is a new blood pressure medicine you can try."

Laughter from *The Smothers Brothers Comedy Show* cut through the tightness in the air. I squeezed my eyes shut, trying to block it out, but the unease wouldn't go away. Da was my rock—he couldn't be sick.

"The president has authorized use of American ground troops to support the South Vietnamese army. Over 100,000 Chicago students protest segregation by staying out of school. And difficulties from rising production costs and competition with television contribute to strike threats by workers against newspapers." The newscast droned out the headlines, having just come on the air.

"Oh, no," Da groaned, his voice low and rough. "All the guys at work are talking about this. We're worried the paper may shut down or merge. There's talk of a strike."

Ma's voice tried to soothe, but it didn't sound convincing. "Jack, let's see what happens. We'll figure it out."

The words tumbled out before Da could stop them. "What if I lose my job?"

I tossed and turned in my bed, panic creeping up my spine. I wanted to cry, but I couldn't. I had never heard them sound like this before. It was always my mother who was off, unable to shake a fog, but Da pulled her back. Never the other way around.

I felt anxious; I didn't understand. I didn't know how to make sense of the change I could feel in the air.

This was the first time I felt the ground shift beneath me—the first time I realized that grown-ups don't always have the answers.

It wouldn't be the last.

Chapter 13

New York, New York, 1984

Two decades later, the ground shifted again—but now, I shifted with it.

Armed with my new degree, I headed to Wall Street—a true male bastion for sure, but one where I hoped performance would be the only thing that mattered. Because I knew how to perform. With a sense of vindication, I found that I could finally speak up and be heard. The culture was certainly macho, but I found space to breathe. My ideas were met with nods and my presence acknowledged. I was being noticed. I was finally *somebody*.

This was new to me. I was still young, still figuring out who I was in this world, but there was a shift. I could feel it with every day that passed. I no longer needed to shrink or hide. I could take up space. And I wanted more space, more opportunities, more of everything that had been denied to me in the past.

For the first time, I felt like I had some control. After a lifetime of hand-me-downs and bargain clothes, for example, I had enough money to buy nice clothes for myself. I could have dinner at a restaurant anytime, not just at my family's once a year outing for Easter. The shift was profound, not just professionally but personally. I was no longer stuck in anyone else's idea of who I should be. I could live life on my own terms.

Citibank's Capital Markets training program was an incredibly high-pressure environment that immersed recruits in the complexities of global finance, including fixed income—municipals, US Treasuries, mortgage-backed securities, and derivatives—as well as foreign exchange. Among forty trainees, fewer than a handful were women. We had to not only prove our competence but also deal with deeply ingrained gender biases.

I adopted a strategy of blending in by dressing in dark suits with blouses tied at the neck, wearing my long hair restrained in a tight ponytail, keeping my opinions concise, and always being prepared. I became adept at reading the room, understanding when to speak up and when to remain silent. I earned the top spot in the program and was given my choice of positions.

It wasn't the first time I worked hard, hoping to be seen—not just for what I'd done, but for who I was. That yearning for recognition started long before I ever stepped foot on a trading floor.

Long before Wall Street, there was an apartment on Sixty-First Street. And a little girl begging to be noticed.

Chapter 14

Brooklyn, New York, 1965

The knot in my chest tightened over the next three weeks as I lay in bed, listening to Ma and Da whispering when they thought I was asleep. Something was wrong. I knew it in my belly but had no words to convey what I sensed. I tried to push away the uneasiness the last Friday in June when Thomas, Peggy, and I joined Da at his desk—a ritual he had created to celebrate the last day of school at Our Lady of Perpetual Help. I was too young to read the deeper meanings behind the name back then or even pay attention.

I was so excited. Finally, I could celebrate all that I had learned in my first year of elementary school. I felt proud to stand before Da's desk, an equal with my brother and sister. As a journalist, Da spent a lot of time at that desk, which was painted black and sat in the front room of our Brooklyn apartment, facing Sixty-First Street. It felt like an altar, a sacred place where Da's thoughts and writing combined, expressing his brilliance—and secret despair.

On top of it rested a polished, cedar wood humidor, where he kept his cheap cigars, topped with a small inlaid metal rectangle engraved with my father's initials—JMR, John Matthew Redding. Da went by Jack. Next to the cigar box lay the heavy, algae-green glass ashtray Da used when he smoked and a lamp with a thick black base in the shape of a rearing horse. Sometimes when no one was looking, I'd open the top of the cigar box and stick my nose inside and sniff, inhaling cedar, tobacco, and traces of lemon polish. Smells of my father.

That day, Da stood with his bulky reel-to-reel audio recorder, the color of oatmeal, and a handheld microphone attached by a cord. It came in its own plastic suitcase with a brass clasp, which made this look and sound professional.

He cleared his throat and winked at me.

"And you, Joanne, what a fine job you did in first grade!" his deep voice boomed, wrapping around me like a warm embrace. I had gotten all A's and was so proud I thought I might puff up like a blowfish. He interviewed each of us, passing around the microphone, making a big deal about our accomplishments, pretending to present us with tall golden trophies and boxes of chocolates. "Thomas, you did very well this year! What is your favorite thing about third grade?" he asked.

The answer wasn't surprising. "Recess!" Thomas shouted. We all laughed.

"And Peggy," he probed, sounding all formal. "What do you have to say?"

"I can't wait to start seventh grade! We won't have to share the cafeteria with the little kids anymore. They're so annoying," she answered, full of preteen snark.

My smile was as wide as the Hudson. It always felt so nice to have him pay attention to us. And the entire summer lay ahead.

Chapter 15

Brooklyn, New York, 1965

Five days later, a sharp knock on the door shattered the morning quiet. School was finally over, and we were sleeping in. I was confused. No one ever knocked on our door.

I twisted my body under the threadbare blanket, the rollaway cot creaking beneath me. Sunlight crept through the thin curtains in the front room where Thomas and I slept. I propped my head up on the pillow to see what was going on. From across the living room, Ma emerged from the bedroom where she and Da slept in their separate twin beds, simple metal frames without headboards.

Eyes guarded, Ma opened the front door to the apartment. There was a cop standing there, a young guy. My eyes went wide. *Why was a policeman at our door? Why so early in the morning?* Ma hadn't even had her coffee yet. I peeked through the blanket, trying to pretend I was asleep, my eyes glued to the stranger in the hallway.

I watched the way his hands fidgeted, as if he felt something slipping through his fingers. *Why was he so nervous?* It was so weird to have the police in the doorway of our apartment.

In the mirror on the living room wall, I watched his dark eyes flick up to meet Ma's wary gaze. His feet shuffled, almost imperceptibly, looking like he wanted to be anywhere but here. *What happened? Was Grandma okay?* My thoughts twisted around in my head. I knew Ma's mother was old, and I worried that something had happened to her.

"We found your car abandoned on the bridge," the officer said, his voice low and careful. "We're looking for your husband."

My mother didn't flinch. Her face was unreadable, like she'd been bracing for this moment all along. "Thank you, Officer," she said calmly.

As the door clicked shut behind him, her composure held firm. She did not turn to face me but instead looked out the window to the uncertain horizon.

"Get up and get dressed. Wake your brother and sister up," she instructed, her voice even, catching my eye in the mirror.

I swallowed the lump growing in my throat, my heart thudding hard against my ribs. The world had just tilted, but Ma moved like nothing had changed at all.

My hands were shaking, and I felt a pit in my stomach as I put on my favorite teal-colored short set with its matching top, the one my mother and I had bought at John's Bargain Store the week before. Somehow, I knew to make an effort that morning, to wear something special, though I did not know why.

We rode two buses to Grandma's house on Seventy-First Street and Tenth Avenue. Ma sat silent, her lips tight, eyes far away. Peggy, Thomas, and I exchanged worried glances, staying quiet. We knew this was one of those times when she definitely didn't want to engage with us. Yet somewhere deep within herself, my mother knew that today even she would need some support.

When we got to Grandma's, the grown-ups pointed us to the living room and went into the kitchen, where they spoke in hushed voices. We sat there for what felt like an eternity, even after the adults came out to join us. My mother, whose hair still held the waves from the pink foam curlers she slept in at night, perched stoically on the couch, its upholstery faded to a pale shade of green, like that of a drought-stricken field. My sister, her scrawny preteen legs folded underneath her like a pretzel, looked distraught huddled in a chair next to Joan. My blond-haired brother looked bewildered, his light blue eyes round and red. And my grandmother, Herminia, settled in her usual armchair, the one no one else was allowed to sit in, wearing her typically unreadable mask. As hours passed waiting for news from the police, my mother remained silent, her face inscrutable.

Aunt Joan tried to console her. "Dot, maybe he stopped for a drink somewhere and is sleeping it off. We'll hear from him soon." Her voice was not terribly convincing. "Maybe he got hurt and is in a hospital. They'll find him. You'll see. It will be all right," she offered, trying again to hold back the tsunami that was about to sweep over us.

We waited. From time to time, my brother or sister would wail or weep, to then be consoled by my aunt in her back bedroom, the one with the gold-flecked wallpaper and pink shag carpeting. But mostly, we just sat. No one moved. No one spoke.

The grandfather clock the family brought with them from Hamburg decades before ticked away, marking each passing minute. The hourly chimes clanged like a death knell intruding on our private hell. Suspended in time, I was aware that something momentous had happened, but we weren't yet acknowledging it. It wasn't yet a fact.

Head bowed, I looked around from person to person hoping to see in someone's eyes the key to burst this frightening bubble, to have the day go back to normal. But that wasn't possible. We bided time, everything on hold except my breath.

I just wanted Da to walk in the door.

After what felt like many hours, the doorbell finally rang. My mother pushed herself wearily off the couch and descended the stairs to get the news.

After a while, she climbed back up, slowly, as if she were dragging his body behind her.

"Your father was driving across the bridge and had a car accident. He is dead." Her voice flat as the plains.

My pinkie rubbed back and forth on the frayed piping of the armrest on the chair where I sat, desperate to hold on to something that wasn't crumbling. The smell of stale rosewater clung to Grandma, suffocating me. I could almost taste it. I wanted to gag.

Inside, my stomach lurched like a boat torn loose from its anchor. I didn't want to be here. I wanted to be with my da.

I hated them both right then—Ma and Grandma with their coldness. I looked at Ma with the patch of dry powder on her nose and wanted to smack it. I didn't want them there. I wanted Da.

A lifetime of silence filled the room for the next thirty seconds.

Then the room exploded.

My sister, hysterical, ran shrieking to my aunt's bedroom with my aunt trailing behind. Joan looked distraught; emotions etched deep across her face. She was the one who always let you know how she felt. My brother started sobbing softly, his small hands trying to block the world from his eyes. My grandmother awkwardly extended her arm around his shoulders. She was not one to show emotion.

My mother shed no tears. Not then, not ever. She sat dry-eyed while telling me it was okay to cry, and I knew it was. "Go ahead, cry," she prompted matter-of-factly.

Although I knew crying was what was called for, even as a six-year-old, I couldn't. I didn't want to. I wanted the world to stop. The movie to rewind. To have a do-over. To start the day again. I squeezed my eyes tight to make it all go away. Silently screaming, pleading that I could open my eyes and be anywhere but there.

No tears came when I finally looked up at Ma.

I knew they all thought I didn't understand what was happening, that I was too young. But that wasn't it. It was like I sat on a cloud, watching it all from above. I had dissociated from my body but was well aware of what had happened.

I knew what it all meant. Da wasn't coming back. Ever.

Almost twenty years would pass before Ma spoke of him again.

I just felt flat inside. I was silent, learning from the best.

Chapter 16

Brooklyn, New York, 1965

The day my childhood truly ended, the smell of Ivory soap lingered on my hands as I sucked my thumb. It was just a few days after my father died when my mother sat me down on the living room couch, springs groaning as we lowered into the indents. The whine of the window fan filled the silence as she folded her hands tightly in her lap, knuckles whitening. I braced for what was coming.

She cleared her throat, that sharp sound that meant something serious was coming. Matter-of-factly she said, "From now on, you're going to have to take care of yourself."

My breath caught in my throat. My brain was scrambled like when I tried to do a word problem in math. I couldn't figure out what she meant. I wished I could ask Da. I wanted to escape. I wanted her to tell me she'd make me pancakes the way that Da did.

Her words floated in the air, sharp and jagged, slicing through the remnants of hope. I blinked fast, stunned, waiting for her to say something more, to explain it, but nothing came.

What . . . what do you mean? I wanted to ask, but the question just sat on my tongue. I couldn't push it past my lips. She never liked to be questioned.

Then, just like that, she stood, dusting imaginary lint off her skirt. Her steps were brisk as she walked away. She didn't look back, not bothering to grant me a glance. I sat stunned, like I had been whacked in the head with a bat, for the second time that week.

The air was suddenly too thick to breathe. I could feel the sting of tears rising but shoved them down. I knew better than to cry. She wouldn't comfort me; she wouldn't hold me. She never had. The only person that had was gone. Oh, I missed him so much.

My heart thumped, my ears roaring like they did when the boys held me under the waves at the beach.

I had to take care of myself. *What did she mean? Was she sending me away? Was she leaving?* I was dizzy with questions. I wished with all my might I had someone to talk to. *Did she only tell this to me, or did she tell Thomas too? Would she get rid of me if I didn't do a good enough job taking care of myself? Would I disappear from her heart like my father seemed to have?*

All that night I lay awake, staring at the cracked ceiling. Shadows danced on the plaster, ghosts of what was and what would never be again. The only sound was Thomas softly breathing in the bed across from me.

Time passed, and I figured out that taking care of myself meant making sure I ate, bathed, and did my homework. It meant learning not to be tucked in or have tangles brushed from my hair. But there was more. And it was harder.

I learned to silence the ache for things I couldn't have—the soft touch of reassurance, a hand to guide me, a voice that promised I was not alone. Da, who saw me.

Chapter 17

Brooklyn, New York, 1965

I jolted awake the next morning, hearing my mother's words echoing in my head. *From now on, you're going to have to take care of yourself.* They hit me like a punch in the gut. Everyone was already up, moving quietly, getting dressed in the haze of early morning. I jumped out of bed, slipped a dress over my head, and quickly brushed my teeth and hair. Today was my father's funeral. It was also the twelfth birthday of my sister, Peggy.

Ma ushered us out the door, leading us up the few blocks to the church, without uttering a word. The air was heavy with humidity and what was about to happen. The massive wooden doors at the front of the church groaned open and we filed in, the only sound our footsteps echoing on the marble floor, marking time. The cool, dim interior swallowed us as we made our way up the aisle to the front pew. Behind us, a soft shuffle indicated others were settling in, but I didn't dare turn around.

Then, the music began. Slow, mournful. It hung in the air like a fog, each note pressing down on my chest. Men in dark suits wheeled the coffin up the aisle, its polished surface gleaming too brightly. When I caught a glimpse of it out of the corner of my eye, it seemed so unreal. *How could my da be shoved into a box?* The thought hit me like a smack in the face. None of this made sense.

The incense hung in the air, sharp and bitter, mixing with the murmur of prayers. Every intonation, every whisper, stretched the pain out further, making it more unbearable. Pain attached to me like a shadow.

My mother refused to allow us to attend our father's burial; instead, my great-aunt Dora took us to a diner across the street from Our Lady of Perpetual Help. We slid into the booth, with its cracked vinyl banquettes that scratched the backs of our legs and the Formica table that was bolted to the wall. I heard the sizzle of bacon on the grill and the clang of the spatula as the cook pushed the grease aside. We all ordered pancakes, swimming in a pool of Aunt Jemima's syrup, with crispy bacon on the side.

I was always *so* excited the few times Da took us to the diner after Mass, but today was different. I just wanted to cry.

Dora picked at her plate quietly, struggling to not look at us. She was a sweet old lady and Grandma's sister. She was plain-looking, her hair harnessed by two big bobby pins that met in an X, gripping curls tightly against her temples. Her clear, pale-blue glasses, dotted with rhinestones in the corners, magnified her soft kind eyes. Her feet were the biggest I had ever seen, like Ronald McDonald's without all the color. She lived with a hot plate in a room that smelled like dust in the basement of Grandma's house.

That day, her hands shook as she dabbed her lips. I looked around, hoping something, anything, would make sense. Nothing did.

I shot a look at Thomas, who sat next to me. He pushed a bit of pancake, speared on his fork, around and around in the syrup, holding his breath. Peggy's eyes kept darting out the window, looking at the church, maybe hoping to catch one last glimpse of Da. But he was shut in a wooden box that was going to be buried underground. She kept kicking her feet under the table, and she looked really mad. Her eyes were wet, a single drop slowly making its way to her chin.

The table had a small jukebox on it, with a push button to flip pages full of song choices, but we didn't play any music that day. No one felt like singing.

When the plates were cleared away, Aunt Dora herded us back to the apartment like abandoned kittens, where we sat waiting for this new life to begin.

After Da died, our apartment got really quiet. Not just regular quiet, like when it was bedtime, but heavy quiet, like when you hold your breath too long and your chest hurts. Thomas didn't say much anymore, even less than before. He sat with his drawing book a lot, scribbling with colored pencils as though the pictures would tell us things we didn't know. It felt like Peggy yelled at me and Thomas a lot when Ma wasn't around. About nothing and everything. We were too loud, we were too quiet, we were too slow, we were too fast. Sometimes, she seemed to explode like a volcano, only to then go to her room and sob. It was very confusing. I just tried to become very small.

A bubble enveloped us all—we were together, yet completely apart. Now it was just Ma, Peggy, Thomas, and me. I watched how their hands moved, and where their eyes went, how they breathed. I tried to guess what was going on in their heads.

Did their faces hurt like mine did, like it might crack in two? Like their skin was going to rip off their faces? Would they trade anything just to hold Da's hand one more time? The silence was suffocating, but none of us wanted to disturb Ma. She went out, came back, and closed the door to her bedroom. Day after day. We kept waiting for her to say something, anything, but she never did.

With nowhere to go, my frustrations bottled up all day and spilled out at night. After the funeral, I started wetting my bed, the shame leaking out of me with every drop. I dreamed I was taken away by a monster with green teeth and woke up screaming. I was afraid. Ma never mentioned Da. It was like he never existed. This terrified me. *Would Ma never mention me again if I disappeared?* I wondered. *Would she just forget about me, like she did with Da?*

I felt my world was different from everyone else's. *How could everyone else act as though nothing had changed?* My friends still chose sides for stickball, still played leapfrog and ran through the fire hydrant. They still cheered when Mr. Softee came down the street. And they still got to hug their das, to sit on their laps. I didn't understand. I tried really hard to act normal, to act like the other kids, hoping maybe the good feelings inside of them would seep into me. But they could still sit on their das' laps, and I couldn't. Just beneath my skin flowed a river of sadness.

A week after the funeral, I beat up a boy. Badly.

A bunch of us were playing stoopball, taking turns throwing the Spalding against the chipped concrete steps. The rules were simple: Catch it on the bounce or on the fly to score. I was winning, feeling the welcome satisfaction of something going right.

"Hey, Joanne, I hear your da's dead. How'd it happen, huh?" He smirked, somehow thinking it was funny. This kid was annoying on his best day. He kept at it as I pretended not to hear him, biting the inside of my cheek.

I felt heat rising through my neck and face.

He wasn't done. "C'mon, aren't you gonna tell us? What happened?"

The words sliced through me, igniting a rage I didn't realize was in me. Before I knew what I was doing, I whipped around and grabbed him, drove him to the pavement, and straddled him. My fists rained down, a blur of knuckles and fury. Blood smeared across his face, his nose crooked and swollen. The kids pulled me off him, their shouts distant and meaningless in my ears.

I wanted the world to stop. I wanted to scream and rage and sob but I couldn't. It felt like I wasn't allowed to. And if I did, no one would hear me.

Hours later, the doorbell rang—a rare sound in our apartment where no one ever visited. My heart thudded as my mother opened the door to the boy's mother, her face red with rage.

"She's crazy!" the woman screeched. "Look what she did to my son!" She pointed at the boy, whose tears mixed with the crusted blood stuck on his broken nose.

My mother's expression didn't flicker. She stared at the woman with a granite-cold gaze and, without a word, slammed the door in her face.

I stood behind her, my knuckles aching from the fight. Ma didn't say a word to me, didn't ask why I did it. To address it would mean confronting what none of us spoke about—my father's death. He was gone. Everyone knew it, and everyone else was talking about it. Just like this kid did. But silence had become our family's language, thick and suffocating.

Although Ma went to a Lutheran church, a priest from the Catholic church we went to with Da came by a few times after he died. He tried talking to Ma, offering some comfort and support. He seemed kind. He was persistent. But Ma was impenetrable; she stonewalled him.

Eventually, he gave up. Everyone did. Friends drifted away, understandably, since their concern for us was met with icy indifference.

Our apartment became a place of pain, a monument to what we had lost but refused to confront. A house of pretend.

That day on the pavement, my fists had spoken the words I couldn't articulate—the fury of unexpressed grief, the chaos and confusion of a world turned dark and unyielding.

I missed my da.

Chapter 18

Brooklyn, New York, 1965

It was late August with a haze in the sky; almost two months had passed since Da died, and it was time to buy shoes for school. We walked up Fifth Avenue to shop. The front windows of the shoe store displayed sneakers in assorted styles, shoes of tan suede so soft I yearned to rub my cheek against them, shiny polished leather penny loafers, and fuzzy slippers in colors of sherbet. The shoes were balanced on boxes and box covers, and the side walls were decorated with cut-out letters and numbers glued to a fake chalkboard background.

I gripped a pair of last year's knee socks to try on new shoes that Ma expected to last the entire school year. It was a big outing for us, and I hoped we might get to go across the street to Woolworth's afterward for a treat. I crossed my fingers behind my back and prayed for Ma to be in a good mood.

The bell, attached to the top of the doorframe, clanged as we pushed open the door and sat down in a row of red chairs molded out of plastic, screwed together in groups of four. It was late in the day, as we had to wait for Ma to get home from work. She started working right after Da died, getting a job as a crossing guard. It brought in a little bit of money while she figured out a better plan. The other kids and their moms had come and gone already, but it didn't matter. The store had a full stock of hideous brown oxfords for us Catholic school students.

The salesman strode over. Standing tall, sporting a crew cut, he smiled, crinkling his eyes, greeting us like we were special. He had us stand, one by one, on the large metal foot imprint to see what size we had grown into. Being the youngest, I went last. I squished my foot back against the heel plate and stood as tall as I could, stretching my neck toward the ceiling. The salesman pushed his thumb on my big toe, eyeballing the lines on the guide and announcing my new size. I felt like a princess. I hated the shoes, which would be stiff and charmless, but I loved the fuss he was making over me, just me. He made me feel important. He reminded me of Da.

After measuring each of us, he disappeared into the back of the store, where rows upon rows of brand-new crisp cardboard boxes lined the shelves. He searched for the right style, color, and size. Then he reappeared, balancing boxes. He opened the lids, unwrapped the paper, and held out the shoes for us to try on. They were brand spanking new and smelled of fresh leather. It felt like Christmas in August. He slipped the cold silver shoehorn behind my heels and helped slide my feet into the shoes. Just like Cinderella, except they were not glass slippers.

We walked to the counter clutching our three pairs of shoes. The lady at the counter, bifocals dangling from a rainbow-colored beaded chain, rang us up, pushing hard on the black keys poking up from the cash register. When she tapped the last key, the drawer flew open, and she slipped my mother's cash under the weighted lever into the bill compartment. She put the shoeboxes in a bag with the handwritten receipt, and off we went.

Fortunately, Ma was in a decent mood that day. She didn't shake my hand out of hers when I reached for it as she normally would.

I smiled, hoping this would last. I liked feeling the warmth of her fingers wrapped around mine. I hoped to draw her closer to me and tried hard to be more helpful and less in the way. But it wasn't working. There must be something I wasn't doing right, but I just couldn't figure out what. Ma's moods were as unpredictable as Chicago weather, but we kids could detect the shifts the way animals sense changes in air pressure.

We crossed the street at the light and headed toward Woolworth's, a five-and-ten-cent store, where the aisles held everything I could ever want, or so I thought. There were spools of thread in every color lined up like an extended rainbow caterpillar, big wooden clothespins that looked like little people, ironing boards and mops, plastic plants, puzzles, and board games. There were potato peelers, knitting needles, kites, and ribbons spooling off cardboard circles dangling toward the floor. Dust motes danced in the afternoon sun, landing on faded boxes of nails and screws like Tinkerbell anointing the goods. Roaming those aisles was an adventure rife with possibilities. Woolworth's was a wonderland, and I loved every second in it.

My mother gave us each a few dimes to take a spin on the bucking horse or the space capsule rides in front of the store. The space capsule was my favorite. I rushed outside and slid the coin in the slot. I squished my eyes together tightly as the ride rattled and shook and made weird launch noises, and I imagined myself blasting off into a brand-new world, one very far from where I was.

The very best part of Woolworth's, though, was the ice cream parlor. Stools were bolted to the black-and-white diagonally tiled floor, with stainless steel poles holding up round red vinyl seats. I sat on a stool and spun, around and around, ignoring my mother, who kept saying I was going to throw up. I tilted my head back, seeing five pendant lights dangling from the ceiling, spotlighting the ribbed glass canisters that sat on the counter holding straws that looked like barber shop poles—red stripes spiraling around them. The ladies behind the counter wore black-and-white uniforms with small white paper hats on their heads and served ice cream in fancy fluted bowls.

But today we weren't having ice cream sundaes. We had to wait for our birthdays when they gave you a sundae for free. I had four long months to wait. But even if it were snowing and ten below zero, I'd walk up to Woolworth's, just not in the oxfords, and have a hot fudge sundae on the house. I was happy just to be there, although I wished Da was too.

Chapter 19

Brooklyn, New York, 1965

I clung to that moment of sweetness, anticipating my free sundae at Woolworth's, which seemed years away once school started the following week. I felt excited to be starting second grade as we got our school uniforms out of the closet. Da was the one who insisted the three of us be baptized and paid money we didn't have to send us to Catholic school. The nun in first grade taught us that only Catholics could get into heaven, so there was no way Ma was making it in; she was Lutheran.

The uniform for girls was a hideous green plaid skirt, a white polyester blouse with a Peter Pan collar, green knee socks, and the new Buster Brown oxfords that pinched our toes. My brother's uniform had an additional piece to it—a tie in the same ugly green plaid pattern.

At eight o'clock that Tuesday morning, the day after Labor Day, we stood awkwardly in silence in the living room, staring at the tie in Thomas's hand. We realized Da had been the only one in the family who knew how to tie it.

I stared hard at the floor. I didn't move a muscle. Not even to sneak a peek at Thomas or Peggy. I couldn't even breathe.

No one said a word. No one dared mention his name. We knew better than to shatter the thin glass box in which our grief sat.

My mother stood rigid, her lips pressed tightly together, always unable to admit she needed anything from anybody. But she needed help and was forced to go down the hallway and knock at the door of our elderly neighbor.

We waited. Nobody spoke.

A few minutes later, sweet, kind Mr. Finnerty, whose sparse tufts of white hair stuck up from his scalp, shuffled unshaven into our apartment in his gray terry cloth bathrobe and bent down to gently tie my brother's tie around his little neck. No one moved, not wanting to undo the quiet act of kindness.

When my mother came home from work that day, she brought with her two clip-on ties she'd bought for Thomas. She had fixed that problem, but the truth lingered like a hungry dog. The silence held his absence.

Da was gone and nothing could replace him.

Chapter 20

Brooklyn, New York, 1965

As I began second grade, things felt strange. Like the air had changed without anyone telling me why. At school, kids laughed like they always did, played tag at recess, and swapped sandwiches during lunch. I tried to laugh too, to act normal, so no one would think anything was wrong. But everything felt wrong.

During art class, I gripped the red crayon so tightly my hand began to sweat. Sister Veronica had asked us to draw our family. All around me, kids were already drawing happy moms and dads with stick arms holding hands. I stared at my blank paper, and my mouth felt like sandpaper.

"You okay, sweetheart?" the sister asked, crouching by my desk. She was young and smelled of peaches.

I nodded fast, my cheeks hot. "Yeah. Just thinking."

At home, I knew how to keep quiet, to match Ma's silence. Her face was always tight now, like she was trying to keep something from spilling out. I learned from her—keep your head up, keep your mouth shut, and nobody will see inside.

When the other kids asked me what I did over the weekend, I made up stories of trips to the park and baking cookies. No one needed to know that most weekends were just Ma staring blankly out the window while Thomas and I played quietly on the floor.

That day in art, I drew a picture—Ma, Thomas, Peggy, and me. I left out Da. The paper felt heavy when I handed it to the nun. She smiled and pinned it to the wall. My stomach twisted as I saw it hanging there with the others. Maybe nobody would notice what was missing. Maybe they'd believe my family was just like theirs.

There was a new girl in class that year: Debbie. She looked just like the girl on the cover of the Trixie Belden books—chin-length hair that was blond, streaked with hints of strawberry. Sister Veronica sat her next to me, and I was glad she did. Debbie had an infectious giggle that made her nose crinkle and scrunch up, causing two tiny dimples to appear in her cheeks every time she laughed. Also she was not from my neighborhood, so she didn't know about my father.

We were to make our first communion later that year, and each week, the class went together to confession so our hearts would be clean when the big day came.

When it was my turn, I slipped into the confessional booth, smelling the aged wood and incense lingering in the air. The rich aroma had seeped into the burgundy velvet curtain that parted to reveal the priest's shadowed profile. The priest's voice was gruff and distant, as if he were bored.

I was nervous and whispered some sins I had committed. My lips trembled and the words spilled out in a rush. I told him, "I miss my Da so much. I wish Ma was gone instead. I wish I lived with Joan and Grandma, so I didn't have to come home to no one."

A long, awkward silence sat between us in the confessional booth. I shifted uncomfortably on the hard wooden bench. The priest took a long time to say anything. I was afraid I was in trouble. Had he fallen asleep? The booth felt suffocating, and panic began to rise in my throat. Finally, he murmured softly, "I'll pray for you, little one."

His words whistled through the hole in my heart. He didn't say anything to make it better. He didn't tell me how to fix it. Just told me to pray ten Hail Marys.

Dismissed, I knelt before the communion rail, the cool marble hard against my knees, and started my penance. I said one full Hail Mary but could not see how this was going to help anything. I closed my eyes and, in my head, said, "Times ten." That was it. I lingered long enough to satisfy the nuns who were watching over us little sinners before returning to my pew.

I returned to church a few days later with my sister and brother. Peggy ran ahead, her footsteps light and quick, while Thomas and I dragged our feet behind her. I wished we didn't have to go to church, but Ma had insisted, her voice sharp. She made us go by ourselves every Sunday while she went to her own church. With Da gone, it just felt weird.

Everything felt different—like the earth had tilted.

As we approached the street corner across from the church, the smell of bacon hit my nose, rich and familiar, reminding me of mornings when Da would fry it up and tell us stories about his day. My stomach rumbled loudly, and for a moment, I could almost forget we were headed into church. At the entrance, I reached up for the cold, hard metal banister, climbing the wide stone steps one by one. The railing wasn't warm and soft like Da's hand that I used to hold. I swallowed hard, pushing the thought aside.

We followed a sea of families, groups of five or more, laughing and talking as we all made our way to find seats. I watched parents holding hands with their children, guiding them toward the pews where Peggy, Thomas, and I would be sitting alone.

We had just passed through the massive wooden doors when a man asked, "Are you lost? Can I help you find your parents?" His voice was kind but carried a subtle edge of concern. His question made it feel as though we were intruding.

Thomas looked at me, confusion in his eyes, and I could see the tension in his shoulders. I darted my eyes to Peggy. Her face turned red, the flush creeping up, and her lips pressed into a tight line like Ma's sometimes did.

"No," she shot back, grabbing our hands, her fingers tight and firm around mine. The man stood there with his family, their faces soft, eyes lingering on us like we were something broken. We were. The ache inside me for Da made me feel lost.

After enduring the entire service, we rushed out, wanting to escape the crowd. Others were already drifting toward the diner, their laughter rising above the hum of the street. We had just been there, not that long ago, on the day of Da's funeral.

We stepped onto the sidewalk, where people parted like the Red Sea, giving way to us as though we might be contagious with death. We were different, and I hated feeling like we did not belong anywhere. I felt like a spy stealing glances at the dads, arms around their daughters' shoulders, holding hands as they crossed the big street. If I closed my eyes, I could almost feel the pace of Da's steps, his hand on mine, steady and sure.

My chest tightened.

We kept moving beyond the crowd, determined to get back to the apartment before Ma got back from going to her Lutheran church alone. I began to loathe Sundays. I did not find comfort in the church or sermons or in prayer. None of it brought Da back.

The next day at school, an alarm blared through the hallways signaling a nuclear attack drill. We loved drills. Class was interrupted, and Debbie and I loved having to crawl down and tuck our bodies under our wooden desks. "*Zzzz, zzzz,*" I snored, pretending to be a bear in a cave. Debbie giggled, a little too loudly.

"What is going on back there?" Sister Veronica asked, slapping the ruler on her palm as she paced the aisles. The nuns told us cowering under the desks would help us avoid fallout from any nuclear bomb the Russians might launch. *Who were the Russians? What kind of bombs? How did they know the Russians dropped a bomb?* It didn't make sense to me, but the nuns didn't like to be questioned. This cowering tactic seemed as ridiculous as damning to hell anyone who wasn't Catholic. *It wasn't Ma's fault for not being Catholic, so why should she be punished? Didn't God say to forgive others?* I wondered. And the more I wondered, the more confused I became.

Later that week, I invited Debbie to play with me after school, and we walked to my apartment by ourselves like I always did. We skipped along the few blocks, swinging our arms, jumping over cracks in the sidewalk.

"Do you have any Barbies?" Debbie asked.

"I do! I have a bunch I got from my sister. They used to be hers, but she's too big for them now. She's twelve," I told Debbie.

"Wow, I wish I had a sister," she said.

When we got to my building, I ran in to grab the dolls. Ma wasn't home, of course. It seemed like she worked all the time. Right after Da died, she started working as a crossing guard, and now she had a second job as an aide at a school nearby. I knew not to bring anyone inside the apartment. No one was ever allowed in there, even when she was at home with us.

"Come over here." I waved Debbie down the steps that led to the back alley and spread the dolls out on the cracked concrete. "This is where you play?" she asked, her face pinched as if she smelled something bad. She lowered herself slowly, as though afraid of what might be on the ground. "Okay," she said, her voice quieter than before.

We played for a while, Barbie speeding off in her convertible as Ken fell out when it flew down the steps. Debbie giggled but kept glancing around. "I should probably go home," she said after a while, as she stood brushing off her skirt. It seemed like a short playdate to me, but I smiled and said, "Okay then. See you tomorrow."

She waved as she retraced her steps out of the alley. I followed her and watched until she turned and disappeared around the corner.

Ma never asked about the playdate when she got home. She never asked about much. I didn't tell her that in all likelihood Debbie wouldn't be back, that I thought she was probably used to backyards and pink bedrooms, not alleys and concrete steps.

In my head, I imagined Debbie's life was like those of Trixie Belden and Nancy Drew, characters from my favorite books. Girls in those stories could do anything. And they lived in houses with window seats and fireplaces. And people who called them honey and ruffled their hair. It's not what I had, but knowing it was out there made me feel hopeful. Maybe one day I could have that too.

I locked that day with Debbie away in a box in my head, a place where I stored my secrets and shame and, sometimes, if I allowed them, my dreams. It was where I kept thoughts of how much I missed Da, how much I wished Ma would smile, how much I wished she'd love me. Sometimes, when I was alone, I'd peer in it, trying to sift through all that confused me—and all that kept me searching for someone to keep me safe.

Chapter 21

Brooklyn, New York, 1966

Though I secretly wished we could move—away from the concrete steps and away from the memories that made me miss my father so much—Ma kept us living in our same apartment after Da died. The apartment building on Sixty-First Street was a four-story walk-up, identical to the others lining the street like soldiers at attention, all the same dull shade of ocher. In the summer, box fans checkered the windows, poking out from under bent metal venetian blinds. When Da died, my grandmother had invited us to move in downstairs from her and Joan, but my mother said no. I guessed Ma was trying to keep things the same, although nothing would ever be the same again.

My brother and I still shared the front room facing Sixty-First Street where, next to his bed, we kept a wooden toy chest full of treasures: his Matchbox cars, Tonka Toy trucks, and comic books and my dolls, colored pencils, and Silly Putty. My folding cot was across from his bed. Between the windows hung an old bevel-edged mirror with scratches on the silver backing and little glass florets that covered the screws. Beneath it was a folding metal card table, its surface covered in contact paper decorated with clusters of red cherries, the edges curled up at the corners, trapping specks of dirt. Sticky to the touch when we'd rub our fingers along it.

There were no more weekend breakfasts of pancakes and Aunt

Jemima syrup, when Ma would say we had enough and Da would pour more syrup when her back was turned. I missed the itch of Da's face when it would brush against mine, scratching me as he leaned over to kiss my cheek. When the stiff stubble of his five o'clock shadow stroked my delicate skin, rubbing in a bit of love.

When I lay on my cot, I could squeeze my eyes tight and still smell the stale Pabst Blue Ribbon on his breath when he'd bend down to whisper in my ear in his deep voice, "Sweet dreams, my little princess. I love you." His black hair and blue eyes, dark as the ocean depths, holding so much in them.

I remember one Saturday after breakfast when my mother was busy dusting furniture in the living room. The lemony smell of Pledge tickled my nostrils, making me smile. Thomas and I, nine and seven, played in the front room, screeching around.

"Vroom, vroom!" We squealed as the tiny metal cars flew off the table, skidding to a stop in the puffs of dust that lived under the beds, awaiting banishment as my mother progressed from room to room, like a soldier, armed with her dustcloth and mop.

We had laid out a whole city with paperback books as streets that we drove through and practiced parallel parking, keen on getting our driver's licenses someday.

I'm sure we were annoying to my sister, who could usually be found reading on her bed in her tiny room. We were little, loud, and in the way, trying to create some kind of joy in the midst of our wreckage. We were kids who desperately needed to play.

We sought more excitement outside, where our street became our playground. Lots of kids lived on our block. The Smiths were behind us, the Sullivans were across the hall, and the Halpersons had thirteen children stuffed in a two-bedroom apartment.

Mostly everyone was a churchgoing Irish Catholic, with a few

Italians sprinkled in. Halfway up the block was an invisible line, on the other side of which the Puerto Ricans lived. They spoke Spanish, fast and hard, in staccato syllables that exploded in the air, spicy salsa sounds. Latin music blared from speakers the size of carry-on luggage that fit in the windows. It excited me and was so different from the staid upbringing of the rest of us. From down the block I watched with curiosity as men entwined with women, hips swaying to the beat on hot summer nights. I was reminded of the summer before last with Da at the lake, dancing with the spatula in his hand. I smiled to myself, before I remembered to be sad.

One day, I sat on the curb with my friend Jane, examining bottle caps we had found. We were debating whether or not they were good enough to save when we heard some boys' voices approaching. Walking next to my brother was a kid I didn't recognize, a boy his age, about nine, wearing scuffed black sneakers and a Yankees shirt.

Jane said, "Hey, who are you?"

"His name is Tony, he's from around the block," Thomas offered as they joined in to be picked for a game of tag. My brother was quiet, but kind. "I told him he could play with us."

Sometimes one or two of the boys in our group would be mean to me or Jane; it was usually when we were beating them. The boys gathered around us and started arguing over teams. Jane tugged on my sleeve as we sat on the curb waiting.

"They're gonna pick us last again," she grumbled.

Tony turned to us and pointed. "I want to be on a team with those two. They look fast," he said, smiling our way. My cheeks got warm. I liked him already.

Tony played with us a few times a week. The days he came around were my favorites, and I felt the warmth of a crush.

We were kids exploring and evolving every day on the streets.

The alley behind our building lured us in with suggestions of adventure and refuge, but sometimes it held real danger. It was a place for people to do things they didn't want anyone to see.

One day when I turned the corner onto my block, I saw an ambulance and a police car in the middle of the street, blocking traffic. Lights flashing, but no sirens. I ran down the block, my book bag flopping against my knees. Thomas had gotten home earlier than me. He stood in front of our building, head hanging.

"Thomas, what happened? Are you okay?" I panted. I couldn't bear the thought of more loss.

Thomas pulled me to him awkwardly. "It's bad, Joanne," he gasped, struggling for air as if he were having one of his asthma attacks. "Tony's dead. The super found him in the alley." He hugged me close.

Tony had overdosed in the back alley. Dead at nine years old. They said he must have found some pills and swallowed them.

After his body was taken away and the police finally left, I sat on the steps leading to the alley, my eyes counting the specks in the sidewalk, my insides screaming, and I sobbed. Why did these people I love have to leave? No priest and no Hail Marys could ever fix the hole that kept widening in my heart.

Chapter 22

Brooklyn, New York, 1966

After Tony was found dead in the alley, coming home alone after school felt even worse. I always hated it, and now my hands shook a little as I put the key in the door of the apartment. Every time my mind went quiet, Tony entered my thoughts.

This silence smothered me when I walked into the living room. The apartment always felt too quiet, like there was something missing. It was just me, the empty room, and the silence. I always felt a little scared, like something might jump out at me from the shadows. Thomas did that a lot, thinking it was funny. But most days now, he didn't come straight home from school. He hated it too.

Before I even threw my book bag on the couch, I flipped on the TV, craving some noise to fill the empty space. The voices from the screen made me feel less alone. *The Andy Griffith Show* was on, and there was Aunt Bea in her ruffled apron making a snack for Opie as he came in from school. Longing strangled me. I wished that were me, coming home to Grandma and Joan's house.

I really wished we could live there. Even though Grandma was kind of cold, Joan was different. She was the best. She wasn't like Ma, not at all. She wasn't grumpy or always too busy to notice me. I wondered what kind of snacks she liked.

Joan was fun, like a big, shiny surprise you never expected. She had a passport, and she'd go to faraway places, places I could only imagine. She'd always come back with a bag full of souvenirs—red and blue shoe pins from Greece, little cloth dolls from Peru, and paper fans from Japan. My treasures. Each one a tiny window into a world that seemed so big and exciting, a world where you could go anywhere if you wanted. Joan made it seem possible, as though maybe one day I could also travel to those places, just like she did.

Joan never got married. She didn't need to. She was strong, like a superhero but without a cape. She'd say anything, even if it wasn't what you wanted to hear. Once, I heard her tell Ma, "Dot, let me lend you a blouse that doesn't look like you stole it from the Beverly Hillbillies. That look was never in style!" I laughed so hard. Ma didn't laugh. Ma didn't laugh at anything Joan said.

Ma wore those pink snap curlers in her hair every night, and during the day, it looked like a big wave on top of her head with curls bouncing everywhere. My aunt didn't have waves in her hair. Hers was straight, all the way down her back, the way everyone's hair was supposed to look, just like in the magazines. Joan was always put together, like she didn't care what anyone thought but still looked perfect. I saw how she loved herself, and she didn't seem to follow anyone else's rules. She made up her own. Even when we played board games. That was called cheating! I hoped that maybe one day I could be as tough as she was.

Sometimes Joan's words were a little scary. She didn't care what anyone thought. If she didn't like something, she'd say it. Loudly. She yelled at the TV, calling people "idiots" or "asses" when she disagreed with them. But when she liked something, she'd say that too, loudly and full of excitement. Joan didn't have a quiet voice.

She seemed to have strong feelings about everything, like there was no middle ground. She didn't sugarcoat things. But she wasn't just tough—she cared about the things that needed help. Like animals. Joan loved animals more than anything. I did too. She'd bring home stray cats and take care of them, even the ones who needed extra care. Ma didn't let us have anything with fur, nothing to snuggle. I could play with Joan's animals if we lived at Grandma's.

Joan worked with a big boss at Macmillan Publishing who owned racehorses. He named one of them after her—Miss Callahan. She showed me a picture of her standing next to the horse. That horse was beautiful, long-legged, and strong, just like Joan. It was the coolest thing ever.

I really wished we could live at Grandma's house.

Chapter 23

Brooklyn, New York, 1966

Growing up, we stuck to our block. Sometimes, while playing hide-and-seek, we would go around the corner, but that felt risky. Today I took the risk.

I found a good spot hidden in a small nook next to the entrance of a dilapidated shed. The kind of place you'd never notice. I squeezed myself into it, folding up like an origami crane, trying to disappear into the shadows. The sounds of the street were alive with the usual chaos—shouts, laughter, kids calling out as they found each other.

"Joey! I got Johnny! Nice try!" The voices echoed down the street, but they were already fading, the sounds muffling as the kids scattered in different directions.

After a while, the cold of the concrete began to seep through my pants, biting into my legs. I didn't move. I just sat there, glued in place, my breath shallow and quiet. The light was starting to shift—thickening, turning the air around me heavy and soft, like gauze. All around me was dark now, that deep gray that settled in just before the sky turned inky black.

I had won. They hadn't found me. But a feeling crept into my chest, and I couldn't shake it. Would anyone notice I was gone?

I sat still, the silence around me deep and consuming. Unfolding my arm, numb from being scrunched up too long, I stretched it out in front of me. My fingers grazed the air, but I could barely see them, like I was just a part of the shadows.

I thought of the playground. The one we never went to. Maybe they were there. Just a few blocks over, on the edge of Sunset Park, plopped under pylons holding up the highway that shut out the sun, sat the playground. A sad afterthought, no doubt checking off a box for lower-income recreation requirement to make some politician feel better. The playground was always gray, like a damp, dank, dreary day, the slides and rusted swings coated with a fine layer of grime. The lone tree, a sycamore, its trunk peeling like the paint in my apartment, shrugged its shoulders, arms drooping down. It was a place where it was hard to smile. I hardly ever went there.

But where was everyone? The longer I waited, the more I realized that no one had noticed. No one had called out for me; they hadn't even realized I was missing.

Then, just when the stillness felt like it was swallowing me whole, I heard it—Thomas's voice, calling my name, tight with fear.

"Joanne? Joanne, where are you?"

"Marco? Marco?" Voices echoed down the street, desperate, pleading for a response. Everyone was looking for Marco. They had noticed he wasn't around.

It was just a few weeks after the hide-and-seek game that a little boy went missing. The police combed the street searching for him. They knocked on every door to see if anyone knew or had seen anything. No one had.

Late that summer afternoon, as moms were rounding up their kids for supper, he was finally found in a vacant apartment up the block, locked inside a new refrigerator. He'd gone in to hide and couldn't get back out. The large cardboard box the refrigerator had come in sat by the curb for days after. So did his mother, weeping.

That fall when school started, I was eight, and my mother began taking night classes after work, so she was home even less. I was scared and wondered who might notice if I went missing.

After school, I came home, let myself in, and did my homework at the table in the front room. I saw Mrs. O'Leary out the window. She was heading out with her broom.

I loved Mrs. O'Leary. She made me think of what Grandma could be like if she were nice to me. Mrs. O'Leary was a grandma too. She owned the building we lived in. She always dressed in her frayed housedress topped with a faded cardigan sweater or a scratchy wool coat in the winter.

When it got cold and the fuel was delivered, Mrs. O'Leary was in charge. She told the pair of big burly men who funneled the flow of black coal down the chute to the boiler in the cellar what to do. Black soot floated in the air, sticking to everything. I watched from a distance so as not to get enveloped in the cloud of dust that rose up from the chute. She was no-nonsense, used to taking control.

I packed my papers up into my schoolbag, locked the door to the apartment, and ran out. Sneakers slapping on the floor, I pulled open the outside door.

"Mrs. O'Leary? Can I help you today?" I yelled, eyes pleading. I loved being with her; when I helped her, I always stuck close by.

"Of course, Joanne. I'll get you a broom." She smiled at me, though her eyes looked sad. "Have you had a snack yet?" she asked, as she pulled some Tootsie Rolls from her pocket.

My favorite thing to do was to help her sweep the front stoop and sidewalk. The rhythm of the broom, the soft bristles brushing against the concrete, was soothing. I swept one step at a time, until I hit the sidewalk, then one concrete square at a time, making sure each was free of dirt before moving to the next. It felt like an act of control. I craved that sense of order, that feeling of contained calm. She stood near me, her movements slow and deliberate. Although she never spoke much, I felt her kindness. She was a calm, quiet presence. I loved to help Mrs. O'Leary.

She offered me more than just praise for a shared chore. In a way, she offered me hope. She didn't ask for anything and didn't seem to need much. She took care of herself, just like I did. I admired that, maybe more than I realized at the time.

I remembered that no one had noticed I was missing that day—until Thomas finally did. That feeling stayed with me. That ache. The realization that disappearing came easy, and being found didn't. So I learned to make myself useful. To stay close. To sweep one square at a time. To find rhythm in repetition. To be helpful, quiet, controlled.

Years later, I walked into a different kind of storm—one filled with shouting, deals, ambition. I knew how to survive chaos. I'd trained for it since I was a kid.

Chapter 24

New York, New York, 1984

After the months of intense training came to an end in early 1984, I slid into a coveted spot: a seat on the Citiback Capital Markets Treasury bond trading desk. US government bonds were as close to risk-free as money gets, but that didn't mean the job was. I felt like I had stepped onto the high wire, with no net beneath me.

From the moment I walked onto the trading floor, it was sensory overload—a frenzy of shouting, cursing, flashing screens, a chorus of voices barking orders, and phones ringing and being thrown, either in frustration or to get someone's attention. Testosterone fogged the air like secondhand smoke. The room smelled faintly of coffee and strongly of ambition.

However, what seemed like a maelstrom of chaos was actually choreographed—as well as competitive, cutthroat, and precise. This was the Treasury Desk in the '80s. Not a place for the faint of heart.

No one cared that I was new. I rolled my chair forward in the trading pit, heart pounding. I was fresh meat in a sea of sharks. The air crackled. *How the hell had I made it here?*

Deals were done in the blink of an eye, sealed by a single word: "Done." Just like that. And with that one word, millions of dollars and securities changed hands. No contracts, no paperwork—just a word. A promise.

They put me on the short coupon desk—treasury notes with two years or less to maturity. Fast, relentless trades. My seat faced a wall of blinking lights—direct lines to brokers, other desks, rival firms. Hundreds of voices, all urgent, all competing. The two-year note trader, a seasoned veteran, showed me the ropes. His voice low and clipped, he introduced me to the brokers on the other end of the direct lines, most of them frat boys with connections, with fast mouths and faster fingers. They were the ones who matched sellers and buyers, executing trades at breakneck speed.

That morning, the economist had run through the numbers. The room buzzed with theories, traders pitching ideas, each one trying to nudge the herd. I learned quickly: Trust no one's confidence. Everyone was selling something, even their own certainty.

Seventeen traders. Three women.

I felt all of their eyes on me. The entire sales force, boring holes into me from their tiered seats, ready to pounce. I kept repeating to myself: "Price up, yield down, thirty-seconds, sixty-fourths, one-twenty-eighths," trying to burn the pricing structure of bonds into my brain. I couldn't afford any mistakes. Not here.

Then the Chicago futures market opened, and the games began. "Give me a bid on ten eight-and-a-quarters of Augie eighty-five!" The voice over the intercom crackled with urgency. My eyes darting back and forth as I checked the screens, I barked back a price within ten seconds. *Phew, first one done*, I thought, adrenaline surging through my veins.

"Done!" The first time I said it my mouth went dry. There was no undo button. No second chance. My word was all that mattered. Thankfully, I had perfected my poker face, having worn it so often growing up. It was like my second skin. My face looked calm, although inside my body adrenaline pounded like a monsoon on a tin roof.

I had just traded ten million dollars.

For a split second, I couldn't quite believe it. I couldn't even process it—*me*, trading ten million dollars. Before the day was over, I was moving hundreds of millions at a clip. And for the first time, I realized I was here. I had arrived.

There was no hand-holding. No apologies. No soft edges. I already knew the rules: Blend in, laugh at the jokes, never flinch, never fold. I'd been shape-shifting my whole life. Living in discomfort, adapting to my mother's ever-changing moods and others' expectations, blending in like a chameleon. This was just another skin to wear. I was unfazed.

Despite the challenges, I began to find my rhythm. Over time, I earned the respect of my colleagues, not through confrontation, but through competence and resilience. Looking back, those early days were a crucible, forging a strength I hadn't known I possessed. I had entered the program as an outsider, but I emerged as a force to be reckoned with.

And I liked it. I had earned my spot, and I didn't just survive, I thrived.

On the trading floor, I knew how to control the chaos. But I hadn't learned my fierce survival skills on Wall Street. Long before I barked bond prices or sealed multimillion-dollar deals with a single word, I stood in a cramped apartment in Brooklyn, dusting book spines and breathing in wood polish, hoping for a glance, a nod, or any flicker of praise from my mother.

Chapter 25

Brooklyn, New York, 1966

The pushcart rattled over the cracked sidewalk as I gripped the handle with both hands, the metal cool against my fingers. The air was sharp with the bite of autumn. Ma's coat flapped in the wind as she walked ahead of me, her eyes focused straight ahead like she was on a mission. She didn't say much, but in the way she handled everything you saw she didn't need anyone to take care of her—like me and Mrs. O'Leary. The part missing was the warmth, and I was determined to draw that out of her.

This was our Saturday routine, the A&P grocery run. Just the two of us. I stayed close, wanting to be near her. Ma hooked our push-cart to a shopping cart, then pushed open the door, and we headed down the first aisle in search of bargains. Her eyes shifted between the shelves and the list she had written in pencil before we left the apartment.

In Aisle 2, just past the produce section, where we only picked up potatoes, Eight O'Clock Coffee bags were stacked one behind the other in rows of red, yellow, and black. My mother always chose the red bag. She grabbed a box of Uncle Ben's Minute Rice and turned it over, checking the price. I watched her hands move. They seemed sure, unhesitating. I tried to be like that, knowing exactly what I was supposed to do.

My favorite part of the trip was checking out. The clerk, an old woman—but I guess everyone seemed old to me—decisively pushed buttons on the cash register to record the prices, then carefully placed each item in a paper bag. There was artistry in it. In went the six-pack of beer, then the cans of vegetables and the potatoes, then the pound package of chopped meat. "Can I help?" I begged, but Ma swatted my hand away from the counter. I loved the orderliness of packing. My life's goal was to be a grocery checkout clerk.

At the far end of the moving belt on the checkout counter stood an impressive-looking Atlantic & Pacific coffee grinder, gleaming stainless steel with bold red lettering. As the clerk pried open the bag of coffee beans to pour them into the wide dark mouth of the grinder, I leaned forward and inhaled deeply. Placing the bag underneath the spout, she pushed a button and, *grrrrrrr*, out spilled grinds, flooding the air with the glorious scent of coffee. It was magical.

"Mmmmm, that smells good," I murmured.

"Back up. You're too young for coffee," my mother said in a sharp voice.

Oh, no, I thought. *I don't want her to be mad at me.* I moved back quickly, catching the clerk wink at me, and lowered my gaze to the floor.

We stacked our bags in the pushcart with the beer on the bottom, as long skinny strips of S&H green stamps spat out of the register offering up dreams of a small appliance in our future.

Back at the apartment, as my mother unloaded the bags, I grabbed the S&H booklet. I wanted to stretch my time with her, with her acknowledging me, for as long as I could. As I licked the back of the stamps and lined them up in the empty spaces in the stamp book, I pored over the catalog that was a collection of treasures like toasters, punch bowls, tie clips, heating pads, watches, draperies, and toys. I got lost in the glories that might come, seeing a future full of possibilities that were just beyond our grasp.

Turning away from the kitchen, my mother put the radio on as she worked her way around the small apartment with a vacuum. Her tastes varied from the likes of Frank Sinatra and Tony Bennett to Elvis, the Philharmonic, and opera. Jonathan Schwartz was her favorite radio host. I liked the music—the sultry crooning, the lush instruments, and the occasional shot of rock 'n' roll.

I stuck nearby, shadowing her. Cautious and alert, I dusted as she vacuumed.

We had two short black wooden bookcases in the living room, matching the desk set in the front room where Thomas and I slept. I clutched a piece of a soft old T-shirt, sprayed just the right amount of Pledge on it, and dragged it across the tops of the book spines and under their lips, clearing away the week's worth of dust. The books—paperback mysteries and outdated Encyclopedia Britannica volumes—looked important to me.

I wondered where the dust came from, these tiny particles of dirt. They floated in the air, too small to be seen except when hit at a particular angle by the light, and then they'd dance in the rays of the sun that snuck in through the venetian blinds. I wondered how they got in with the windows closed and the door shut tight. So many questions swirled in my head, but that's where they stayed. I didn't want to bother Ma.

The scent of lemon lingered in the air as I stood back to admire my work, hoping for a moment of recognition from Ma, a smile, maybe even a word of praise. But that rarely happened. Instead I turned away from the quiet of the apartment to the outside, where the street could offer me the attention I craved.

Chapter 26

Brooklyn, New York, 1967

The street was my whole world when I was eight. Coming home from school, I threw my schoolbag in the apartment, changed out of my uniform, and raced down the stoop, eager to get outside. The block was alive with kids running and shouting. No one had any scheduled after-school activities or camps to go to.

For as long as I could remember, an empty lot sat across from our building, littered with rusted oil cans and broken car parts. Spiked iron rails, broken sections of a chain-link fence, and splintered chairs were strewn about at random, with rats playing tag. I wouldn't go in there alone. It was scary. On cold nights older kids made fires in oil drums and huddled around them roasting potatoes on sticks until the cops showed up and made them leave.

Last week, a few trucks pulled up to the curb. Big men with bulging arms, packs of cigarettes rolled up in their T-shirt sleeves, unloaded piles of wood into the lot. A group of us kids sat on the stoop watching every move. Finally, one of the boys shouted, "Hey, guys, what are you doing over there?" "Buildin' a house," one of them yelled back.

Stunned into silence, our jaws dropped in amazement. We were shocked. *Incredible.* A whole house, just for one family. I couldn't believe it—a house with its own garage, like something on TV.

Next to the house being built sat a shoe repair shop run by an ancient Italian man, his back a question mark, who spoke no English, weaving stitches with his weathered hands splotched and smelling of leather oil. And then, a pharmacy with a bell that clanged when the door opened, offering a rush of rare and welcome air-conditioning that hit your nose with that weird drugstore smell, with hints of camphor and liniments.

And now there'd be a house. A real house.

Chapter 27

Brooklyn, New York, 1967

Just as this house would be different from all the other buildings, I always knew Ma was different from the other moms on the block. She worked, and none of the others did. Ma didn't have a husband anymore, while they all did. We never ever talked about Da, but I really missed him.

Sometimes Ma told us stories about Grandma and her childhood. Grandma was a seamstress before she married my grandfather, a handsome, charming Irish American man who dragged behind him his own bag of horrors. My grandfather grew up in an orphanage, born to a mother who as a child left Ireland, and who as an adult left her children at a Catholic orphanage like a load of dry cleaning that she never reclaimed, leaving them to grow up on their own.

Against all odds, Ma said he grew into a man of warmth, so much so that it was only in speaking of him that my mother, a person who didn't seem capable of affection or of speaking well of anyone, lit up.

Every once in a while, after she had a few whiskeys, she'd talk about her dad. Her eyes would glimmer, the edges turning down as she spoke. She loved her father, which was confusing as she didn't appear to love anyone else.

"All the kids on the street would come sit on our stoop when they saw my dad outside. He was like the pied piper, regaling us with stories true and made up, entertaining us for hours."

"Tell us more about him," I begged, hoping to keep her talking to us. Peggy shuffled closer, and Thomas looked up expectantly.

"He was a great man," she began, voice getting quieter, her gaze glassy. "He volunteered for World War I when he was thirty, a lieutenant with the New York Fire Department. He didn't have to enlist; he was old for the war. His fire station was in Lower Manhattan. His crew was one of the ones that witnessed the horror of the Triangle Shirtwaist factory fire in the spring of 1911, when close to one hundred fifty souls were lost."

"Anyway," she said, already losing the strength to continue, her mind clearly far away. "He wrote a bunch of letters when he was in the war to a woman here in New York. Although he barely graduated from high school, his letters were magnificent. They are in the Library of Congress."

Peggy, Thomas, and I caught each other's eyes, trying hard not to giggle. By now we were used to Ma making things up, like telling us about the great stuff we did as a family that never happened, or swearing she never said she wanted to shoot herself while she was in one of her moods. She said anything to make herself look better. We were used to that, but this was ridiculous. *The Library of Congress! No way*, I thought.

She got melancholy when she spoke of her brothers. Ma's two older brothers, born just thirteen months apart, fought in the next war, World War II. One came home, one didn't. The eldest, John, arrived at his brother Charlie's base in England one December day in 1944 to surprise him, but missed him by just a few minutes, only to see the wings of Charlie's bomber lift off the runway on a mission. It turned out to be his last.

Charlie was shot down over Germany, his whereabouts unknown for a long time. My grandfather, having survived the trenches in France in World War I, was all too familiar with the horrors the Germans inflicted on their prisoners. He tortured himself with every imaginable scenario of what his son might be enduring. When the dreaded knock on the door came months later, bringing confirmation of Charlie's death, it was, in a way, a relief. But my grandfather never recovered. His heart stopped beating a few years later, worn down by grief. My mother was only twenty-one.

I learned that the weight of the loss smothered what remained of her family. The flames of hope and possibilities were snuffed out, leaving behind the cold ashes of grief. With my grandmother unable to offer much comfort, my mother turned inward, swallowing her dreams. My mother passed that silence to me. The air in our apartment felt thin, like something was missing.

But just outside our apartment, life had a different rhythm. Our block pulsed with energy, loud and unpredictable, with scraped knees, bottle caps, and the click of jump ropes against the pavement. And right down the hall, there was Jane—my best friend, my escape, my safe place.

Chapter 28

Brooklyn, New York, 1967

Jane's door was next to the cream-colored marble stairs, treads worn smooth and gently sloped like the indent of a woman's waist. We were two peas in a pod—tomboys who stuck together and played with the boys on the bottom half of the block. The kids up the block were mostly Puerto Rican, while down the block we were mostly Irish. We never mixed, except for an occasional bottle fight in the alley.

Jane and I sat on the steps to the alley, lighting matches we stole from her dad's nightstand, the swoosh of sulfur catching fire fueling our adrenaline rush. As we melted wax, dripping it into bottle caps to play skellzies in the middle of the street, we debated which game we wanted to play. Skellzies entailed flicking your middle finger against your thumb, shooting bottle caps around a grid drawn with chalk in the middle of the street. We had to duck between the parked cars when cars came barreling down the street, but that just made it more fun.

"If a lot of the boys are around, we could play Wiffle ball or stoopball," Jane said.

"Yeah, but only if they have a ball with them. Or we could do leapfrog or hide-and-seek," I suggested.

On Sixty-First Street, we spent hours playing ring-a-levio, red light–green light, hit the penny, and buck, buck, how many horns are up. Sometimes we even got the boys to play jump rope and hopscotch with us. And we were always hopping over chain-link fences as we were chased by the building supers, who suspected us of doing shady stuff in the back alleys.

The afternoon stretched on, and the humid air sat thick on top of us. One of the builders from across the street walked over, muscles bulging, sweat drenching his shirt, and wrestled open the Johnny pump. That's what we called the fire hydrant.

"Yay!" The shouts of glee were deafening, drowning out the *slap-slap* of the sneakers on the pavement. Everyone came running from all sides, even the teenagers, flocking to the gush of water like moths to a flame. We all ran through and around the thick jet of water, shrieking in joy and getting soaked to the skin. It was the best afternoon. The only thing that could possibly make it better was the jingle of the Mister Softee truck coming down the block. Then we scattered, yelling to our mothers for ice cream money.

The very best days of all were when the trucks with the rides came down the block, pulling along a portable amusement park. For a dime, you could spin around on the Whip or swing back and forth on a pirate ship.

The next Saturday morning it rained, and Jane invited me to play in her apartment. As always, her father sat in his brown faux-leather Barcalounger, reading the sports pages and sipping coffee out of his NY Yankees mug.

We were playing a new game Jane had gotten for her birthday called Twister. When we flicked the spinner, it whirled and clacked, and our limbs twisted and tangled as we tried to stay upright. In the chaos, we collided, collapsing in a tumble and a blast of laughter.

Jane scrambled to her feet, brushing herself off as she headed to the kitchen to get us a snack. As she passed by, her dad grabbed her by the waist, pulling her onto his lap and tickling her. She squealed, laughing and protesting, both of them descending into a fit of giggles.

The middle of my forehead hurt. I tried hard not to look but my eyes kept returning to him. I didn't want to stare but I was unable to look away, like a dog eyeing a bone he knew he couldn't have. I wondered whose lap I would sit on now.

Jane's father looked up every once in a while and flashed a smile that caused my stomach to swirl with confusion. I wasn't used to being smiled at, let alone by a man, never mind a dad. It felt nice though, like *maybe* this was how things were supposed to be. Even better than playing with Jane those days was knowing her dad was nearby.

Chapter 29

Coney Island, New York, 1967

A few days later, the sun burst out, shoving the clouds aside and spreading its warmth on the city. My mother took a bunch of kids from the block to the beach, to a world far removed from the cozy, quiet moments at Jane's house. I wish I could say the joy of that beach day was uncomplicated, but with my mother, nothing ever was.

The subway lurched aboveground, clattering onto the elevated tracks that separated neighborhoods. Light flooded the car, and the air was sharp, salty, filled with the promise of freedom. I gripped the sweaty steel pole, steadying myself against the jolts. Danny, from the building next door, a scrawny blond kid with a voice deep as the sea, slipped to the center of the car, wrapping one wiry arm around the pole. A grin stretched across his face as if this moment was made for him.

The train wheels screeched, part of the city's chaotic symphony. Danny cleared his throat dramatically. Then, puffing out his chest, he belted out an impressive rendition of "Hello, Dolly!" Passengers blinked, startled, then burst into hoots and hollers, cheering along.

"Sing it, kid!" a man in a Mets cap shouted.

We laughed, giddy with anticipation. The trip to Coney Island felt magical. Swapping asphalt and concrete for sand and surf. When the train finally pulled into Stillwell Avenue Station, its gears grinding and squeaking, we tumbled out, hauling coolers, striped umbrellas, and canvas bags bursting with towels. My mother led the way, a general marshaling her troops. Kids, some from our block and others we barely knew, trailed behind, each carrying something. It was known in the neighborhood that any kid was welcome to come to the beach with us. "Stay together!" she barked over her shoulder.

The boardwalk shimmered in the heat, its planks worn smooth by generations of feet. It ran the length of the beach, home to mom-and-pop shops hawking plastic souvenirs, miniature versions of New York landmarks, and hats of all kinds—Yankee and Mets baseball caps; tall, felt multicolored Dr. Seuss hats; even cotton bonnets decked with riotous flowers. We traipsed past candy stores, palm readers, and magic shops. We passed the fortune teller encased in glass, her turbaned head nodding mechanically as coins clinked into the brass slot. I wondered what future she'd spit out for me on her small square of paper.

The wooden planks ran diagonally from stores to sand. Humid summer air hung heavy with the greasy smells of fried clams, taffy, Shatzkin's knishes, burgers, hot dogs, fries, and slices of New York's finest pizza. There was puffy pink cotton candy with its sugary tease, dozens of flavors of Italian ices, and ice-cold sodas in huge paper cups. Our bellies rumbled as we raced by, eager to flex our toes in the sand. Families lined up for the Parachute Jump, the Cyclone roller coaster, and penny arcades with skeet balls and water rifles for squirting at balloons. And there were bathhouses with signs reading "For Your Pleasure." We were at Coney Island, the Riviera for low-income Brooklynites—home to Steeplechase Amusement Park and the world-renowned Nathan's Annual Hot Dog Eating Contest. Sweet scents, sour smells, bright flashing lights in every color of the rainbow, and barking voices trying to rope in customers all battled for our attention.

The sand burned our feet as we claimed a patch of beach, spreading out our blankets like flags staking territory. The frayed red quilt, part of the patchwork of fabrics in a potpourri of colors and patterns, looked like a page in a stamp collector's binder. Blankets and towels lay so close to each other they almost touched, forcing us to walk single file. As we settled in, I looked around and noticed all the dads—tossing footballs, lifting their kids above the waves, and cracking jokes as they rubbed sunscreen onto freckled shoulders. There were so many. I missed my da.

We built castles, dug moats, and let the sun bake our skin. My mother sat upright, watchful but distant, feet half-buried in sand, her attention drifting somewhere beyond the waves.

A sharp whistle cut through the air, piercing the screeches of children playing. The lifeguard nearest to us, a kid of maybe sixteen, just starting to sprout hints of facial hair, screamed "Floater! Floater!" He leaped from the high white lifeguard's chair and raced frantically toward the ocean, kicking up sand in his wake. So did we—all twelve of us kids who had come to Coney Island that morning, shepherded by my mother. We scrambled toward the water, deserting the castle we were building, to see what was happening.

It came closer, propelled by the rhythm of the surf, bobbing up with each wave. A large globe shape was discernible, almost translucent in the glaring sun, pearly white with a tinge of pale blue, like a robin's egg just before the baby bird cracks its way out. But this was no sign of birth. It was the bloated body of a middle-aged man, dead. He was spat up onto the sand with a final push of the sea. Women screamed and sobbed; lifeguards surrounded the corpse. "Get back!

Get back!" they yelled, directing people in the deepest voices they could muster.

We stood frozen, a cluster of wide eyes and pounding hearts, until my mother's voice cut through. "Come on," she said, not unkindly.

We stumbled back to the red blanket where my mother sat, her face a blank. She opened the cooler and began handing out sandwiches without a word. Peanut butter and jelly with gritty sand stuck between the bread. Liverwurst with relish slick with warmth. We ate in silence.

My mother's lips were drawn tightly into a thin dash, as if underscoring her refusal to speak of what we'd just witnessed. She didn't flinch or falter, just chewed methodically, as if swallowing every terrible thing she refused to say.

I stole glances at her face, searching for a crack in that stoic mask. Nothing. Just the rhythmic crinkle of plastic bags and the hum of distant carnival rides. Whatever thoughts she had, whatever memories clawed at her from the past, she buried them deep. That day lingered, not in words but in heavy silence, our questions swallowed whole like waves returning to the sea.

I knew better than to ask. But I wanted to. The words clawed at my throat. *Did it remind her of the morning the cop knocked on our door? Of the moment her world shattered?* I imagined that knock echoing in her head, louder than the lifeguard's whistle had been today. I wanted to ask if she ever thought about Da, if she missed him. *Did his absence gnaw at her the way it did me?* But I knew better. Instead, I took another bite of my sandwich, the taste flat and gritty. The sea breeze tugged at her hair, shaking it loose, but she didn't flinch, didn't move. Her silence was a fortress I had learned not to breach. So I sat beside her, my questions swallowing themselves whole, flat and gritty like the sandwich, while the waves carried away everything we wouldn't say.

The day dragged on, heat heavy on our skin. I could hold my bladder only so long; I didn't want to pee in the ocean. Ma sent me up to the squat cinder block buildings by the boardwalk that housed the toilets. "Jane, come with me to the bathroom!" I pleaded, reaching for her hand. I didn't want to go up there alone.

Deep in shadows smelling of urine, disturbed lonely men with grizzled faces greeted us, offering a peek at their sad shriveled dicks, suggesting various things they'd like to do with us. "Hey sweetie. Want to touch this?" We scurried past, hoping the stench of their sickness didn't stick to us. We didn't mention it to my mother.

We stopped for Italian ices on the way home—little balls of heaven scooped into pleated paper cups. The tart taste of lemon and the sweet swirls of rainbow flavors dancing on my tongue. My mother quietly looked around to see if there were any kids who didn't have an ice, as there were always a few without money. "Hey, what kind do you guys like?" she asked, and just like that their hands were wrapped around a cup. A quiet act of kindness you'd miss if you blinked, her face softening for just a moment.

By the time the subway rumbled back underground, the smell of salt fading into steel and soot, the questions inside me remained heavy, unanswered. My mother sat with her hands folded, eyes fixed on the window as darkness swallowed the light. She never spoke of that body, and neither did I. Some things, I learned, were meant to be buried deep. I was becoming a great secret keeper.

Chapter 30

Brooklyn, New York, 1967

No other adult ever came on these trips to the beach. Ma was almost always alone. She drank alone in our apartment, usually cheap beer, sometimes whiskey. She never socialized with the neighbors or other parents. Maybe that was easier for her. Unwilling to let anyone get close to her, unwilling to face the personal questions that might be posed, to be forced to speak of what had happened. To be judged. *Who knew?* I tiptoed around her, ducking and weaving as if in a never-ending boxing match.

She acted superior, as if the women around her—those housewives, those "lesser" creatures—could never understand her. You could feel the eye roll she'd suppress as they discussed their children or their husbands, poking holes in their happiness with a sneer. "They have no idea what they're blabbing about," she'd say as she shut the door to our apartment, her tone dripping with disdain. "They're all idiots. They don't know what real life is."

Our apartment was a minefield. I tiptoed through the rooms, never knowing when it was safe or when things were about to blow up. Sometimes it was quiet—too quiet, like when you're holding your breath in a scary movie, waiting for the monster to pounce. Then the monster *would* appear.

Some days, her meanness was a sharp, cutting blade, an icy chill that would slice through the room without warning. Her words came at us like shards of jagged glass, leaving us reeling. "Why can't you do anything right?" she'd snap, her face twisted with an emotion I couldn't quite name but that made my bones hurt. She'd hiss at us, her voice low and venomous, eyes narrowing with a viciousness that said she'd rip you apart if you so much as looked at her the wrong way. It didn't matter if the crime was crumbs on the kitchen table or a school uniform not put away. We never knew what would set her off—just that when she exploded, everything in her path shattered.

There were days when it felt like her anger had been building for years, fed by resentment and pride, bitterness seeping from every word, every glance.

But just as quickly as the storm would hit, the shift would happen. I believe she wanted acknowledgment, wanted someone to see the weight she carried, but she'd never ask for it. Instead, she let her bitterness hang there, like an accusation. "None of you appreciate what I do for you," she'd mutter, self-pity drenching her accusation. She played the martyr, accusing us of taking her for granted, but pushing away anyone who got too close. Her bitterness was so thick it stifled any chance of warmth. She was simultaneously a hero and a victim, but neither role seemed to bring her the peace she so desperately sought.

And we, her children, were caught in the crossfire, trying to survive her shifting moods. I tried hard to navigate her fury in a vain search for love. I tried to navigate the chaos, to hold out hope that if I just got it right, if I just did the right thing, maybe she would love me. Many times I stood watching her, knowing deep down that nothing would ever change, yet still I'd try to make the paper towels we used for napkins look nice by folding them, hoping she'd notice. I'd put the sneakers into a straight line so the hallway looked neat. I'd scrub the toothpaste out of the sink, trying to be helpful. But no matter what I did, her storms rolled in just the same, sudden and punishing.

But it seemed she was aware, on some level in the elevator of her mind, of these gaping emotional deficiencies. She'd pull a veil of normalcy over us whenever others were gazing in our direction. She held up a screen obfuscating our dysfunctional reality.

A thin veneer of respectability surrounded us. We projected an image of normalcy. We were clean. We were dressed. We were fed. Clearly, she had a blueprint of how things should be, but she only unfurled it when necessary.

She sat at the kitchen table, the fluorescent light buzzing overhead, grading the stack of papers spread before her. I watched her as I did my homework. After getting a master's degree from her night classes, she became a reading teacher in struggling schools, and every morning drove the Volkswagen to Bed-Stuy and Fort Greene, underprivileged neighborhoods in Brooklyn, to help kids who had learning challenges. As she rustled through the pages, she spoke of their struggles, her sympathy evident. She described how they'd sit in her office and how she'd listen, offering words of comfort, a gentle hand on the shoulder.

Hearing her speak hurt like a weight crushing my heart. *How could she show them such care and empathy? Did it not occur to her that I needed her to take an interest in me? To ask about my fears, my hopes? Even just how my day went? My grades?* The space between us remained as vast as the ocean. She looked up from her papers, proud of herself, her story, and looked right through me.

It was the same with everything. She dismissed not only my emotional needs but my physical ailments as well. One morning as I knelt, doubled over the toilet, puking my guts up, she called out over her shoulder, "You're fine. I'm leaving. You're not sick. Get yourself together so you're not late for school," and let the door slam behind her. I hated her telling me I was fine when I clearly wasn't. My mother, sympathetic to her struggling students, within our own lives locked shut the door to her heart, unable to muster a scintilla of kindness or affection for her children. Over time, her profound neglect steadily eroded any shred of hope I had of being seen.

I wondered if she even realized what she was doing. Could she feel the gulf between us? Was it intentional? What kept her from offering us the care that was so easily offered to others? I sat in the corner, watching her at the kitchen table, poring over a pile of papers, hoping she'd see me too. And whatever thoughts she had about the dead body that bubbled up to the surface, she kept buried, never speaking to me about what I had seen.

Chapter 31

Brooklyn, New York, 1967

One evening just before the start of school, as the sands of summer were swept away, the street hummed with the last breath of heat. After the suppers of meatloaf and mashed potatoes, Chef Boyardee ravioli, canned franks 'n' beans, and tuna casserole had been cleared, the amber light sat low in the sky and the streetlights buzzed to life. The sky shifted from crepe-paper blue to a sultry, deep azure, tinged violet at the edges. Parents perched on stoops sipping cold cans of Pabst Blue Ribbon, trying to escape the heat. We played tag, racing around, shrieks of joy piercing the layer of humidity that stuck to us like glue.

A few months had passed since the family of eight moved into the new house across the street from my bedroom window. They spoke only Spanish and mostly played with each other in their backyard. But tonight, the younger kids, laughing and breathless, took turns jumping rope on the sidewalk, their sneakers tapping rhythmically against the cracked pavement. One of the older girls adjusted her ponytail, her eyes watching the younger ones as they tumbled over each other in playful chaos. A quiet smile tugged at her lips, the kind that spoke of the comfort found in their new life, in their new house, on this new street.

A car came barreling down the street, a chocolate brown sedan, its tires screeching as it skidded to a halt right in front of the house. The driver's side door whipped open, and a man bolted out, his face tight with rage. It was their dad—he never came home this early. He charged up the steps to the house, past his kids playing on the sidewalk.

The shot popped like the snap of a whip, silencing all, including the woman's screams. He flew down the stairs, hopped into the car, and was gone as quickly as he had come.

When his wife had met him at the top of the stairs, he shot her in the face.

The street was still. Too still. Silent.

Everything felt heavy and suffocating. Her blood dripped down to the sidewalk, step by step, a steady little stream rolling over, keeping time with the final beats of her heart.

And then came the kids' screams—frantic and raw, like small animals being ripped to shreds. I couldn't move, frozen in the horror of it all. My chest tightened and my breath grew shallow, as my eyes remained glued to her body, crumpled and lifeless on the steps. The world felt like it had stopped spinning. Now the only sounds were the *drip-drop* of her blood, the kids crying, and my own breath, raspy and thin.

The crowd on the street slowly shifted, still hushed, rearranging itself into close family clusters. Children were clutched tightly by their parents, life rafts in a churning sea.

The murmurs began rippling through the crowd, low whispers mumbled by the women. "She was sleeping with another man. He found out."

I found my way to our stoop and sat down next to my mother. My brother and sister came over too, squeezing between us on the step below. We huddled, pushing our bodies against hers. "Ma. Ma," we said softly, seeking comfort and protection. Anything. "Ma," I whispered, desperate for her to pull us close, to tell us it was going to be okay. That she'd keep us safe. I was only eight, and my Da had been gone two years. I really needed her to comfort me.

She didn't move. Her face stayed still, blank. Her arms folded tight across her chest. Silence wrapped around us like barbed wire.

I sat there, staring at the pool of blood that had formed on the sidewalk. My thoughts were all mixed up. How quickly people can disappear—just be gone. Da had been with me one minute, hugging me as he walked out the door, and then—nothing. Gone forever.

The evening bled into a hot sweaty night, with swarms of mosquitoes circling, searching for prey. I thought about Tony and the boy up the block—how they'd just vanished, like they'd never existed in the first place. My da and the man at the beach. And now this woman across the street, gone, shot down in an instant.

I shivered, in spite of the heat. The terror of it was overwhelming. I felt a terrible pressure, a hard rock in my chest.

Hours passed before the dark van marked NEW YORK CITY MEDICAL EXAMINER pulled up. Men with gloved hands placed the dead woman's body into a black rubber bag, the grating pull of the zipper echoing in my bones. The van drove off, leaving the air thick with a sadness so deep it felt like the stars had gone out.

My head swirled with the horror of the blood, the body, the bag. I didn't know what I was supposed to do. The screams stayed wrapped around me, pressing into my ears, my chest, my bones. The horrifying high-pitched screams of the six kids ricocheted in my ears. I knew those screams. It was the sound of having no one, of realizing the world won't catch you when you fall. My heart broke apart again.

Chapter 32

Brooklyn, New York, 1967

That summer rolled to a close, and school started again without Da. School felt like a safe place, a place where I could be good at something and be noticed. I was ready for fourth grade. Math, spelling, reading—I found them easy, and people noticed.

Standing in front of the school gates waiting to be dismissed, I was jarred by the sight of Ma rounding the corner. I was lined up with my class, finally being sent home after having been kept late because one of the boys clapped the erasers inside the classroom.

Normally she wasn't home yet. My stomach dropped, and a bit of dread crept up my spine. Had something bad happened? She had never before come to pick me up at school. Maybe her class was canceled.

I could sense the smoke rising from her as she got closer. She had that small smile on her face, the one that didn't reach her eyes. My ears started ringing. *Oh, no.* I cringed, knowing rage was about to erupt. The fake smile, the tight shoulders, the crisp tap of her walk. Mrs. Corrigan turned her head as my mother's hand touched her shoulder from behind. "Oh, hello," she said kindly, unaware of what awaited her. I braced for what was about to happen. I wanted to disappear, to be swallowed up by the sidewalk.

"Are you the teacher?' my mother asked, the calm before the storm. We hadn't yet had our parent-teacher conference.

"Yes, I am." Mrs. Corrigan responded with a smile.

"Well, clearly you shouldn't be! What the hell is wrong with you? How dare you keep my daughter late without letting me know! Don't you dare ever pull a stupid stunt like that again!" she spat, her voice full of venom. The kids looked on, terrified. She grabbed my hand and stormed off, as other parents began arriving.

I was embarrassed and confused. Normally my mother would never have known I was kept late since she was never home this early. *Hmmm, maybe she did care*, I wondered. *Maybe she was worried about me.*

No, that was not the case. Her anger had nothing to do with being concerned about me. It was just about her. "I'm so mad I had to walk up to school to get you," she snapped, only angry about being inconvenienced.

A few days later I was home alone. Ma came home and saw I had spilled some milk on the kitchen floor and off she went, exploding again.

"What the hell did you do? You are useless. You can't do anything right! I am sick of this, you, all of this!" After exploding and screaming at the top of her lungs, she retreated to her room. She reappeared, having packed a suitcase, and headed for the door. She had done this before, and it terrified me. Panic shut down my lungs and sped up my heart. I lunged forward to grab hold of her. I didn't want to be left alone again. I threw myself on the floor and clung to her lower leg, clutching desperately, as she dragged me prostrate across the floor of the apartment, my knees skinned, begging her not to go.

"Please, please don't leave me. I promise I'll do anything, better than ever. Pleeeease," I pleaded, hysterical. I didn't want to lose Ma too. But my begging fell on deaf ears. She didn't utter a single word. She picked my arms off her leg like specks of lint and walked out the door, the door slam echoing in the marble hallway.

I dropped down on the floor and wept, sobbing until my eyes ran dry. Stillness slowly lowered itself on top of me like a weighted blanket, the ticking of the kitchen clock the only sound. Curled into a ball, the rug scratching my legs, I lay there, finally realizing no one was coming to help me.

From now on you're going to have to take care of yourself kept repeating in my head. I thought I had been doing a good job at it. But I guessed it wasn't good enough.

Time passed. I pulled myself off the floor, moving to the window to peer out between the blinds, to see if she was coming back. Thomas and Peggy still weren't home yet. Growing tired, my mind wandered, thinking that maybe Joan would worry if I didn't come for dinner on Sunday. Maybe she'd come get me then. Maybe she'd keep me.

Hours later, Ma came back. She didn't say a word to me. She didn't need to. Her silence said it all. It was as if it never happened, as if I hadn't just been abandoned by the one person who was supposed to stay.

Something inside of me went still. A part of me stopped hoping; instead, it started to get filled with resolve. I told myself I'd be all right, no matter what. I knew I had to prepare for more. More of her mood swings, her anger, her withdrawals. For the next time she might leave, or the next time she might come back. I tried to keep my distance—physically and emotionally. I tried harder to stay quiet when she was angry, to wait for the storm to pass. I tried to shrink even more and lock away my feelings. It was easier that way. I wasn't sure it was possible, however, to become any more invisible than I already felt.

From now on, you're going to have to take care of yourself circled round and round in my head. I stopped hoping for her to take care of me at all. I'd try hard not to rely on her for anything.

I realized that I might have been better off if she hadn't returned.

Chapter 33

Brooklyn, New York, 1968

It was a few months later when the door clicked shut behind me as I stepped inside, the quiet of the empty apartment swallowing me whole. I wasn't scared, not anymore. The scar of my mother's departure that day was still apparent, but it was softer now. Not gone, just dulled. Peggy wouldn't be home until supper, so I was on my own again. I was used to it.

I sat on my bed debating which new book to start—Nancy Drew or Trixie Belden—when I heard my brother barge in, sparks of excitement shooting off him. "Look, look! Look what I can do!" he gushed, unspooling his fingers, flexing his white knuckles, to show me an M-80, a serious firecracker. "I've been practicing in the alley and can light it and put the wick out before it goes off," he bragged, his face flushed, grinning.

I acted aloof but was really dying of curiosity. I walked into the living room, sat in my mother's chair, the plaid one with tan piping and the skirt that hid its legs, and said, "Show me."

Thomas pulled a pack of matches from his pants pocket, hands shaking just a bit, and struck one. The rush of sulfur as it caught flame, *swoosh*, whizzed by my ears, and its bitter smell filled the air. He quickly licked his thumb and forefinger to snuff out the flame, but the fire kept eating the wick. The flame crawled down the length of the fuse.

Panicking, with eyes as wide as dinner plates, he dropped the M-80 on the rug—the murky green eight-by-ten that Ma had bought with S&H green stamps—and turned his head away just as it blew up. It burned a hole straight through to the wooden floor.

The boom echoed through the hallway of the apartment building, bouncing off the marble floors and walls. The explosion was earsplitting. Momentarily paralyzed and deaf, we looked like cartoon characters, hands over our ears and lips frozen into little round *O*'s. Yet there was not a single knock at the door. No one bothered to check on us, not even after that blast.

Thomas started to freak out, breathing heavily like he was about to have one of his asthma attacks. Panic gnawed at my stomach, and my eyes darted between my brother, who looked like he might pass out, and the hole in the rug.

We had to fix it. Had to cover it up.

Not wanting to suffer the wrath of Ma, we panicked. This would be *bad*. I was never sure if the stupid stuff that made her mad would make us disposable like Da. Or would she simply leave us forever, like he did? Terrified, Thomas and I leaped into action.

Ears ringing, hearts pounding, we knelt to inspect the rug. It was ruined. Being only nine and twelve, we weren't very strong, but the adrenaline that was pumping through our bodies worked in our favor. We tugged the furniture, hands scrambling, dragging it off the rug to one side. We wrestled the rug from under the legs of the couch and recliner, grabbing a corner of it and yanking it around in a circle. We pushed and pulled, moving the chair over the hole, hoping she wouldn't realize we had changed anything.

An hour later, the key rattled in the lock and the door squeaked as she pushed it open. We froze. Thomas and I, heads bowed low, pretended to be engrossed in homework. We didn't dare breathe. She went straight into her little bedroom without a word. We heard her grunt as she dropped her bags on the bed. Our ears on high alert, we heard her yanking on the door of the metal closet, hangers rattling. She reappeared a few minutes later, and we tensed up. She had changed into one of her usual faded floral housedresses. She strode into the kitchen, donned her apron, and started pulling food from the refrigerator to start supper.

We could barely stand the suspense. We held our breath. Finally, she turned, glancing through the living room to acknowledge us, nodding silently. She paused, like a pointer sniffing out birds in the brush. We were stiff with fear. Her head turned slowly, eyes scanning the room. A slight hint of sulfur still hung in the air, or maybe it was the smell of fear. Would she notice the couch was an inch or so to the right of where it had been when she left in the morning? Would she see the indents made by the feet of the furniture, now exposed?

Her eyes finally settled on us. We could feel them without looking up.

She said nothing. Silence sat heavy and frightening, like an abandoned tombstone.

We never knew if she noticed and just chose not to address it. There was so much she never seemed to notice. There was so much she never addressed. Like how miserable we all were.

Chapter 34

Brooklyn, New York, 1969

It was a humid evening in July, when I was ten, that my mother dropped the bombshell, her voice casual as she passed the peas across the table. She found a way to add to our misery.

"We're moving," she announced, as though it was just another bit of conversation. "In three weeks."

The fork slid from my hand, clattering onto the plate. "What?! Why? Three weeks! Where are we going?"

"To the top floor of a two-family house owned by someone I know from church. It's on Seventy-Second Street. We'll have more space than we have here."

"Seventy-Second Street? That's so far away! What about school? What about our friends?" Thomas, Peggy, and I spoke over each other, frantic.

Ma's tone remained matter-of-fact. "Peggy, you'll keep going to Bishop Kearney; Thomas, you'll take the bus back to finish your last year at O.L.P.H. before you go to high school. Joanne, you'll switch schools."

The announcement was like a gut punch. She just dropped this on us without any discussion. She didn't ask or care how we felt.

"I don't want to go to Catholic school anymore!" I blurted out, desperate for some victory in this nightmare.

"You are," she said firmly.

"But Da's gone, and he was the one who wanted it. *He* was the Catholic. The nuns said you're going to hell because you're Lutheran. So why do you care?"

Silence took a seat at the table. The three of us didn't dare breathe. It was a risky move to poke the bear. Would you face the storm or the silence?

She surprised us this time. Maybe it was the thought of saving money that swayed her.

"Fine, you can go to public school if you want," she said. "Now start packing. We're out of here in three weeks."

I stood in the hallway, hugging a box labeled "Joanne's Stuff," watching two sweaty men hoist the old black couch up the narrow stairs. Ma was at the top, arms crossed, directing them. "Living room is that way. Watch the walls!"

I hated leaving our old neighborhood. I felt like I was leaving parts of myself there in the scuffs on the linoleum floor. Leaving behind the place where I could still see the shadow of Da. But Ma insisted this place was nicer, that this was "a step up."

Unpacking, I searched, glancing around, for any trace of my father. A photo, a trinket. The only thing that remained was the wooden humidor that had sat on his desk. She left the rest of him behind.

Thomas got his own room by claiming the small one just off the living room, facing the street. It had a window and a door he used to shut himself off from everyone. He slammed the door when the movers left, locking it shut. Ma said nothing; she just kept unpacking.

For a while after the move, Thomas went back to the old block every day after school, sitting on our stoop for hours before finally taking the bus home in time for supper. After a few months of this, one of the mothers from the old neighborhood noticed and grew concerned. She called Ma, suggesting that Thomas might need someone to talk to. But Ma didn't listen. We never had anyone to talk to. And that didn't change.

A lot did change, but so much stayed the same. No one was ever looking out for us on Sixty-First Street, and that didn't change on Seventy-Second Street. Neither place was a "home"—all I ever felt was rejection radiating from both places. I was there because I had no choice. There was food and there was a bed. An actual bed now. The cot was left behind on Sixty-First Street.

That year was a turning point, one full of changes we never saw coming. After one of the women from the old block called about Thomas, Ma made him come straight home. He did, but he was different. His face was closed off, like he was hiding behind some kind of wall I couldn't climb. He didn't even say hello. He'd just walk past me without a glance, his jaw tight, eyes focused ahead like he was seeing something only he could understand. He used to talk to me and hang out with me, but he didn't anymore. When I tried to ask him about it, he just brushed me off, his voice sharp, like he was trying to push me away without saying it out loud. Day after day, he'd shut himself in his room, locking me out.

By the following summer, I realized he had started dealing drugs. I was heading into junior high, and he was starting high school. He started with pot and hash, but it didn't stop there. Soon, it was pills, cocaine, anything he could get his hands on. Kids in the new neighborhood who had barely acknowledged his existence were suddenly flocking to him. The power he held was palpable, and I could feel it in the way they looked at him—like he was someone to be admired, feared, maybe even envied.

Every evening after supper while Ma sat on the couch, a cold can of beer in her hand, watching game shows, tendrils of smoke slowly curled under Thomas's bedroom door, swirling around the living room. You couldn't avoid smelling the earthy, pungent odor of weed. She'd crinkle her nose, but she never said a word. She just sipped her beer.

Maybe she was too drunk. Or too stoned. Or too scared.

Thomas was no longer the chubby kid who used to buy pants in the husky section at Robert Hall's anymore. He shot up, taller than Ma, and his shoulders got wide, while his voice got deep and gruff. He was fourteen but acted older, slamming doors hard when he got mad. I wondered if she noticed all the changes—how tense everything felt, the smell, the money he suddenly had, and his red, glassy eyes. I wondered if her stomach was always in a knot like mine.

We settled into a rhythm of ignoring each other and pretending our life was normal, while the three of us were each trying to navigate the haze of changing hormones. Ma went to work and school and came back with nothing to say, no questions to ask. We all showed up for supper and then disappeared. And I still kept trying to figure out how to have the white-picket-fence family.

A few months after school started that fall, Ma sat on the couch in front of the TV, her hand cupping a glass of cheap Scotch. The people on the screen laughed and hugged like a happy family. My sister was out somewhere—she was seventeen and always somewhere else—and my brother was in his room preparing baggies of weed to sell that night. Ma sat staring at the flickering screen.

I tiptoed across the living room, careful not to bump into the black metal shelves that Ma slept behind. She called it her "bedroom," but it wasn't much—just a twin bed shoved behind the shelves, and two metal cabinets stuffed with all her worldly possessions. The cabinets' doors needed to be yanked hard; like her, they seemed hesitant to reveal their interiors.

A squeaky plastic folding door separated my space from my sister's room. The magnets on it never stuck quite right, so it barely stayed shut. Still, it was more privacy than I'd ever had on Sixty-First Street. I didn't have a window, but I had my first real bed and my own closet with a door I could close.

But there were mornings when the door couldn't close enough—the mornings I woke up having wet the bed. I was confused and embarrassed that this was still happening. I was almost twelve. Maybe Ma's rule of no visitors and no sleepovers at anyone else's house wasn't so bad.

I slid into my closet, closing the door behind me. This was the only place that felt truly mine. My jacket and a few shirts hung overhead, sleeves brushing my shoulders like a gentle hug. I sat, knees tucked under my chin, thinking about my bedwetting. The mornings I woke up with wet sheets, I hid them in a plastic bag until laundry day, when I'd bring them to the laundromat. The fact that Thomas and Peggy never teased me about my bedwetting somehow made me feel worse.

The air in my closet smelled like musty sweaters and a faint trace of paint. I pressed my back against the wall, wishing a new wall color or a new address could fix everything. But it didn't. I could hear laughter from the television, and I closed my eyes, imagining a different place where families liked to hug each other.

I finally got up and went into Peggy's room, careful not to touch the plants in the macramé hangers. Purple coleus spilled over the edges, shading the view of the backyard. My sister didn't like me in her room, but I had no choice. I had to walk through it to get to the kitchen and bathroom. Peggy had a fish tank that I hated. The constant gurgling of the filter, and the buzzing of the flat white fluorescent light, drove me crazy. Ma wouldn't let us have real pets, pets with fur. She swore she was allergic, but I just think she hated anything cuddly or comforting.

Our new block was lined with attached three-story houses, each with a tiny patch of concrete posing as a front yard, enclosed by a short wrought-iron fence. Behind each house was a postage-stamp-size patch of grass. On some, families plopped down aboveground pools, obliterating the little bit of greenery. We could look out the windows and see the backyards, but we were not allowed in.

I watched our new neighbors: the Murphys, the O'Briens, the Reillys, families that seemed so different, yet somehow all the same. Their kids, the street full of them, were part of a world that I could see but never quite enter. Their station wagons, their endless backyard games, their big family meals—they were close, but always just beyond my grasp.

I stared out Peggy's window at the backyards, listening to the endless bubbling of her fish tank, staring at a world I couldn't quite reach but wanted desperately to be in.

Chapter 35

Brooklyn, New York, 1970

Later that week, I lay on my bed waiting for Peggy to come home so we could head to Grandma's. I thought back to what Ma told me in the deli earlier that afternoon. As we shopped for cold cuts, my mother reminisced about something that had happened when she was my age. It was a rare glimpse into her world growing up.

Back when she was a kid, she had gone shopping with Grandma at a neighborhood German delicatessen, one that smelled of vinegar and brined meats. The shop was an assault on the senses: Open tubs of mustard lined the counters next to vats of sauerkraut with their sour tang, and links of blood sausage hung from the ceiling next to yellowed flypaper. It was the kind of place where the owners knew you by name. To them, and to my mother, Grandma was Mrs. Callahan, a woman who only spoke English.

The radio droned on in the background analyzing the war in Europe. Wielding a sharp knife to slice some meat for Grandma, the owner turned to the cashier, uttering, in his native language, words of praise for Hitler. My grandmother—always so composed, so distant, so quiet—exploded, hurling a barrage of words at him in fluent German. Her two sons had flown sorties in Europe, and one of them had been shot down by the Germans.

My mother told me she hadn't ever heard her mother speak

German before. What else did she not know about her mother? What else did I not know about mine?

My grandmother seemed to move through life on the edge of something, never quite crossing over into openly conveying emotion. To me she was cold and silent, like a piece of furniture. She never laughed, never cried. It wasn't until later that I realized how much she had buried under the surface, how much pain she carried in those tightly clasped hands.

At four, she lost her twin brother to poison. And in her forties, the war took her eldest son, and then grief took her husband. The war that seemed so distant to me had shaped everything about her, and about our family.

Ma inherited her silence. I saw it in the tightness of her jaw, the stiff edge to her smile. She cracked after Da died; the breaks in the stoic surface began oozing anger, jealousy, and disgust that bled through everything.

It was like an unspoken rule passed down: Don't feel it. Don't show it. Grandma lived by it, Ma followed, and I was left struggling to understand it. Was it the grief that crushed their spirits? Or something more ingrained, etched in the bloodline, that made them cold?

I didn't know. But the silence stretched on, generation to generation—a thread of survival. It was a hard-hearted sorority, and the price of membership was steep. They only showed the minimum emotion necessary to survive. It made me wonder: Did they ever truly feel anything? Did they ever truly feel alive?

We kept going to Grandma's every Sunday for dinner, even after Da died, even after we moved. The routine never changed, the smells never changed, and, in a way, I really liked that—the predictability.

This Sunday, I opened the door to her house and smiled, comforted by the familiarity of it all. It was the same every time—a roast loin of pork, encased in a crusty layer of juicy fat, sprinkled with paprika. Running up the stairs, I called out for Snoopy, desperate for a snuggle. I squeezed into the tiny kitchen to peek in the oven, the smell so strong I could almost taste it. There were baked potatoes, with the skins nice and crispy, and green beans too. At Grandma's, the beans were fresh and actually green, not the canned ones Ma heated up at home. It made the meal feel exotic.

Given Grandma was German, it was always a pork roast and there was always red cabbage and sauerkraut—red cabbage out of a jar, sauerkraut from a can. One kind of cabbage was not enough.

Sitting at Grandma's table felt different to me from when we ate supper at our place; it felt special. Snoopy burrowed under the table, draping himself across my feet. Wiggling my toes into his belly, I ducked under the table and swore I saw him smile. Hoping for some scraps, he was disappointed. The food was the best of the week. I could have licked the plate.

Grandma's dining room had an actual dining room table, made of wood, draped with a tablecloth, with matching carved mahogany chairs surrounding it. On the chairs sat needlepoint cushions, made by Grandma. It all felt much sturdier and fancier than the Formica table and chairs in our kitchen. Dinner was served on real china Grandma's parents had brought over from Germany, and everyone had a cloth napkin. I never wanted to dirty my napkin, knowing what a pain doing the laundry was.

At home, I did everyone's laundry. I hated that job and the endless, thankless cycle of it. But when we moved to Seventy-Second Street, it became my job, twice a week, from when I was ten until I left for college. Given our age difference, my sister and I had no real relationship. Not sure if she had any chores, but my brother was exempt. He had male privilege, or maybe Ma was afraid of him. Since he started dealing, he didn't allow her into his room. And she didn't question him. Sometimes he was pretty scary—over six feet tall with a short fuse.

So, it was just me dragging a pushcart, stuffed with two bulging bags of wash and an extra-large tub of powdered laundry detergent, up and down two flights of stairs and back and forth across three city blocks to the laundromat. Twice a week, when I came home from school, I trudged to the laundromat, my pockets clanking with quarters for the machines. I washed, dried, and folded everyone's clothes, sheets, and towels, hating every minute of it.

When Ma disappeared for the weekend, as she often did, leaving us to fend for ourselves, I told my sister and brother to do their own laundry. I don't know how my sister coped, but Thomas had it figured out. He went to the Army Navy Store around the corner and bought a stash of Hanes underpants and crew neck T-shirts in various colors. The kind with the little pocket on the chest. Enough to last until Ma came back, paid for with the cash from dealing drugs. Genius. And lazy. A perfect combination.

I slunk past the corner of Ovington and Fifth Avenues where my friends hung out, headed to the laundromat. Trust me, they weren't doing anything too exciting, but it was better than doing the laundry. They loitered around the poolroom during the day, the corner bar once the sun went down.

"Hey, how ya doin'," they muttered, exchanging nods. Most of them were older, my brother's age or even older than that. It was impossible for me to look cool while lugging loads of laundry, but they never teased me about it. And I tried really hard to make up for it when the sun went down.

After supper I walked a few blocks to the park, having folded and put away all the clean clothes. Everyone was sitting on squeaky rusted metal swings that were either freezing cold or scorching hot, and benches that were a faded green with chipped and peeling paint. The park was gritty: Graffiti covered the cement supply building, and the hum of the highway was audible in the distance. There were tennis courts, but they were in ruins—nets long gone, metal brackets bending to the ground like broken arms. Puddles of piss and jagged shards of broken beer bottles filled the cracks in the asphalt court.

At seven o'clock, we all crowded around one of the benches. "Five bucks each," Chris said, throwing a crumpled bill down onto the slats of the bench. We all coughed up some cash as Chris lit a cigarette. I saved money from a few jobs I had. During the school year, I walked dogs; in the summer, I groomed dogs and made calls for newspaper subscriptions for a friend's father.

"I'll go get the stuff from Otis," he muttered, looking over his shoulder. "He told me he'd be down by Bliss Park." My brother, Thomas, went by the name Otis with his customers, a nod to the legendary musician Otis Redding. This way, if anyone ever tipped off the police, they wouldn't know his true identity. Every evening, he made sure to vary his location to minimize the risk of being caught.

I glanced around at the others. Noreen was leaning against a pole, twisting her hair, not a care in the world. Mary was yakking away with Sally and Gary. Timmy was squatting against the building, staring into space like he was seeing something the rest of us couldn't see. It was an eclectic group. I was the youngest by a couple of years, granted access because my brother was the dealer. And my cynical view of the world combined with my too-old-for-my-age attitude earned me my staying power. Most of them were in their late teens, some as old as twenty.

Chris reappeared, tossing a bag of weed and some papers on the bench. Donny picked it up, sniffed it, and started rolling joints. Lighting up, he took a deep drag and passed it around. Strains of Jimi

Hendrix filled the air. Gary had brought his boombox. He took a toke and blew out a cloud of smoke that hung over us like fog. "You guys ever wonder what we're doing?" he asked, eyes glazed.

"Wondering is for people who think life's gonna get better," Donny said, shrugging. "We're fine. We're just here."

And that was it. No big speeches, no deep thoughts. Just the way it was. No one really expected much else from a group like ours—no plans, no ambitions, just the next hour, the next joint, the next time we could all pretend this was something worth doing. They seemed content with this life, never questioning what was next.

I took a hit, sat back, and tried to blend in. The park, the group, the buzz—it was all temporary. Just like everything else in my life. I was counting down until I could bail. I felt like an impostor.

Buzzed, we headed over to the bar where middle-aged men stopped off on their trudge from the subway to their homes, steeling themselves for the monotony of their lives. I wondered if my father would have been there, or some version of there, if he were still alive. I tried not to look at these men; they seemed draped in disappointment and despair.

The men had assigned stools and bar tabs they paid off on Friday evenings when Jack, the bartender, tallied up what they owed. Jack reminded me of the scarecrow in *The Wizard of Oz*, scrawny with legs attached by puppet string, flicking outward when he walked, the gait of a seasoned alcoholic. These men, with their weary expressions, reinforced the feeling I had that I was a stranger in my own skin, in my own neighborhood, passing through a world that wasn't mine. They all seemed trapped, stuck in sad routines. I felt disconnected from them, but at the same time, just like them. I wondered if I'd make it out or if this was my future too. I stood at the edge, watching life move on without me.

Chapter 36

Brooklyn, New York, 1970

The year after we moved, everything changed. I was entering uncharted territory: junior high, with its lockers, long hallways, and changing classrooms. Stepping into a whole different world, I wasn't the same anymore, either. I could feel it even before I understood what was happening. I couldn't ignore it. School began, and I got my period.

I stood in the kitchen doorway, feeling uncomfortable in my body. It wasn't just the physical changes, it was everything—I felt ever more distant from Peggy and now Thomas. Unable to talk to Ma, I wished I were closer to Joan. I was unsure of who I could turn to, having learned to keep my distance from everything and everyone. My whole life started to feel like watching the men in the bar, disconnected from whatever was happening around me.

I watched Ma moving around, transferring plates from the drying rack to the white metal kitchen cabinet.

"Hey, Ma?" I hesitated, then blurted it out. "I just got my period and I need something for the bleeding. Not sure what I should do."

Her back was to me, and she didn't turn around. She went to the hall closet without a word, rummaged around for a moment, and then handed me a stretched-out sanitary belt and pad. No explanation, no instructions.

I stood there, holding the strange items in my hands, feeling more isolated than ever. Of course there was no heartwarming chat about my changing body and what it meant. She left me to figure it out for myself.

As if on cue, Thomas came up the stairs. He was changing too, but in his own way. He'd just started at Brooklyn Tech, a prestigious engineering high school, and was starting to feel different as well. He'd sometimes call me into his room, when Ma wasn't home, feeling kind of full of himself, like a big shot. He'd show me the new weed he had or the small notebook where he kept his ledger, details noted in his tidy handwriting. He was proud of himself and the money he was making on his own.

I was curious—how could I not be? It all looked impressive, like a glimpse into an adult world—a mysterious one of bags of weed and wads of cash. He liked showing off and I liked someone paying attention to me.

It all felt strange though. Everything was happening to me and around me, but no one was really talking about it. We were all just stumbling along, trying to figure things out on our own.

The following spring, the air felt charged, as if the earth was holding its breath. A hint of coolness still lingered in the air, but there was a subtle shift, a reminder that spring wasn't far off. I was in my room when Thomas called me.

"Hey, Joanne. I've got something I want to show you," he said. His tone was casual, but it felt like he was inviting me in on some secret.

Ma wasn't home yet. It was one of her late days, when she went straight from work to her classes at Wagner College in Staten Island. Peggy wasn't home either; she had a job at the A&P after school.

I was twelve and feeling awkward. Thomas was almost fifteen and seemed way cooler, like he knew things I didn't. There was a distance between us now. I walked into his room, feeling curious but cautious, like I was stepping into something that wasn't entirely meant for me.

He shut the door and turned the lock. He pulled down my pants and said he wanted to look at me.

He said it was no big deal.

I froze in place, my feet unable to move. My eyes remained glued to the blinds pulled halfway down the window. A flush of adrenaline raced from my head to my toes, but I couldn't move. I wanted to scream but was so used to no one hearing me I didn't bother. I don't know if I could have. My mouth went dry like when the dentist sucks the saliva out with the little hose, but I thought I was going to wet my pants—the ones that were now around my ankles. I wanted desperately not to be there.

The wind sighed through the crack in the open window. In my head a long, low moan howled a chorus of *no, no, no*, but even that couldn't drown out my racing thoughts. Thoughts that I couldn't erase. The strong earthy smell of his weed stash suddenly made me want to vomit. I didn't know what to do.

I felt very small and very dirty. I wished I were dead. I was so ashamed. It must have somehow been my fault.

We both struggled with navigating affection, as we had experienced so little of it. We had no idea what healthy love looked like. He was at the age where he was aching for a girl to simply notice him. He was awkward and shy.

I hated what he had done yet felt sorry for him. I felt pity. My eyes, when I finally pried them from the spot on the window and looked at him, must have given it all away. I could see shame and regret drift like a cloud across his face.

Afterward, I felt bad for him, so I excused him, minimizing his invasion. I felt complicit, like it was somehow my fault. I didn't tell anyone because I didn't want him to be mad at me; I was desperate not to have another person ignore me like I felt my sister and mother did. And the same thought kept returning: *Maybe it was my fault.* Shame silenced me once again, eroding my core a little bit more. Chipping away at my soul. I didn't say a word. I couldn't bear having him shut me out. Ultimately, it wasn't really a decision—after all, I had no one to tell.

Chapter 37

Brooklyn, New York, 1971

My body felt like it was betraying me that year. I couldn't control it. I couldn't even figure out what was happening as it changed in ways I wasn't ready for. It kept changing, without asking, without warning. Every day, my emotions exploded out of nowhere, swirling inside me like a storm I couldn't outrun. I wanted to escape it all—escape my house, escape my neighborhood, escape the people around me. Everything felt wrong.

But then something started to shift—something that both terrified and confused me. And made me feel ashamed. It was subtle, at first. A bunch of Greek men who had recently moved into the neighborhood hung around a new gyro shop down the street, and their eyes began to roam over me as they licked their lips, while the meat turned slowly on the spit. They didn't try to hide it, their stares lingering longer than they should have.

It made my skin crawl, but it also made me feel something else. *I felt seen.* I was something they noticed, something they wanted. Even if it made me uncomfortable, it meant I existed. I wasn't invisible anymore. Maybe that was the only thing that mattered.

Then there were the holy rollers. The Catholic mothers who went to Mass daily, clutching their rosaries. They began to narrow their eyes in judgment as I passed by on my way to school, muttering about the "sluttiness" of my jacket, unbuttoned by one notch too many.

I felt their disdain burning into my back as I passed them, my head held high.

Distracted by their piety, they failed to notice their own daughters genuflecting for blow jobs until one of them got pregnant. The girls' jackets had stayed buttoned, but it didn't matter. Their hypocrisy was as clear as the gossip they spread.

But there was another truth settling in—something I couldn't ignore. I was smart. And that intelligence, I decided, the thing I had buried under the weight of everything else, was going to be my escape. I didn't want to stay in this suffocating neighborhood, these cramped streets where no one dared to venture beyond the few blocks they knew.

I wanted to break free, to escape to a world I had only experienced in books—where homes were full of laughter and smelled of cookies, where mothers kissed their children goodnight and tucked them into bed, where families loved each other. Where they fought, yes, and then made up.

The street hummed with the rhythm of daily life. In the morning, I watched the men shuffle down the block headed to the subway, to Manhattan. Each day just like the one before. I saw the wives do their shopping for food and clothing, do their banking, and go to church, day after day, week after week, all within the safe zone—a perimeter of three or four blocks in each direction. They really didn't go beyond that.

Were they lacking curiosity? Or were they afraid of what they might find out there? I couldn't figure it out.

I sat on my stoop watching the husbands retrace their steps in the evening and their wives greet them with supper and cocktails. "Welcome home, dear," they'd say, smiles fixed, offering a peck on the cheek, having dabbed on some lipstick as they came to the door. Some of the men came home later, having stopped at the bar—for a drink, for a break, for a moment to dream, fortifying themselves for another evening of small talk and television.

After supper, I imagined them on their couches, slumped and silent, eyes glued to the television. Dishes cleared, the only sounds the low murmur of sitcoms and the clink of ice cubes melting.

My friend Kathy had showed me one day how her mother's hair-sprayed bouffant was propped up on a scaffolding of pillows each night. She mimicked her father with his back turned away from her mother, only to wake up the next morning and repeat it all over again.

Weekends, for the other families on the block, might include Chinese food and a movie at the Alpine, just four blocks away. A movie, a brief escape until the lights came back on. But thoughts of Manhattan? Of venturing out of the safety of the surrounding few blocks? It apparently never crossed their minds. The city seemed as far away to them as the stars.

I also realized that in order to survive, I had to work hard not to appear too smart. I had to fit in with everyone else, those whose heads were not always calculating an escape, working on an exit strategy. Not, like me, constantly preoccupied with thoughts of getting out of the world I felt stuck in.

I had to find a strategy, a way out. I cut class but kept up my grades. I hung out in the park, did drugs, but didn't let them consume me. I had sex but avoided getting pregnant. I watched friends drop out, get pregnant—and one even leaped off the highway overpass thinking they could fly, confused by a tab of LSD taken on a random Friday afternoon.

I finished seventh grade, with my mind already racing toward freedom. I didn't know how far I could go, or how I'd get there, but I knew I was not going to spend my life in this world of confined space and narrow minds. I believed college was my way out. I struggled to understand the choices my siblings made. Peggy graduated that summer and went to Brooklyn College. Being much younger, it seemed to me that she had never really been around much since Da died and hated to be anywhere near Ma. Her decision to not go away to college baffled me. I couldn't understand that at all. *Why didn't she escape when she could?* I'm sure she had her reasons. I would have asked her, but we never spoke.

I was already counting the days, waiting for my chance to leave.

My brother, too, stayed in our small-minded neighborhood. He continued dealing drugs, a routine that felt strangely normal in the space where we lived. Everyone seemed to be getting high, so why not? My brother was the "smart" one, making money from it. He began to carry himself as though he had found some shortcut to life that others hadn't figured out. School and a future job didn't seem so important anymore. He started to put on weight, and at sixteen, he turned to amphetamines to combat the weight gain.

The pills changed him. He wasn't the same person anymore, his shy kindness erased by paranoia. His body had already grown imposing, and now he became belligerent and scary. He was always on edge. Friends started to pull back, frightened and concerned.

I was afraid to confront him, but no one else would. Not quite a teenager, I was no expert on addiction, but I realized I needed to try to get him to face reality. I knocked on his door one evening, when no one else was home. My hands clammy from nerves, I confronted him. I told him he had a problem. That he was losing control.

"Hey. You gotta stop what you're doing," I suggested, trying to sound sympathetic, not accusatory.

"What? What are you talking about?" He got defiant, but I could see a hint of fear in his eyes.

I didn't back down. "You're taking uppers and you're scary! You're getting real paranoid. People are afraid of you. You know you're fucked up."

"Shut the fuck up. Who are you to tell me anything?" Despite his words, I could sense his defiance fading. He seemed hurt.

"I'm your sister. I'm the only one who gives a shit enough to try to help you. You have to stop. We need a plan."

I tried to sound confident and offer him a way out. I knew if I were him, it would have meant so much to me to have someone care about me, to go out on a limb to help me, to be there for me. Thankfully, it seemed to mean the same to him. Weeks went by and I checked in with him daily. Slowly, he weaned himself off the pills.

But me? I was still lost, still trying to figure life out. I felt like I didn't belong anywhere. I felt trapped, and I wasn't sure where to turn.

A few months later, school started and I began eighth grade. Mr. Calendo, my homeroom teacher, was fresh out of college. He infused the class with energy and enthusiasm. And he somehow saw me—really saw me. Not the lost girl I had become, but someone else, someone worth guiding.

One afternoon, I went to him, with a crack in my usual veneer of confidence and a bit of panic in my head. I thought I might be pregnant, and I didn't know where else to turn. Without a flicker of judgment, he directed me to Planned Parenthood. His eyes never wavered, never flicked to the side with embarrassment or pity. He was just helpful. But it wasn't just that moment. There was more. He called me "spunky" in front of the class and cheered when I beat Marty Cohen for the best grades. He didn't just acknowledge me; he acted as if I mattered. Like he could see past the mess of my life to something I hadn't even recognized in myself. He told me I could rule the world. Maybe it was a silly thing to say, but right then, it felt like the first time anyone had given me permission to even think about it.

That moment, his belief in me, stuck with me. *I could rule the world.* It was the only piece of recognition I held on to, the one thing that kept me going through everything else.

Years later, I ran into Mr. Calendo in a bar in Manhattan. I was in my twenties, just starting to make my mark in the world. It was a random encounter, one of those brief, fleeting moments in life. I pulled him aside and thanked him. I told him how much that one moment, that one small gesture, had meant. How it had kept me moving forward when no one else seemed to see me.

I didn't get out in one smooth move. It was messy. I was messy. I stumbled, hid parts of myself, and took risks I didn't fully understand. But I kept going. Each step forward, each moment I chose not to give in, not to give up, added up. I held tight to that belief—maybe I could rule the world, or at least escape the one I was born into. By the time I landed on Wall Street, I was no longer the girl who clung to teachers' praise and cleaned bookshelves for attention. I had grown a new skin—tough, sharp-edged, and polished just enough to pass. But that hungry girl was still there, just beneath the surface, watching everything, keeping score.

Chapter 38

New York, New York, 1984

Wall Street was in a decade of debauchery. Money rained down like ticker tape, and egos grew as huge as the bonuses. Brokers showered us with front-row concert tickets, dinners at Manhattan's best—Le Bernadin and Il Mulino—and limos as ubiquitous as yellow cabs.

That year Citibank's Christmas party was at the Palladium, a former concert hall turned nightclub. It was a blur of flashing lights, pulsating music, and flowing drinks. And it was very hot in every way. Amid the frenzied madness, a shy young assistant slipped off her sweater, forgetting she had nothing on underneath. She resigned the next day, too embarrassed to face the guys on the floor. That was Wall Street—no room for mistakes, and no mercy when you made one.

A month later, Eddie, a lacrosse player from Manhasset, mentioned he was feeling sick. He shuffled to the men's room, sniffling. As he flushed and exited the stall, he was accosted by Spidey, a short, obnoxious trader with a Napoleon complex, who ran the desk. Shoving Eddie up against the putty-colored metal door, spit flying, he snapped, "What the hell are you doing? No more cocaine in the office!" Eddie, caught off guard by Spidey's absurd accusation, played along for a bit by pretending to be high before telling him to back off.

"I have a cold. I wasn't snorting anything in the stall!" he finally snapped, pushing Spidey away. But Spidey wasn't convinced. So Eddie blew his nose, holding out the tissue to prove his point. "Yellow mucus, not coke."

It was nine o'clock in the morning.

That was not unusual. Rolexes adorned every wrist, complementing cuff links and monogrammed shirts. Big bonus checks were spent on big toys—boats, snowmobiles. Wives got mink coats with shoulder pads, and Cartier bracelets. My bonus was laughably small in comparison, something I'd discover the following year in a conference room where I was being deposed by a lawyer holding salary sheets during a sexual discrimination suit. Three women on the desk. Three numbers that didn't match the others. I hadn't expected equality, but the gap was insulting.

I deposited my bonus check and left it to sit. I kept looking over my shoulder, half expecting someone to take it back.

One evening, feeling stuffed like the pork dumplings I had gobbled up at a greasy Pearl Street dive, I wandered along Canal Street. I passed windows with shellacked burgundy duck carcasses hung up by their necks. Men, shouting in Cantonese, hawked dried cod stacked high like sheets of cardboard. My eyes caught those of a round Chinese woman with a wide smile, her gold tooth glinting in the gaudy neon lights, her age indeterminate. On her table, rows of watches were laid out on scratched Lucite trays, wedged between jars of plastic trinkets depicting New York City landmarks. Pegboards hung with fake Prada and Gucci bags leaned against the wall.

"How much?" I asked, pointing at the fake Rolex. Twenty-five bucks and some hand gestures later, I had one on my wrist.

The next morning, Spidey spotted it. "Hey. Redding. Where'd you get that Rolex?"

Without taking my eyes off the screens, I responded, "A broker gift. Eamonn at Cantor."

"You can't do that! You can't accept a Rolex from a broker."

"Why not?" I said, my head still flicking back and forth, focused on the screens. "I do a shitload of business with them. You guys go on free golf trips all the time. I got a Rolex."

"No. No. It's not the same. That's not okay! It's too much money. You have to give that back."

"No, I'm not going to," I smirked, enjoying pissing him off. I let him stew for a while. "It's a watch," I said, eyes still on the blinking screens. The Treasury bill auction was minutes away, and I had to hedge. My guy was already standing by at the Fed. I didn't have time for Spidey's insecurities.

Spidey wouldn't let up. "I'm serious. You have to give it back."

Finally, I relented. "Okay, fine. It's a fake." I sighed.

He grabbed my arm, turning it over. "Let me see it again."

I held up my wrist. "It's fake. Canal Street," I said dismissively, thinking that would be it. Spidey kept at it, twisting my wrist, inspecting the bezel. "It's not a fake, Joanne. Stop bullshitting me. You need to give it back."

"Don't be an ass. It's a fake."

"I'm not kidding. You've got to return it."

I sighed. The desk had gone quiet, with all eyes on us. "Okay. If you really believe it's not a fake, let's swap. Mine is a more expensive model and it's brand-new. You give me yours and I'll give you mine."

The entire room waited for him to make his move. Put up or shut up? Salespeople shuffled papers, eyes peering over their reading glasses.

Spidey hesitated, calculating. Finally, he muttered something derogatory about my market position and being a woman and slunk back to his seat. The Rolex could've been real. In those heady days of the '80s, it wouldn't have been out of the question. But it wasn't about the watch anymore. It was about power, and I had held my ground with a smile.

Despite such triumphs, there were still moments, even in the midst of the chaos of Wall Street with its blinking screens and pounding trades, when I'd be whipped back to life with Ma: the clatter of hangers in the coat closet, the smell of coffee, the feel of polyester upholstery under my fingers. No matter how far I had climbed, something in me was still that girl—trying to earn a nod, a moment of acknowledgment. Trying to be seen.

Chapter 39

New York, New York, 1972

It was one of those rare afternoons when my mother and I went shopping, just the two of us. The fluorescent lights hummed as we stepped into the store, smelling freshly polished linoleum and hearing the clank of hangers. I walked close to her, trying to bridge the space we shared. But the distance still felt impenetrable. Ma was always busy, always somewhere else—at work, at class, or at home grading students' homework or doing her own. I tried to fill the dead air with something, anything, but nothing worked. All I could do was wait for her to see me.

I picked up a top, a pretty blue that I thought made my eyes pop. I held it against my chest and stared at myself in the mirror, trying to picture who I really was. I turned to get her opinion, but she was lost in her thoughts, off in the distance. I waited, again, hoping for her to turn my way.

"That's nice," she muttered, finally noticing me, before moving on to the next rack of clothes.

The stores we frequented—Abraham & Strauss, E. J. Korvette's—were staples for families like ours, the lower middle class, just scraping by. We scoured the sales racks, hunting for treasures or at least something functional and cheap. Sometimes we'd head over to Manhattan, taking the N train to Herald Square, and paw through the racks at Macy's and Lord & Taylor. Laser-focused, like a retriever flushing out game, Ma led the way to pieces hidden in the recesses, the deeply discounted clothes.

Maybe it was growing up during the Depression that shaped her relationship with money. She pinched every penny, wasting nothing. Growing up, I almost exclusively wore my sister's hand-me-downs—stretched-out sweaters covered in pills, in colors I abhorred. Shirts that didn't quite fit but I had to wear.

I wanted to ask her about life, about everything. But I didn't. Instead, I just followed her, pushing aside all the questions that bubbled up inside me. Her long hours away from home made it hard to shrink the distance between us. It seemed to grow wider the more I reached for her.

"Let's stop for a hot dog," Ma suggested. It was our routine when we went to Macy's. Exhausted from our hunt for bargains, we made our way to our usual spot—Chock full o'Nuts on the corner of Thirty-Fourth Street and Broadway, its sign beckoning us in. We scooted up onto the black, backless stools at the shiny Formica counter, the hum of conversation and clink of coffee cups filling the air. My mother always insisted on this detour before heading back to Brooklyn. It was a tradition, and to me, it always felt like a small luxury.

Looking over the plastic menu, my thoughts drifted to our annual family Easter meal in a real restaurant. I could almost taste it all again.

The smell of marinara sauce and garlic hit me as soon as we walked into the brightly lit Italian restaurant, its red-and-white checkered tablecloths so cheery, a sharp contrast to the drabness of our apartment. Ma led us through a maze of tables to the back, where a round one was already set for us, as though we were special. The murmur of voices and clinking of silverware buzzed around me.

I took a seat across from Joan as she laughed loudly at something my grandmother said, and I felt happy. The sound was comforting, familiar, in a room where I felt like we didn't quite belong. A room of tablecloths and stemmed wine glasses.

The waiter, tall and a bit too serious looking, strode over, all business in his black pants and vest. I couldn't help but notice a few black chest hairs peeking out from under his stiff white shirt with the top button undone. I watched as he set plates down in front of us: lasagna, chicken cutlets, and a mountain of pasta and sauce, dishes that were such a contrast to the bland food we got at home, where we'd get just enough to stop our stomachs from growling. *What a feast!*

I could see the steam rising from the plates, the mozzarella melting, the smell of basil wafting in the air, and for a moment, everything felt perfect. I dug in, the sauce rich and thick on my tongue, savoring every bite as though it were some rare delicacy. This was the best meal of the year, no doubt about it.

Then came the moment, as it did every year. The waiter, having hovered just long enough to make sure we were taken care of, handed my uncle the check with a flourish. I watched him—my uncle John, the only one who had any real mystery about him, the one who came in from Saint Louis each year for this one meal with us. He glanced at the check and stood, slapping his hands on his knees.

"Be right back, folks," he said, with a smile. "Gotta hit the terlet," he added, still with the Brooklyn accent. And just like that he was gone, leaving the rest of us to stare at the check in the middle of the table. The women's eyes flicked nervously from face to face as the weight of the bill hung heavy. Every year, without fail, John would escape to the restroom, and every year, his sisters would be stuck with the bill.

But for me and my mother, our meal that day at Chock full o'Nuts was different. It wasn't grand, but it was a treat for us. It felt like what dining at the 21 Club was for Upper East Siders. Ma and I each had a hot dog. The skin snapped as I took my first bite. I smiled then, looking at Ma. "Hey, thanks for this, Ma. I love coming here with you, whether we find any bargains or not." I may have glimpsed a slight upturn of her lip, as she sipped her black coffee.

She left a generous tip for the woman behind the counter, a small kindness that felt big in that moment. It made me proud. It wasn't fancy, but being served outside our home, even if it was just a hot dog, made me feel like we were sharing something special.

This was the closest we got, these moments when we were together but still so far apart.

Chapter 40

Brooklyn, New York, 1972

Meals at home were never very exciting. They were an unremarkable routine that we all sat through whenever my mother was around. Supper was always at five thirty, no matter what. We ate in the kitchen—the only option—at a rectangular table with a flecked Formica top and ridged metal edging.

When she got home from work, Ma would always change into a floral "housedress," as she called it, which clashed with the apron she tied on top, with its competing floral pattern. As I remember it, the kitchen always smelled slightly rancid, with a hint of desperation in the air.

Ma was, without question, the worst cook ever. But at least she fed us, trying to offer a semblance of stability by sitting together at the table every day at the same time.

Every dish she made, except for one, her so-called Swedish meatballs, was cooked in the oven at 350 degrees. Every meal included a baked potato. Every meal. Even when I came back from college and tried to expand her horizons by making rice as a side dish, she still insisted on having a baked potato. I never figured out if it was the Irish or the German in her.

We always had a protein, usually meat, and the potato and a canned vegetable. The meat was always cooked until it was brownish-gray and stringy. The potato was always baked. The carrots were always perfect little squares and always mixed with peas. The corn was always creamed. And the string beans were always "French," which meant really skinny and brown-tinged.

Called to the table with a bellow, we slunk into our usual seats, my sister closest to the window with its tattered, ruffled half-curtain. My brother got the spot closest to the exit, and I was against the wall. Ma settled in across from me, stationed by the stove.

"What are we havin'?" Thomas asked. Sometimes it was hard to tell. Being a teenage male, he ate whatever it was anyway.

"Peggy, put down the book!" my mother snapped. I had the impression that my sister did anything to not have to engage with or look at any of us. She lowered it to her lap and continued to read.

Every meal was bad, but the worst nights of all were when she made bluefish, just plain oily bluefish, or tongue. The slab of tongue sitting on the chipped beige plate, looking exactly like a cow's tongue, somehow did not inspire an appetite in me. It didn't matter how hungry I was.

I longed for a dog for many reasons, not the least of which was to be able to feed my food to it covertly. I tried everything to not have to eat many meals—the vegetables-under-the-canned-gravy trick, or the meat-under-the-potato-skin—only to be lectured about the starving kids in Biafra. But I swore they'd choose to starve rather than eat what was put in front of us.

The nights Ma wasn't around for supper, Peggy was in charge. She had to make food for the three of us. Although I felt she had absolutely no skills, it was still a step up from my mother, partly because we could just not eat it. Peggy had two dishes in her repertoire. If it was a Friday, we had tuna straight from the can slapped on a hamburger bun and put under the broiler for some unknown reason. Other days it was hamburgers, cooked black on the outside and totally raw in the middle. Doused with a ton of ketchup, they could be made edible.

The other families on the block, the Catholics who'd risk eternal damnation if they ate meat on Fridays, had pizza. I didn't taste pizza until I was eleven. Ma said it was too expensive. Pasta, or as everyone called it back then, "spaghetti," another popular Friday night choice for others, was off-limits to us. Too "foreign," my mother said.

Thomas and I, despite—or maybe because of—the endless monotony of those disgusting meals, became excellent cooks. Maybe it was our way of showing my mother that we could do something better. My sister still doesn't like to cook.

Chapter 41

Brooklyn, New York, 1972

It was a Thursday afternoon, the sun sitting low in the sky as I walked home from school, the weight of the day settling on my shoulders. I had stayed late at school working on a project for the eighth-grade science fair, and then I walked my aunt Joan's dog. Grandma wasn't around to let him out anymore. She had died a few weeks before. She had a stroke and passed away in her sleep.

Peggy had supper duty tonight, again. I wasn't in the mood for another one of her rushed, burned meals. My stomach rumbled. I needed something real, something that could fill me up, so I wouldn't be hungry again an hour later.

I walked a little slower as I approached my corner and then made a decision, instead heading left toward Gino's on Fifth Avenue. I had a few dollars in my pocket from my dog-walking gig. Whiffs of melting mozzarella and roasting tomatoes drifted into my path, making my belly smile.

I pushed open the door, walked past the crowd at the counter, and took a spot at the back of the line. A few people ahead, I spied a man with a fedora on his head, clipped black hair peeking out below the brim. A tan raincoat was belted around his waist, and underneath were dark charcoal cuffed suit pants. His polished black shoes caught the glow of the fluorescent lights. I could see the hint of stubble on his right cheek, and it hit me like a punch in the gut: It was Da. I swear. I was certain it was. He was as tall as I remembered and the same width. My ears caught the low rumble of his voice as he placed his order. My heart skipped a few beats like double Dutch jump rope, and my pulse pounded in my ears.

He's alive, I thought, my mind whirling. *Oh my God, he's alive!* My gut lurched, jerked by the weight of loss and the desperate ache of longing I had buried for so long. Time slowed to a crawl. The big man with the mustache behind the counter twirled circles of dough in slow motion, as puffs of heat blasted from the oven that October afternoon.

I stood, frozen, willing the man in the raincoat to turn around. I wasn't sure I wanted him to, yet I wanted him to more than anything else in the world. In my head, I was convinced it was my father who had been gone for so long. I was so happy he was alive, yet I was crushed he was here and hadn't come to find me. I was painfully aware of how irrational the whole thing was, but in that moment, it felt like the truth.

I advanced, little by little, in the line, inching closer, hoping he would sense me, his daughter, behind him and turn around. Hoping he'd see me and this nightmare of him being gone would be over.

The big man with the ribbed white T-shirt, tight around his biceps, sweat beading by his temples, slid a hot slice off the huge paddle onto a paper plate, into a bag, and took the twenty-five cents from the man's palm.

The line advanced, I turned my head for a moment, and then he was gone, along with all the hope I held that somehow he had made it out alive. Out of our life into another.

Chapter 42

Brooklyn, New York, 1973

A few weeks later, I opened the apartment door to the smells of supper: meatloaf, baked potato, and something canned. *Good, somewhat edible*, I thought.

"Hi, Ma! How are you doing? Sorry I was late after school." It was unusual that she was home before me.

I glanced into the living room and saw her body doubled over, sunken into the sagging couch.

"What's wrong?" I asked, hurrying toward her. Grandma had died a few weeks ago; what else could have happened now?

On the coffee table was a torn envelope and, in her hand, a thick document—my grandmother's will.

"How could she do this?" she moaned, her shoulders slumped forward. Her hands trembled reading a copy of the papers she had received from the attorney. Her voice, usually so confident, was a whisper, ragged with disbelief. Her agony quickly turned to fury. "How could she do this?!" Her words hit me like a slap, though I knew it wasn't me she was angry at. It was Joan. In her eyes, Joan had done this.

I was thirteen, and Grandma's will threatened to tear our remaining small family apart. Grandma had left half her house to my aunt Joan and split the other half between Ma and her brother, John.

My mother didn't mourn—she raged.

"Joan must have talked her into it. We should all get the same. She was our mother too," she kept murmuring, as if trying to make sense of it.

She couldn't let it go. Ma was convinced Joan had manipulated Grandma into doing this, shortchanging Ma and her brother. It was the same old story—Joan's birth, when my mother was eight, shoved my mother into the background, and now here she was pushed aside again. She thought herself a good daughter and felt betrayed by her mother. Old wounds were reopened.

The accusations started. Joan's defense came out cold, almost rehearsed, as though she had said it a hundred times before. "I stayed with her," she said. "I took care of her."

But Ma, raw and bitter, couldn't contain her fury. "You took advantage of her!" She flung sharp words like rocks.

Joan, herself full of fire, spat back, "I should have gotten the whole house! Damn you! You both deserve nothing!"

"Bullshit! This was what you wanted." My mother's voice cracked like a whip. "For most of your life *she* took care of *you*! Cooked, cleaned, everything. You never did a goddamn thing." My mother's tongue, as sharp as a razor.

The air was thick with years of unspoken resentment.

Negotiations dragged on, with offers made, prices countered, each exchange a battlefield of accusations. It grew increasingly hostile. A deal was eventually struck, but not before insults were hurled, tensions escalated, and the relationship was severed.

My uncle stayed out of it, miles away, a silent witness to the chaos. And I decided I was not going to lose Joan in all of this. I knew what happened truly hurt my mother, but I was not willing to lose Joan as a result of their feud. I still found myself drawn to her. She was a glimpse of something else, a thread of connection. The rift between my mother and Joan was wide and deep. They didn't speak for years. But I kept in touch with Joan. And she made an effort to stay in my life. As my junior high was just a few blocks from her house, after school I'd walk her dog, but it felt more like an excuse for us to cross paths. For me, she was a window open to a different life. A reminder that there was still beauty, possibility, and connection in life's mess.

Chapter 43

Brooklyn, New York, 1973

That belief, that sense of something more, stuck with me. When I was summoned into Dean Green's office on my first day at Fort Hamilton High School, I didn't need anyone to tell me how to survive. I already knew. He wanted to let me know that he'd have his eyes on me.

"I know who you are, I know who your brother is. He's a truant," he warned, puffing his chest out, attempting an intimidating stance. His gray metal Board of Ed–issued desk, cluttered with manila file folders, a crumpled White Castle bag, and a paper coffee cup with a cigarette floating in it, didn't scream power. I was unimpressed.

"You don't know me. You have no idea who I am. Save your energy for someone who might actually need you. I don't. I'll make it out of here without any help from you. I'll cut classes from time to time to keep my friends from thinking I'm a nerd but believe me, I can take care of myself. Don't waste your time on me. I don't need you looking out for me." I turned and walked out, my mother's words echoing in my head. The ones she uttered right after Da died: *From now on, you're going to have to take care of yourself.*

By then, a full-fledged teenager, I must have been giving off the scent of a stray—raw, exposed, unattended. In the span of two weeks, two married male teachers in their forties made their move. One of them, smooth-talking and casual, invited me to a concert. I suggested he ask his wife instead.

The other one nearly asphyxiated me, cornering me in the hallway, grabbing me hard from behind. I froze, begging silently for him to release me. It felt like the people who noticed me were not the ones I needed to notice me.

In the morning before I went to school, I started meeting an eighteen-year-old in his parents' basement. School was overcrowded, so my classes began at eleven thirty. We had sex, with me hoping he could fill some of the emptiness inside me. I didn't really understand what I was searching for, but I craved touch and attention. Anybody's touch and attention. I just wanted someone to hold me.

Soon, I found myself hanging out with a twenty-one-year-old. He had a girlfriend his own age, but I was a steady sidekick. Pathetic as it was, it seemed better than standing on the same street corner night after night. And honestly, part of me was flattered.

Vrooom, the tiny Triumph pulled up in front of the poolroom and I slid in, trying to look nonchalant. "Where we headed?" I asked, loving this freedom I wasn't used to. "Sheepshead Bay," he said, smiling at me. "Hungry?" I shifted in my seat. I was always hungry, but he didn't need to know that. Food at home was neither abundant nor tasty. "Yeah, sure. I could eat."

As we roared onto the Belt Parkway, the wind rushed through the cracked windows, cooling the flush I could feel climbing up my neck. We pulled into Randazzo's parking lot. I wasn't sure what to expect. Restaurants still made me feel awkward, my once-a-year Easter dinner being all I knew. Inside, the walls were covered with photos of boats and men holding fish. We were led to a small table, and I quickly scanned the laminated menu, pretending to know what I was doing.

Angelo sat across from me, talking about something I didn't catch. I was too busy trying to figure out what to order. My eyes flitted between the seafood—clams, calamari—and the pastas. I wasn't familiar with any of them, but I wasn't going to admit that.

"And for the young lady?" the waiter asked, expectantly.

"I'll have spaghetti with tomato sauce, please," I answered, playing it safe. I handed him the menu, hoping I sounded confident.

As we headed back after dinner, Angelo steered off the highway to a dark, secluded street. I pretended we were somewhere else. He parked the car and turned to me with a smile. I felt exposed and flattered at the same time. He wrapped his body around me as I leaned into him. I closed my eyes, telling myself it felt good. It was a distraction.

I told myself I was mature, smart, confident. That I had it all together. But deep down, I still felt that hole inside, that emptiness I couldn't seem to fill. I was still that lost little girl, searching for something, someone, to help me feel whole.

From wood-paneled basements to back seats of cars, I searched for love in all the wrong places.

As my sophomore year in high school came to an end, my escape drew closer. Although I was already the youngest in my grade, my grades and course load were good enough for me to skip junior year.

That September, now a senior, I earned an internship at a veterinary hospital in Manhattan and jumped at the chance. The city was a different world, vibrating with a jolt of energy that soaked into my bones. I'd been taking the subway into Manhattan every chance I had. Most weekends I was exploring the Village, roaming up and down St. Marks Place. Everything was faster, brighter, louder. For the first time, I wasn't just existing. I was *alive.*

A few weeks after the internship began, I came home from Manhattan and flung myself on my bed, trying to shut off the constant hum of life. The chaos seemed to fade away as I sank into my pillows, the weight of the world temporarily suspended.

The bookshelves in the living room were crammed with books—some old, some new, their pages filled with words that had become my refuge. It was here, in those books, that I escaped. I found solace in stories where characters triumphed over pain, where love wasn't a distant dream but a reality.

The loss of innocence and the weight of human suffering in *To Kill a Mockingbird* was a journey that pulled me in. *Little Women* left its mark on me, with its focus on the importance of kindness and the support of one's family, lingering long after I'd finished reading. *One Hundred Years of Solitude* transported me to a world that felt like a dream, so full of magic and possibility. Every book was a window opening to a life I could barely grasp but longed for. Each showed me a world beyond the one I knew, where survival was possible despite the odds.

Swinging my legs off the bed, I wandered into the living room to peruse the bookshelves. My eyes scanned the spines, landing on something unexpected—a dusty old yearbook, tucked between a couple of the tattered mysteries my mother loved. My mother's yearbook. The cover was worn, pages yellowed, but it pulled me right in. A relic of the woman who raised me yet was a stranger to me. *Ma's* yearbook.

Her face was front and center in the class photo—president of her class at Bay Ridge High. This didn't look like the woman I knew, dressed stylishly in a simple blouse and skirt, her hair pulled back neatly, her eyes sparkling with something I didn't recognize. She looked happy and alive.

Beloved. Active. She had been the one to lead, to stand tall in front of the crowd, to speak out and command attention. She was a member of the Young Democrats, the Economics Club, and the Fencing Club. This blew me away. She was so closed off now, so antisocial, that these were things I couldn't imagine her doing.

The words under her photo caught my breath: "Fly high and see the world." I could almost hear the young woman she'd been, the girl who had looked forward and seen a future where she would soar. I knew that young woman. She was me—the girl who wanted to break free from what she knew, who wanted something bigger. My mother had felt it and now I did.

I had a hard time understanding these two versions of my mother. The one I knew now was resolute and unapproachable. While the person she had been was popular, adventurous, involved.

I guess I *had* seen flashes of what she used to be. Like the time when Ford pardoned Nixon, and Ma, seething in a rage of indignation, donned her kerchief, slipped on her practical shoes, and stormed out, marching to the Western Union office, where she fired off a telegram to the president, telling him exactly what she thought.

That was Ma. Unexpressive with and about her family, but when she saw something wrong in society, she took action. Whether it was protesting the Vietnam War in Times Square or cutting down a neighbor who dared question why I walked my friend, who didn't look exactly like us, to the bus stop, she was relentless. In those moments, I admired her. But it confused me.

Clearly at a point in her life she had been different. She'd been accepted to Purdue at sixteen, ready to leave Brooklyn and step into the world. And then the war came, World War II.

All her dreams—her ambitions, her future—came to a screeching halt. I could almost picture her, suitcase packed, standing on the precipice of a different life, her heart full of hope. But none of that came to be. Instead, the war came and took away her brother, her father, and her plans for life. She stayed in Brooklyn, living with Grandma and Joan, enrolled in Brooklyn College, and worked in a factory, becoming part of the war effort, the very thing that had snatched her dreams away.

I glanced over at her, sitting on the couch, looking tired as usual. There was no trace of the young woman in the photo, no trace of the dreams that had once glimmered in her eyes. There was just the woman I knew—the one who carried the weight of loss like a heavy cloak. She had never left Brooklyn. And I'd never asked why.

Pain had settled into the crevices of her life and smothered what remained of her family. I didn't know all the details, but I could feel it—how the flames of hope had been extinguished by the weight of all that had been lost. My grandmother never seemed capable of offering much comfort. So, my mother had swallowed her dreams, burying them deep inside, and a part of her was erased. She became unreachable for all of us, and maybe even for herself.

I looked at the yearbook one last time before putting it back on the shelf, suddenly feeling the burden of all that had transpired. A part of me wanted to ask her about that girl in the photo. *What had she dreamed of? What had she hoped for?* But I didn't. Some questions felt too big to ask, too heavy to lift. Instead, I sat there in silence, feeling the space between us grow a little wider.

Chapter 44

Brooklyn, New York, 1974

A few weeks later I pulled open the glass doors of the library, the quiet hum of whispers and rustling pages greeting me like an old friend. This place, with its familiar stacks, had been a refuge for me when I was in junior high. It was where I lost myself in worlds of books: science fiction by Isaac Asimov, Eastern philosophies that spoke of deeper truths, and stories about characters who, like me, were tangled in the confusion of life. I read about families, their complexities, their connections, their fractures. The sweet, musky smell of old paper and the rhythmic shuffling of Dewey decimal cards in their drawers felt like home.

Now nearing the end of high school, I returned to my old haunt with a few hours to kill. The chatter around me was all about college applications and looming deadlines. I caught snippets of conversations as I searched for an empty seat—"I just finished my essay" and "Got my letters of recommendations done last week"—and I felt a pang of panic.

Settling in by the window, with soft light spilling onto the oak table, I pulled a notebook out of my bag. It was time to start figuring out what my future might look like. A whisper interrupted my thoughts. "Do you think we'll get in?" It was a girl a few rows over, talking to a friend. They were comparing schools, debating the best essay topics. I sighed, feeling out of place in this world where everyone seemed to have it all figured out.

I tapped my pen against the paper, trying to force some kind of plan. But all I could think about was how different my life was from theirs. Everyone here seemed to know exactly where they were going and what they wanted to do. Me? Despite my impressive grades, I knew nothing about *this* process, but I had to try. I had no time to waste. I had to figure out how to get out of here.

As far as I knew, Peggy and Thomas had only applied to colleges in Brooklyn, but I needed more. College was my ticket out. As always, my mother was no help. Ironically, she was now a guidance counselor, having received another master's degree, yet she never spoke to me about my plans. The other kids talked about SATs and campus visits with their parents, but for me, I was walking this path alone, as I always had.

I noticed the seniors in the school hallways were clutching copies of the *Fiske Guide to Colleges*, so that's where I started. I grabbed a copy off the shelf and flipped through its pages to see which schools might work for me. It was overwhelming.

The tuition costs were out of this world, so high I couldn't even wrap my brain around them. I didn't know anyone who made that much money in a year. Slowly the reality of what was and wasn't possible began to sink in. *Scholarships? Financial aid?* I didn't have a clue how to get either of them. I scanned the book again, imagining myself in places I couldn't even afford to visit. Ultimately, my options shrank to state schools, whose tuition, although much smaller, was still difficult to comprehend.

This would have been the moment when I could have used some help from Dean Green, the guidance counselor. But he had happily abdicated any responsibility for my future the year before, when I told him I could take care of myself. No one in the school spoke to me of my potential, and it never occurred to me to ask anyone for help. So, I didn't apply for any scholarships or to any competitive schools.

A few weeks later, I asked my friend Mary to come look at schools with me. "I need someone else's opinion, and I trust yours! Come! It'll be fun," I pleaded, not wanting to do this alone, so we hopped the subway to the Port Authority, then caught a Trailways bus for the four-hour ride to Binghamton, New York. Between the two of us, we had ten bucks for lunch—just enough to scrape by. Mary was two years older than me, street-smart and striking with her high cheekbones and blond hair. She had already finished high school and worked as a salesclerk in a clothing store.

Though a solid choice on paper, SUNY Binghamton didn't win me over. The campus was all concrete and brutalist buildings, the kind that made you think of 1950s Russia—stark and ugly. The last place I wanted to be. I wanted somewhere that didn't remind me of what I was trying to escape.

The next weekend, we ventured up to New Paltz, a small town just ninety minutes from Brooklyn that looked like paradise. Getting off the bus at the gas station on Main Street, I already knew. My eyes took in the town, with its cozy bars, organic cafés, and health food store. It was a world away from the hard edges of Brooklyn.

"Wow! You just can't stop smiling," Mary pointed out, laughing. "I think we've found your new home." She was right.

The air smelled different—fresh-cut grass mixed with the sweet caramel scent of Katsura trees. Walking up to campus, we passed perfectly maintained Victorian houses, just like the ones I'd read about. There were freshly painted wraparound porches, brick chimneys, and garden beds full of pink petunias, tawny grasses, and hydrangeas, blue as the deepest ocean. I had found my heaven.

The admissions office set us up with a tour guide, an upperclassman with a full beard and straggly long hair that clearly hadn't been washed in a while. Like a hippie version of Pigpen, he was surrounded by an almost visible swirl of patchouli. The campus, replete with a collegiate quad, spires, and perfectly laid-out bluestone paths, seemed straight out of a movie. As part of our tour he took us to the "tripping field," bordered on three sides by masses of huge oaks with pines and spruces scattered in between. "Get it. LSD," he told me, eyes glazed, and I couldn't help but laugh.

For the first time in a long while, I felt a spark of optimism and possibility.

Chapter 45

New Paltz, New York, 1975

Months later, on a sun-drenched, hope-filled day in August, I finally left Brooklyn. I was ready.

Thomas drove us up to New Paltz in a borrowed, battered station wagon the color of dog vomit, its side chewed up by rust like someone had taken a bite out of it. We shoved my possessions—a few trash bags of clothes, bedding from home, a couple of posters, and a stereo—into the back seat. He had borrowed the car from Bobby, a cop who lived across the street and was one of my brother's regular cocaine customers. As we cruised up the Thruway, the hum of the tires and rock 'n' roll blasting from WNEW filled the car. My attempts at small talk were met with a few grunts; conversation never came easily for my brother.

"Hey, think it's gonna be weird?" I asked, feeling a little nervous, not that I'd ever admit it.

"I dunno," he grunted, staring at the road.

We pulled into the dorm parking lot, the lone brother-sister combo amid a sea of families. Mothers, fathers, brothers, sisters, and even grandparents swarmed the parking lot, carrying piles of stuff into this next phase of their children's lives. In between the hugs and laughter, a few moms stole glances at us, pity pooling in their eyes, their gazes quickly averted when they saw me noticing.

My brother deftly snagged a spot right near the entrance to LeFevre dorm. "Let's get this over with," he muttered, pulling my bags from the back. I followed him into the building feeling my excitement build. My roommate wasn't there yet, so I claimed the bed near the window. *Yes!* Already I was over the moon. The room was exactly as I had pictured it—two single beds, dressers, and matching desks made of particleboard with wood grain laminate glued on top. *Paradise!*

"Well, here we are," I said, looking around, ready to burst. Stepping onto unfamiliar soil, I was unsure where to begin, but excited to make it mine.

I unrolled my posters—Jimi Hendrix, Janis Joplin, The Stones—and thumbtacked them onto the white walls. The floors were parquet, freshly scrubbed, and the large window opened to a gorgeous grassy green expanse, perfect for all-day Frisbee tournaments.

I stashed my toiletry case, a blue paisley one I had bought at John's Bargain Store the week before, in the big cabinet under the sinks. The communal bathroom had three sinks lined up along the wall, a row of mirrors above them, toilets across the room, and two showers at the end. "Wow," I called out to Thomas. "Come check this out! A shower! No more handheld hose in the tub."

I heard him grunt in acknowledgment, but he was busy wrestling with the stereo he was lending me. The turntable, receiver, amp, cassette player, and speakers all had to be wired together. While he did that, I unpacked my jeans and peasant shirts, and put away my Frye boots. "It's done," he said, as the familiar scratch of Pink Floyd's *Wish You Were Here* filled the air.

It had taken less than fifteen minutes to assemble my new life. We looked at each other for a moment, not knowing what came next.

My brother's emotions were always sealed tight, locked up in a mason jar he had closed many years earlier. Growing up, he used to ask me how to talk to people, how to start a conversation. That day, he didn't have much to say, but I knew he cared, and I knew he was proud of me.

"Hey," he said, shuffling his feet as he spoke, eyes downcast. "This seems really cool. It feels good here. Good for you. You deserve it." I wondered if he wished he could have done it too—to escape and maybe reinvent himself.

I was the only person we knew to ever go away to school.

We stood there not sure of what to do. Neither of us had a script for this. Finally, he cleared his throat and raised his eyes to meet mine. "Hey. I'm gonna get going. I've got to get the car back to Bobby." He offered an awkward hug as he left and handed me a large baggie. He said, "Here, this is for you. This'll help you make friends."

It was his going-away gift. Thai sticks, the best weed of the time. He was a drug dealer, after all, and this was what he could give me.

I could feel my heart race with the excitement of it all—my new life, my new freedom. The unknown was right there in front of me, and having waited so long, I was ready to grab it.

After he left, I wandered out into the hallway, following the strands of music spilling out from the suite across the hall. It was the Eagles' *Hotel California*. I wandered into Candi's room, where she sat on her bed sketching, and introduced myself. Already in her second year, she knew the ropes, while I was figuring out the lay of the land. Candi's room became the unofficial meeting place for many of us who arrived that day. We hung out after classes, after dinner, after a night out. We swapped stories, aired complaints, sought advice, and grew friendships. It was the pulse of the floor.

Late in the afternoon of move-in day, my roommate, Debbie, showed up, her mother and father in tow. She was quiet, a budding artist, and covered her walls with Magritte posters. We were as opposite as we could be but coexisted in a respectful way.

Her parents came into the room, their eyes fixed on me. They seemed to be waiting for some explanation. I stood there, alone, feeling exposed, the silence awkward. Then it dawned on me.

"Oh, hey. You all just missed my parents. They left for the store to get some more hangers. The store must be pretty crowded," I said, my voice small, trying to sound casual.

I was hoping they didn't notice the empty garbage bags on the floor—that my clothes had come out of. Her parents suggested, kindly, "We'd love to meet them? If they get back before we leave, maybe we could get a coffee."

With cash and cars, the crew came up from Brooklyn a few weeks later to check out my new place. Sally "Cream Cheese," freckled and full of giggles, who believed blow jobs didn't count as sex, came with Vito, the son of a mob guy who ran trucks distributing mozzarella around the city. Mary, Chris, Donny, Timmy, Anne, and Noreen traded barstools in Brooklyn for ones in New Paltz. And I found myself back in the Triumph, both of us aware on some level that he was too old to bring into the dorm room.

Physically out of Brooklyn, I still had to extract myself in all other ways.

Qualifying for a work-study program, I juggled two campus jobs and picked up a third in a bakery to help me get by. Lots of hours, little cash. Needing to support myself, I quickly found another way to make money. The college food plan came with a book of tickets that could be exchanged for a meal at the food hall or groceries at a small campus store.

Checking out the campus store for the first time, the fluorescent lights hummed above as I looked around at the shelves of peanut butter and Kraft Macaroni and Cheese. And then I spotted them—a large display of bongs, next to the boxes of Oreos. Bongs. A gold mine at college.

I bought the entire inventory—the display items and whatever was in the back storage room. Three weeks into the semester, sick of eating gray-tinged roast beef with gluey gravy on top, a sad reminder of my mother's cooking, I resold the bongs for cash. With the money, I bought much better food, and it all tasted a bit like freedom. I was hustling, trying to make it in a world where others seemed to already know their place.

Chapter 46

New Paltz, New York, 1975

The weeks that followed my move to New Paltz were a whirlwind. I settled into the rhythm of college life: classes, late nights, and new friendships. I began to fill the spaces that were left behind in Brooklyn. Despite the buzz of college around me, the distance and emptiness I felt when I thought about home remained.

I longed to be the kind of daughter whose mother wanted to hear from her. Who could call home and share the newness of it all—the friends, the freedom, the future. But that summer before I left had passed without us speaking about what was coming next, just as we had never discussed things from the past that threatened to stir up old wounds.

Unsurprisingly, it wasn't until I was packing the car for the move up that she had finally come outside.

"Hey. Joanne. Here's a few dollars in case something comes up. You sure you've got everything?"

"Yeah, I'm good. All set."

"Well, I'm sure you'll do fine. Call next Sunday night if you can. Good luck."

I tried for a hug, but as I leaned forward, she bent backward. The famous recoil. My mother didn't do physical touch—never had. The brief embrace was a formality, a gesture she couldn't return. But I was used to that. That lack of real connection. I was used to it, but I always hoped the next time might be different.

My first Sunday at college, I called. Sunday after six was when phone rates were the cheapest. I tried to bring her into my new world but quickly realized she didn't want to come in.

"Hi. Ma? It's Joanne."

"Hi. How are you? How are things?"

"Great. I'm really liking it here. The classes are good. I've met a bunch of people. I'm really happy."

Silence. Then I heard her breathe in, heavy.

"Well, that's nice," she offered, her voice flat, after an uncomfortable pause, as though I'd said something wrong. "Well, take care. I don't want to run up the bill."

The conversation ended quickly; they always did. Happiness felt like a zero-sum game with her. Her annoyance seemed to grow in direct proportion to the happiness I felt.

Our calls petered out after a while, becoming less frequent until I finally gave up. Home at Thanksgiving, I tried again to draw her into my college experience, but she still seemed disinterested. Maybe she resented my happiness, my escape. Or maybe it was the idea that I had left—her *and* Brooklyn.

Ma visited campus twice—once during my freshman year, and again at graduation. The first time, in the spring of my freshman year, she showed up with a strange mix of forced effort and quiet resentment. As we walked across the gorgeous green lawns, her eyes darted around, taking in the distant mountains and the laid-back, hippy-ish vibe of the town. Her lips tightened as she surveyed the students lounging on the grass, laughing, happy. I could feel her scorn, thick like mud.

"Must be nice," she muttered. Her words were clipped and sarcastic, while her eyes scanned the surroundings as though the campus were an alien planet. The freedom I felt there, the space to breathe and to dream, seemed to make her uncomfortable.

It wasn't just that I was living a life she never had, but that I was clearly *loving* it. My happiness seemed to make her bitter. Her attitude felt like the kind of jealousy you might see in a sibling who's been left behind, watching you experience everything they never did.

During that first visit, she made a little bit of an effort. She invited some of my new friends to dinner in town, something I told her other parents did. Ma was always better with strangers. She was extremely smart and had been at the top of her class at Brooklyn College. She read *The New York Times* every single day, so she was at ease discussing current events, politics, and the arts. She held her own in a crowd.

At Barnaby's Steak House, a local pub where you could get a cheap steak and a baked potato, we sat chatting—my mother, my friends, and I.

"So, what are you all thinking of majoring in?" "Where are you from?" My mother asked the obvious questions, listening as my friends gave the same answers they'd given at the dinners with the other parents. I knew that beneath the smooth smile, she was looking for a crack. Something she could sneer about. Something she could chew on and belittle them with inside her head.

But on the surface, she maintained her best behavior, the behavior she saved for the outside world. She drew them into conversations about Jimmy Carter winning the Iowa caucus and the Oscar buzz around *One Flew Over the Cuckoo's Nest*. Topics that pulled them in. She was charming, funny, likable. My friends thought she was great. The woman who could be so warm to strangers. At home, we got the chill of the Arctic.

Chapter 47

New Paltz, New York, 1976

I was itching to get out and explore the world. While Dylan's "Forever Young" became a theme song the following year at school, I found myself fantasizing about a poster in the dorm hallway advertising study abroad opportunities. I sat with a few other friends in Candi's room, passing a joint around while we imagined where we might go: Jamaica for ocean studies, Florence for art history, Mexico City for archeology. The world was ours for the taking.

While some of the girls were joking, I was serious. Why couldn't I find a new place to live? There was nothing holding me in New Paltz. I did not want to stay stuck in the same rut and paralyzed by my relationship patterns: always with an older guy, trying to find a feeling I had never had—the senior with a sly smile and a way of making me feel both invisible and seen; the TA, tutoring me in things other than economics; and, of course, Angelo from Brooklyn, whom I'd been involved with for a few years. He still came to New Paltz to see me when his real girlfriend was busy, with his Triumph and pack of Marlboros in his pocket. Our relationship had progressed a bit from food and sex to conversations.

One night, after he showed up at my dorm, we made our way to our favorite bar, settling into a dimly lit booth. The conversation meandered; we were talking about nothing and everything. The sounds of Neil Young surrounded us, but even Neil couldn't hold my attention. My mind kept drifting. I was seriously thinking about leaving, going to Europe for a semester, following through on the dreams discussed in Candi's room. But when I shared this, he couldn't wrap his head around my wanting to leave. Why I *needed* to leave. I tried to explain.

"I want to escape, to get away from here. To go far," I said, watching him frown, confused.

"I don't get it," he said, shaking his head, his fingers picking at the label on the beer bottle. "Why? Why would you want to leave all of this?"

All this? New Paltz? Brooklyn? I hesitated, not answering right away. I had never really spoken about my family, what it was like to grow up in it, to anyone. The silence behind the slammed doors. The secrets that rattled around like skeletons in the attic. The feeling of being unworthy. I shifted in the booth, uncomfortable.

"My mother has a lot of problems, a lot of issues. She is not easy to be around," I finally mumbled, not looking at him. "And, you know my father died when I was little. He had a car accident and fell off the Verrazzano Bridge." An eternity passed as we sat. "Honestly, I've wanted to get away for as long as I can remember."

I could feel him studying me, his hands moving to mine. Looking at me puzzled, he asked, "Your dad? How is that possible? How did he fall off?"

I didn't know the answer to that. I hadn't really thought about it.

All I knew was that I had to trade these feelings of suffocation and limitation for a world full of possibilities and dreams. I knew I needed to go.

A few days later, I walked into Candi's room. The usual crew was there, still talking about the overseas programs. *Why can't I go?!* I thought. Although I had never left the country or crossed an ocean, the program seemed like an incredible opportunity. As the girls chatted, I evaluated the options.

London felt like a cop-out since I would not have to learn another language. South Africa seemed way too far away to even contemplate. But France, *oh, France*, with its food and beauty, was top of the list for me. The cost was about the same as staying in New Paltz, except for the airfare and extra spending money I would need. I was sure I could figure that part out. I had taken French in high school, hoping it would connect me with my sister, Peggy, who had studied it too. Unfortunately, it didn't help our relationship and I still couldn't speak a word of it, but I didn't let that stop me.

Three months later, I sat on a bed in Grenoble, France, the room a sickly shade of Pepto-Bismol. My hands gripped the pillow as my eyes stared blankly at the ghastly curtains swaying with the breeze. The scent of freshly baked bread wafted in from the boulangerie next door, but it didn't make me feel any less alone. Earlier in the day, I had practiced over and over again in my head *je voudrais un croissant, s'il vous plait* as I walked to the boulangerie salivating for a warm croissant. Pushing open the door, I smiled politely, greeting the imposing woman in her starched, white apron with a "Bonjour, Madame." I followed with my well-rehearsed line only to be met with a blank stare. I had to resort to pointing to get the damn croissant. I sat counting how many Fridays until I'd be back in the States. Sixteen of them. Head in hand, I repeated like a mantra: *I can do this. I can do anything for sixteen Fridays.*

I had just turned eighteen. I wasn't homesick for Brooklyn. I didn't miss my family. I was missing the comfort of knowing what to expect. Everything here was so different—from the language to the food to the light switches.

At that point, the few sentences I could piece together didn't matter, as my pronunciation was so bad. My first evening, I was bending over to take off my shoes when I heard the mother and her two young daughters I was staying with whispering to each other. I sensed they were talking about me, but I didn't understand any of it. What I learned, thanks to the English skills of the ten-year-old, was that I was allowed one meal a day and one bath a week. Not ever a shower, a bath.

Days passed as I tried to adjust. But then, on the tenth day, I came back from class to find both daughters rummaging through my things. My clothes were strewn across my bed. The girls had been trying them on.

"Hey!" I snapped, crossing the room toward them. "What do you think you're doing?" They might not have understood English, but they knew what I was saying. The girls froze, looking very guilty. That was it. I wasn't doing this anymore. I needed something different. Some control, some space. I needed to be alone.

A few days later, I moved. I asked around at the university and found a tiny room on the top floor of a building with a red tiled roof in the center of town. I climbed the six flights and heard the pigeons cooing outside the window, sentinels perched on the edge of time. Everything looked ancient. The room was small. The ceiling slanted so low over the bed I had to crawl out sideways every morning. The walls were chipped, and the floor creaked underfoot, but it was *mine*.

I shoved my backpack into the corner and looked around. The tiny table near the door? My dining room. My office. My everything.

The porcelain sink, a joke of a kitchen. The hot plate, a reminder of how little I needed to survive. The toilet just down the hall was shared by the four other apartments on the floor. Two were inhabited by old grumpy men who seemed to spend an inordinate amount of time behind its locked door.

This was my sanctuary. My space.

The place didn't have a shower or tub, so I became resourceful. My backpack became my portable bathroom, stuffed with a towel, soap, and shampoo. I grabbed showers wherever I could. The girl across the hall became a friend. Her shower was an orange stand-alone plopped in the middle of her kitchen. I brought food; she offered the shower. It was a strange combination of steam—rising simultaneously from the shower and the pot on her stove. Strange, but it worked.

I had arrived in Grenoble, France, unable to understand much, and according to the woman in the boulangerie, my speaking was incomprehensible. But I had high hopes of becoming fluent, as I thought it would be an asset later in life.

Jody, my neighbor with the shower, took me out to mingle, both of us hoping to be able to practice some French. The bar was loud, filled with sounds of clinking glasses and voices, both French and English, shouting orders at the bartender. We were leaning against the sticky wooden bar nursing glasses of cheap *vin rouge*. She had been in Grenoble for a few months already, so her French was passable. My attempts at conversation devolved into awkward stares and a lot of "uhs" and "ums." It was too easy to get sucked into hanging out with the English speakers. I didn't want to do that.

I knew I needed to truly immerse myself in all things French if I was ever going to become fluent.

And then he appeared: Bernard. Leaning against the far wall, a Gauloise cigarette dangling from his lips, I caught him staring at me. His dark hair fell across his face, a face like Richard Gere if you squinted hard enough. He spoke about as much English as I did French.

"Tu veux danser?" he asked, leaning close enough that I could smell the espresso on his breath. His French was fast like a machine gun, and I was lost.

"Um. Je ne parle pas très bien francais," I sputtered. "But I'd like to."

He grinned. "Pas de problème," he answered, offering me his hand.

By the end of the night, it was clear we had a connection. He made me laugh a lot, my French improving with each glass of wine. I was determined to become fluent, and he was determined to be with me, so we started seeing each other regularly. I was soaking up French, as he spoke it, like a sponge. I didn't realize he was speaking a lot of slang, so much so that my professors were appalled. They said I sounded like a street kid from Paris. I took it as a compliment. A true immersion course.

Through Bernard, I learned more than the language. I learned how to live in France as the French do—to eat, smell, hear, and feel the way they do. To love it. And he was kind to me.

I made friends from all over the globe—people from countries I couldn't find on a map, whose stories were so different from mine. Friends who had come there with a similar sense of adventure.

I tasted foods I hadn't known existed—snails and frogs' legs—and loved them. I took a French cooking class hoping to be able to re-create some of the dishes I so loved when I went back to the US, hoping to hold on to a piece of France, to bring it back with me. I hustled, working at the outdoor markets when not at school, to make some cash.

I saw incredibly beautiful sights, from the Eiffel Tower to the trout-loaded streams in the Dordogne in southeast France, from the snow-covered caps of the Alps to some bucolic villages. Living there made me realize how large the world was, how many adventures and opportunities it held. France didn't just expand my world; it blew it wide open. And it was far away from the place I didn't want to be.

My time in France was transformative. I grasped the immensity of possibilities, of choices, of life. I gained confidence in my ability to handle anything.

As the semester drew to a close, I began dreaming in French. Linguists say this signals the start of true fluency. I decided to stay for another year.

Chapter 48

Brooklyn, New York, 1977

One year after I had left the States in search of something more, I stepped off the plane at JFK, my boots hitting the pavement with a mix of excitement and trepidation about coming home. I was back for Christmas break and the air smelled too familiar—exhaust and subway fumes.

I hadn't seen anyone from home in a year, not a single face from the past. Phone calls had been the only connection, and they were short and distant. The French police had figured out the rigged phone lines the international students used, so calls had to be brief. I called the bar from time to time to check in with the crew and sometimes I called home, but my mother never had much to say. The connection felt thin, barely hanging on.

Thomas was waiting for me when I got off the plane. He took me home to drop off my backpack, then led me back to the bar I knew so well. "Come on, let's get a beer," he smiled, taking my elbow.

As he pulled the door open, the place erupted in cheers. People called my name, bottles clinked. "Welcome back, Joanne! We missed you!" The throng of familiar faces crowded around me, faces I'd seen a hundred times before. Hands reached out, hugging me, patting my back.

I should have felt great with this welcome, but instead I felt out of place.

They tossed back shots and snorted lines of cocaine that stretched across the bar like some strange welcome mat, as the music vibrated through my chest. The same songs from the jukebox that were on before I left were still playing. Thomas had rented the whole place out, all to celebrate me, but it felt jarring. The noise and the chaos overwhelmed me.

Though every face was familiar, it seemed I'd outgrown them. The irony wasn't lost on me: Home didn't feel like home anymore. I felt more grounded in France, with Bernard, who was spending the holidays with his family in Grenoble. I already missed him.

The guys around me seemed unchanged, doing the same things they were doing when I left—lines of coke, sloppy drinking, loud talking. I hated how judgmental that felt, but I couldn't help it. I'd seen too much of the world now; I didn't want to go back to numbing myself with the same distractions. I was a different person.

I felt as if I had walked into a familiar dream, with time stuck in the past, only to realize I no longer belonged. This was not my life anymore. This was not my dream. I had moved on and changed so much. Everyone else seemed to have stayed where they'd always been and would always be. I felt like a stranger. I no longer wanted this life, and I couldn't wait to leave again.

Chapter 49

Paris, France, 1978

Christmas had been a letdown with my recognition of how clearly I had moved on from my old life. Nobody seemed particularly interested in what I was actually learning in France, whom I had met, and what I had experienced. It saddened and surprised me that my siblings weren't curious, but it didn't surprise me at all that my mother was disinterested.

However, at my urging, she visited me a few months later. I hoped we might finally be able to bond over this shared experience.

We met in Paris, the city where I'd fallen in love with the cobblestone streets, the wicker chairs at outdoor cafés, the Haussmann buildings with their intricate iron railings—pieces of a dream I wanted to share with her. I hoped to connect with her through the magic of it all.

She had traveled abroad before with my aunt Joan, but this was a first for us. When she walked next to me, her expression was distant, almost dismissive, as she looked around, barely registering the beauty I was so eager to share. I hoped for a connection, a moment when we both could take in the city together, and enjoy it together, but instead, her voice cut through the silence, dashing any hopes. Her mind looped in the prison of comparison.

"If you've seen one castle, you've seen them all," she said with a raised eyebrow, her tone clipped, the words dripping with disdain that I knew all too well. This wasn't anything new. On trips she had taken to Alaska and Egypt, places that should have sparked awe, her reactions were the same. "If you've seen one glacier . . . one pyramid . . ."

Bernard joined us for dinner one night. The dinner was predictable. Bernard tried his best with his limited English to engage her, and she, in turn, put on her public persona—lobbing softball questions at him, complimenting his country, and wearing her smile that never went higher than her lips. I glanced over at her, feeling like she was here only because she felt she *had* to be. That thought hurt more than I wanted to admit. My hope that maybe this time with her could have been different felt almost silly. My heart sank.

The weight of it all pressed on me as I walked next to her, trying to ignore the empty space between us. I knew she loved culture since she went to museums and shows back in New York, but it had never been something she could show me. In France, every new place I went, every step I took, felt like a reminder that my growth, my journey, somehow made me stand even further apart from her, maybe even *against* her. *Was she jealous?*

In my heart, I knew it wasn't the beauty of the city I wanted her to see. It was me.

As hard as it was, in a way I was grateful for this distance she kept between us. It pushed me to keep trying to find something, anything, that might finally make her see me, make her react, make her feel something toward me. I was proud of myself—that my choices to get noticed had been positive ones. That I had the guts to move to France and the determination to stay long enough, and work hard enough, to become fluent. And to find love.

Chapter 50

Brooklyn, New York, 1978

The spring flowers that had greeted my mother on her visit to France were still in full bloom as I packed up my life and returned to Brooklyn a few months later to spend the summer.

Here I sat in the passenger seat of yet another VW Beetle—the same color and model as the one my father had—with the windows rolled down and a hot wind rushing past my face. Bernard was driving, his hands gripping the wheel, eyes fixed on the road ahead. He came to America to take a cross-country trip with me. We were crossing the northern route from New York to California, the miles stretching on forever, which served to remind me of the vastness of America, so different from France. Senior year would start for me in two months, and then I was off to join the workforce.

With a full tank of gas, a tent, a few jars of peanut butter and jelly, and a loaf of white bread, we set out driving west. We were hired by a company that transported cars for people who were moving. This helped stretch our limited travel budget. Stopping along the way at KOA campsites, we wrestled our tiny pup tent erect each night and slept with our legs sticking out, buffeted by noises from the RVs that surrounded us. We listened to the hum of the crickets and the whisper of the wind, as well as the drone of the generators.

One night, Bernard grabbed the pup tent from the trunk and tried to put it together. A man, middle-aged with a sunburned face and a big grin, sat next to his RV in a lawn chair under some party lights.

"Hey there, son. Looks like you could use a hand," he said to Bernard, as he walked over. Bernard looked at me, then back at the man. Bernard didn't speak much English, so he didn't respond.

I stood up and chimed in, "That's really nice of you. He doesn't speak English, but I think he's figuring out the tent situation."

"Well, I can hold that pole for you if you'd like," he continued, addressing Bernard in a much louder voice.

"He doesn't understand you," I repeated, with a smile. "He's French."

The man frowned, then looked back at Bernard, continuing to speak, his voice growing even louder, as if a higher volume could somehow make him understand. It was almost painful to watch. He eventually gave up, heaving a frustrated sigh, muttering something about "foreigners." Bernard and I were both used to this—these moments of disconnection, these times when people couldn't seem to comprehend that not everyone spoke English.

Weeks later, I came back to my old neighborhood in Brooklyn. I hadn't spoken English for so long, and the sound of it hurt my ears. The Brooklyn accent—my accent—felt foreign now and sounded grating. The way people said "youse guys" and "fuggedaboutit," and how they pronounced "caw-fee" and "wawta," made me cringe. In that moment, I made a decision. I would erase it. I would make a conscious effort to enunciate my speech and get rid of the traces of Brooklyn.

Bernard kept in touch after he returned to France, and I to New Paltz, begging me to travel through South America with him after my graduation. He promised more adventures, more worlds. The idea was tempting. But I knew I couldn't. I had to get a job; I had to take care of myself. Who else would?

Chapter 51

Scranton, Pennsylvania, 1978

Before I returned to college for my senior year, I was invited to a wedding. Peggy was getting married. She'd finished Brooklyn College and met Roy when they both worked at the local grocery store.

The Firemen's Auxiliary Lodge in Scranton, Pennsylvania, smelled faintly of Lysol and glazed ham. A few folding tables topped with paper tablecloths sat under the tent, sagging under the weight of plastic bowls filled with potato and macaroni salad. A baked ham adorned with pineapple slices sweated in the summer heat.

I stood by the cooler filled with ice and cans of beer, sipping diluted punch from a plastic cup. Ma stood next to me, arms across her chest, her hair in tight curls from the pink foam curlers she still wore to bed. Thomas slouched nearby, fidgeting with a toothpick, avoiding eye contact.

"They seem happy," I offered, with not much enthusiasm. No one responded. My mother's eyes followed Peggy as she moved through the tent clutching wildflowers.

Roy's family laughed easily, looking like they belonged. As they helped themselves to slices of ham, their voices rose and fell in harmony with the music coming out of the cassette player. Ma, Thomas, and I sat down on a bench, not knowing our part to play, uncertain of where we fit. I wondered if anyone else realized how out of place we felt.

I swallowed hard, past the lump that had formed in my throat. I fought back the urge to weep—not from joy, but from a profound, gnawing sadness. My family had no idea how to celebrate each other.

There were no speeches, no father-daughter dance or brother-sister moment of send-off. It felt pathetic to me.

Catching a glimpse of Peggy in her white dress, I was bulldozed by a wave of grief. I bit back tears. She had always felt like a stranger to me, and now she really looked like one. And she'd always be one. It was the end of an era, the final goodbye to our messy world.

After the wedding, they moved to an apartment in Queens. Roy worked as a meter reader for Con Ed, and Peggy landed a job at an insurance company in Manhattan. At least she made it out of our mother's place. I hoped she was happy.

Chapter 52

New Paltz, New York, 1978

September came and I was back in New Paltz for my last year in college. I signed up for an elective, a sociology course called On Death and Dying—fittingly taught by a professor whose family owned the local funeral home. "There is a reason you have chosen this elective. For some of you the reason may be obvious, for others not. I encourage you to explore what's brought you here," the professor instructed.

Confusion surrounded me when I left the auditorium that afternoon, nagged by his comments. *Why did I take the class?* Years before, when Da died, my mother told us he had an accident in his car—and that was it. He, and his death, were never spoken of again. By anyone. I realized I had questions that needed to be answered.

For several weeks, I traveled the route from New Paltz to Brooklyn repeatedly, riding the bus to the Port Authority in Manhattan, an urban cesspool, and then two subway trains, each time planning to ask my mother about my father's death. But each time, I chickened out.

Instead, I bought tickets for *Whose Life Is It Anyway?*, a Broadway play starring Richard Dreyfuss, which explored the question whether one has the right to end one's own life. The play hit home, but I again lost my nerve that day, not knowing how to even begin a conversation with Ma.

When finally I mustered the courage to ask her, I was armed with the death certificate I received from the New York City Department of Health. My professor had suggested I write away for it. He said it might answer some of the questions I had about Da's death.

When the official-looking envelope arrived in my mailbox a few weeks later, I carried it into my room, my hands sweating as I turned it over and over. Sitting on my bed, I took a few deep breaths. I knew in my bones what the truth was, but part of me dreaded the confirmation. I slowly peeled open the envelope and unfolded the paper.

My eyes scanned the document and fell on the "Cause of Death" line. There, typed in Times New Roman, was the word *suicide.* Startled, I let out a small gasp. I closed my eyes and thought back to that morning, so many years before, with the cop at the door and me, lying on my cot, looking in the living room mirror. I cried for my loss, for all my father had lost, and for all that would never be.

I had to ask my mother. I got a ride down to the city and made it to her apartment just after lunch. Ma was puttering around cleaning up. I realized it was now or never.

"Hey Ma, you have a second?' My palms were sweating, and I could barely hear my voice over the beating of my heart.

"What is it?" She walked back from the kitchen and stood in the hallway with a dustcloth and can of Pledge. She was wearing the usual housecoat and apron even though she wasn't cooking.

"Um . . ." I stammered, feeling the sweat creep up to my armpits. "Um, I've been wanting to talk to you about something for a while."

Her pupils constricted almost imperceptibly, like a cat preparing to pounce. I could feel her dread, and her walls went up. She clearly already grasped that whatever I wanted to talk about was going to be uncomfortable. But talking about anything was uncomfortable for her.

"What is it?" she repeated, her voice rising at the end.

"I want to ask you about Da's death. I got his death certificate from the city, and it says it was suicide." It came out in a rush.

The words had barely left my lips when she started shrieking.

In a swift move, she spun to her right, grabbed a large red umbrella from the metal stand near the front door, and started beating me with it. She rhythmically whacked me on the back, punctuating each syllable as she screamed at the top of her lungs, "It's none of your business!" She spat out her hateful words, which sliced into me like thin slivers of glass. They hurt. Some of them remain forever embedded.

I wondered how she could have kept this hate and pain so deep within her for so long. Was it shame or guilt that made her want to keep any reference to him buried? Was her heart broken because she loved and missed him? I didn't know.

I kept speaking. The questions I had to ask had festered inside me for a very long time. "Why did he kill himself? Why did you not tell us?"

She kept screaming and hitting and I kept asking.

I needed her to tell me now what she should have told me as a six-year-old that fateful day in July, over a decade earlier. The elapsed years had done nothing to soften her. She showed no tenderness, no sorrow, only fury and denial.

Why did he do it? Did she think he might? What was going on that was distressing him enough to take his own life? Did he love us? How could he have done this to us?

My brother, who still lived with her, in a room with a locked door, heard the screams and ran out to pry her off me. She screeched as he held her back, her legs and arms flailing, clawing at the air.

"I wanted to go to my grave with this!" she screamed, over and over. "You have no right to ask me about this! It's none of your business!"

Her entire being seemed to yearn to snuff out any remnant of my father's life. She was intent on denying reality. *None of my business?* How could it not be? He was my father.

She'd never beaten me before. I think beating me would have meant caring enough about something I had done, or who I was, to elicit such a strong reaction. Or maybe it was that it would have meant touching me, and she couldn't bear that. Or she was so stunted, so walled off by her mental health challenges, that she was incapable of expressing *anything*, locked away in her own misery. The distinction may be important academically, medically, but it wasn't important for me.

Her reasons didn't matter to me then, nor do they now. I was the one left injured, the one who would never get the answers I needed. At least now I understood why my father hadn't been buried in a Catholic cemetery. Although he was the only one of us who cared about being Catholic, the Catholic Church had refused to bury him, deeming suicide a "grave offense" against God. I wondered why they allowed the funeral to happen in their church at all. The church judged him disloyal to their God because of his failure to surmount the torment in his mind. He, himself, put out the flames of anguish his faith could not extinguish.

Chapter 53

Rye, New York, 2013

Many years later, I read a book review in *The New York Times* about *After Visiting Friends: A Son's Story* by Michael Hainey. He wrote about his father's secret life, which he uncovered after his dad's death. His father had a relationship with another woman on the other side of the midwestern city where the author had grown up. Mr. Hainey was a magazine editor. Like me, he was six years old when this happened, and his father was a newspaper man. I reached out to him, and he encouraged me to not let the time gone by dissuade me from my curiosity about my father.

I did a bit of research online and learned from *The New York Times* archive that my father was the first suicide on the Verrazzano-Narrows Bridge. Two poor souls attempted before him but didn't succeed. In the final line of the short piece I read, "His wife told the police he was despondent." These eight words jarred me. I was stunned to learn my mother had offered information, an actual observation of his mindset, to someone other than us, to a stranger. For my entire life, no shred of information, no admission of knowledge, ever parted her lips. My stomach dropped. She was still alive when I read this, but I didn't ask her about it. I knew she'd have nothing to say.

I found out that my father had left the car running. He took the time to unlace his shoes, take them off, and line them up side by side next to the car before he jumped. This information shook me to my core.

Studies have shown that even a short fence, one that's easily climbable, drastically decreases suicides. When offered just a moment to pause, most people realize that ending their life is not the best choice.

My father took the time to unlace his shoes and place them neatly to the side, and yet he still jumped. I wonder what he thought about as he did it. Did he think about us? Did he see our faces in his mind? Did he think about the depth of pain that would be inflicted? Or was he in a fog, a trance, beyond reach, when he did a plié over the edge of the earth?

I had grown haunted by thoughts that if I'd only been cuter or funnier as he left for work that day, he might still be alive. *Was it my fault? Could I have stopped him?* Now, I was haunted by the vision of his unlaced shoes.

Chapter 54

New Paltz, New York, 1979

Senior year came to a close, and the sun was a brilliant gold coin that Saturday in late May, warming the campus and hinting at all that lay ahead. We gathered on the quad, where rows of white folding chairs were lined up neatly to accommodate the graduates. I made it. Having arrived as a sixteen-year-old desperate to break free of my home life, I was leaving a confident, self-sufficient, worldly young woman, ready to face whatever came next.

Surrounded by family—parents, siblings, aunts, uncles, cousins, and grandparents—the gathered graduates inhaled the scent of lilacs and mock oranges blooming in the beds that edged the lawn. My brother had dropped me off on my first day, and my mother was here on my last day.

In the months before graduation, I scrambled to find a job. It was not easy, despite the fact that I had worked three jobs while in New Paltz and at the outdoor markets when I lived in France. The day after graduation, I started with Alitalia, the Italian airline, working at JFK Airport. I moved back in with my mother, but there was no room for me in her new place. So I squeezed into a twin bed next to hers, the rhythm of her relentless snoring grating on my nerves like chalk scraping against a blackboard. As I tried to sleep, my mind was already planning how to get out of there, yet again.

The Alitalia terminal buzzed with chaos, a place where the air always felt thick with frustration. I was twenty and eager to prove myself, but it was an uphill battle against my male colleagues, who made it clear I didn't belong. "A man should have this gate agent job!" they said, waving their arms as though they were still in the "old country." "You are young. So pretty. You should be home, barefoot and pregnant. A man should be taking care of you." Little did they know no one had taken care of me for a very long time. But I swallowed my frustration and smiled through gritted teeth. I was tough, and this job, as unprofessional as it was, was teaching me new lessons.

The airline was notorious for canceling flights without warning, and when these dreaded announcements blared from the overhead speakers, chaos ensued. It was like watching a wildfire start with no water in sight. People would scream, cry, and curse in every language imaginable. I could feel the anger radiating from them, their disbelief turning into rage. Cries of "Vaffanculo!" came from a little woman dressed in all black, stockings rolled down around her knees, hairs sprouting from a mole on her chin. I felt like I was being cursed by a witch.

I stood, straddling the luggage belt, to try to calm the storm, attempting to speak over the shouting and the clattering of bags. My voice was a mere murmur against the cacophony, but I did it anyway. "Please, calm down," I said loudly, trying to be the voice of reason amid the madness. At the same time, I called for security, hoping they'd arrive before someone threw something at me. I learned quickly that the anger wasn't about me; it was about much bigger things—the injustices of life, most notably among them the airline and its incompetence. I began to understand that people's behaviors toward me often had nothing to do with me at all—a very good lesson to learn.

Every day brought a new adventure. Mondays meant dealing with parents trying to pass off four-year-olds as infants to avoid buying them a ticket; the fact that they had to show a passport with the child's date of birth on it somehow eluded them. But the real fun was on Tuesdays, when I handled seat assignments, which were done by sticking seat numbers to paper boarding passes. I wielded my little bit of power like Catherine de Medici, seating rude passengers next to nuns, or cramming obnoxious ones between two sweaty, grumpy travelers.

Wednesdays, I greeted arriving flights and dealt with unclaimed luggage. Sometimes I had to break open locked suitcases to clear them through customs. I found wheels of fontina, crumbly blocks of pungent Parmigiano-Reggiano, and phallic-looking dried meats stuffed in corners between socks and underwear.

Despite all the lessons I learned from managing customers and navigating the constant onslaught of misogyny from my coworkers, I knew I needed more. More than just the madness of the chaotic airport terminal. More than the feeling of being invisible to the men around me. I wanted a challenge. I wanted recognition. I wanted more space to grow, to prove myself to the world.

Chapter 55

Brooklyn, New York, 1979

That first summer after college, my mother decided to visit her brother, John, in Missouri—the brother who came to town every year for Easter dinner when my grandmother was alive. On my day off from Alitalia, I woke up thrilled to have the living room to myself. I leaned back on the couch, feet propped up on the rickety coffee table, hoping it wouldn't collapse under me. Ma had left the day before, setting off for the Port Authority to catch a bus to Missouri.

The black phone on the wall in the kitchen began to ring insistently. The kitchen, with its paper calendar advertising the local insurance agent and the stained oven mitts hanging from magnetic hooks, felt suspended in time. I headed in, the drip of the faucet keeping time with the *brrrring* of the rotary phone, expecting it to be my mother on the other end letting me know she'd arrived safely. I grabbed the receiver and pressed it to my left ear, tugging the long twisted black cord into the hallway.

It was John, who was waiting for her at the bus station in Saint Louis. "Um," he began. "The bus from New York arrived and your mother didn't get off. She wasn't on it." He normally called her Sis. This wasn't good. He stopped, silence filling the space between the *pings* of the water dripping from the kitchen faucet.

A thought went through my mind. *Wow, she finally did it. She left. She's gone.* It had been more than a decade since Da died. A few months earlier, I had learned the truth about my father's death, that he made the choice to end his own life. It left me tormented and sad that he didn't instead choose to get on a plane to California and start a new life. Just walk away. Drive. Get on a plane. A train. A bus. Kick restart.

Living in France for a year and a half made me realize how big America is and what possibilities for reinvention it offers. I always wished my father had made that choice. I thought maybe that was what my mother had just done.

That day, as I heard my uncle's words on the phone, my insides felt flat. All these years of anticipation, and here it was. It was a relief in a way. Maybe it was time for her to be gone. We were too old now to be put in foster care, which is what should have happened if anyone had noticed us earlier on. She had disappeared. Maybe this wasn't so bad.

I hung up. My brother had come out of his bedroom and now he looked at me expectantly. "Who was that?" he asked. Although younger by almost three years, I was the one who had already moved away from my mother, physically and mentally. I was only back at her apartment temporarily.

I turned to Thomas, dreading telling him, since I knew he and my mother were still intertwined in a noxious, symbiotic, codependent relationship. I wasn't sure how he'd react.

"That was John. He says Ma didn't get off the bus," I said, warily.

"What do you mean? Was she sleeping or something?" he asked, coming closer to me.

"No. She wasn't *on* the bus," I answered, gently. I knew this would freak him out. His face crumpled, like a truck had smacked into him. He was panicked, I'm sure wondering how he would survive without her.

My mother seemed afraid of him, yet she catered to his every whim—ignoring the drug-dealing business he still operated out of his bedroom, cooking and cleaning as though she were his maid, and paying parking tickets that piled up because he regularly failed to wake up and move the car, the car he had co-opted from her. Was it the fear of his reaction—he was quite imposing with a fiery temper—that drove her to not confront him, or was it the fear of him leaving her alone? She ran hot and cold. It was hard to know what made her tick. I had moved on from his world of drugs and avoided him.

Before graduation, when I was still away at school, I called to check in from time to time. "Well . . . thanks for calling. I couldda been lying in a pool of blood," she sneered, her voice laced with sarcasm.

Sometimes I couldn't help but jab back at her. "Well, then you wouldn't have been able to answer the phone, so it wouldn't have mattered."

Other times, she'd just be annoyed. "Why are you calling? Wudda ya want from me?" she would ask, her paranoia in full bloom, convinced I was only calling to get something from her, when all I wanted was connection.

A few months before her bus trip, I sent flowers for Mother's Day. I called to wish her a happy day and check that the flowers arrived.

"Yeah, I got them," she grumbled.

"Are they not nice?" I probed, confused by the hostility in her voice.

"I'm allergic to flowers. They make me sneeze," she snarled, as if I'd committed some crime. "I threw them in the garbage," she told me.

I was fed up with the confusing push and pull, rejection followed by neediness, neediness followed by rejection. When she hung up on me, I didn't care. She never acted like she wanted or needed to be with me, and if she thought I wanted or needed *her*, she became extremely difficult to deal with.

I began to understand that her intense fear of abandonment, the lashing out, and even the rejection wasn't her choosing to be so mean. It was deeper than that, a symptom of a personality disorder, a mental health illness out of her control.

Despite his bravado as a drug dealer, Thomas was still just a lost boy. He had been shoved aside, never learning how to express his feelings. Never allowed to have any.

My fantasies of my mother disappearing were soon doused. We got news a few hours later; she would still be with us—with us in her way of *not* being with us. The original bus had broken down somewhere en route, with passengers then split up onto other buses and my mother's arrival much delayed.

My brother raced to answer the phone when it rang this time, a big smile of relief breaking across his face. I stood back, quiet, a level of disappointment edging in, wondering what might have been. How it might have been better without her.

Chapter 56

New York, New York, 1979

Ma returned home from Saint Louis two weeks later without much to say about her adventure. I, however, was setting off on my own and, having saved up some money, got an apartment for myself in the neighborhood. And the following spring, having had enough of the misogyny at Alitalia, I landed an interview with one of the French firms in the city. My mind drifted back to all the job applications I had sent out before graduation that were widely ignored, in what felt like a million little rejections. I'd reached out to the French Embassy in the process of sending résumés far and wide across Manhattan, hoping something would stick. But every response came with the same question: "How many words a minute do you type?" It grated on me. I knew the young men with their bachelor's degrees were never asked that question, never scrutinized over a skill that seemed beneath them. But it was 1979, and I had to play by the rules, whether I liked it or not.

I had swallowed my pride and signed up for Betty Owen Secretarial School while working at Alitalia, forcing myself to walk into that uncomfortable classroom a few times a week. The *clack-clack-clack* of the typewriters and the stiff metal chairs gave me the willies. All of it felt wrong. It was humiliating, but I did it. I practiced, even though I sucked at typing even after weeks of trying. I hated that I felt compelled to do it, but I added it to my résumé.

So it was under false pretenses that I showed up at the offices of Neyrpic Engineering, presenting myself as a candidate for the secretarial position they were seeking to fill. My French was flawless, and the president, Martin Blanchet, who interviewed me, was clearly impressed. Bernard would be so proud of me. We hadn't dated since I left Grenoble for New Paltz, but we were still in touch. He was my biggest cheerleader.

Finding out I went to school in Grenoble, the city where Martin grew up, seemed to seal the deal. We bonded over patisseries and bar tabacs in neighborhoods we both knew. The conversation was effortless, a connection between two people, and for the first time in a long time, I felt like I belonged. The job I thought I was applying for didn't even matter anymore. This connection, this unexpected bond—it was like it was meant to be. I could already feel the door opening just a crack, and I wondered if this could be the beginning of something that changed everything.

As we stood up and walked to the doorway of his office, Mr. Blanchet smiled and said, "I think you'd be a great fit." Then, gesturing to the typewriter that sat on a desk in the outer area, he asked, "Could you just type up a letter?" *Shit.* My stomach dropped. I was *so* close.

Putting on my best game face and most hopeful smile, I told him I really couldn't do that. "In a pinch, I could peck out a letter, but I really don't type very well. I top out at thirty-five words a minute, which apparently isn't very good at all."

The clock on the desk ticked. The silence stretched on. He just kept his eyes on me as if trying to decipher the next move. I tried not to blink. "If you hire me, we"—yes, I actually said *we*—"we would *have* to hire a secretary." It was bold, but it was the truth.

In a stroke of enormous luck, he hired me. And *we* hired a secretary. Martin had seen something in me. My determination? My confidence? My intelligence? My intense desire to be offered an opportunity to grow? I don't know, but over the next few years, he gave me the space to prove myself, to show him what I was capable of. He gave me the freedom to shine. He proved to be a true mentor.

I had an office and a secretary. I oversaw project management and marketing, traveling to places like Ketchikan, Alaska; Wenatchee, Washington; and Twin Falls, Idaho. The work was challenging and engaging. I finally felt like I was using my brain.

The job allowed me to continue to rent my tiny apartment in Brooklyn, finally free from the cramped twin bed next to my mother's. It was a relief to have my own space, even if I shared it with a family of roaches. I had my own set of Revere pots and a color TV—everything I needed. Parked outside was an old VW Beetle bought with money I had saved, red, just like the one my da left on the bridge.

I was still figuring life out, but I was living it on my own terms.

The job kept me busy, sometimes too busy to date. Or maybe I just used that as an excuse. I'd been told that I came off as intimidating, which I really didn't understand. I was certainly self-sufficient. Thanks to my mother's directive when I was six, I had no choice. Maybe men needed women to seem needy. I found most guys my age childish, inexperienced. Outwardly I appeared closed off, but deep down I craved connection. I was afraid of being hurt, being rejected, but I always had hope.

Chapter 57

New York, New York, 1981

I was proud of how far I'd come: my independence, my career, my hard-won freedom. But self-sufficiency had a shadow side—it didn't leave much room for letting anyone in. Still, no matter how guarded I seemed, I always carried a quiet hope that connection might find me anyway.

Vickie, a friend of mine from my days at Alitalia, and I signed up for a tap class just for fun; I didn't expect it to lead anywhere. After class, we stopped in a bar on the Upper East Side with our black tap shoes and towels in bags draped over our shoulders. As we sat down, a man spotted us across the crowded room. He flashed a smile as he jostled his way over. Tall, with thick dark wavy hair and a full throttle smile—Don was his name. He bought us beers and chatted us up.

At twenty-two I was already afraid my life was passing me by. Everyone else seemed to be moving forward, full of purpose. My job was amazing, but the rest of my life felt at a standstill. Then Don showed up. I had literally tap-danced my way into his life, and he seemed to notice everything about me. He made me feel like a new chapter might be beginning.

He was ten years older, smart, funny, and, *incredibly*, into me. I wasn't used to that kind of attention. He wined and dined me, ushering me through crowded restaurants by the small of my back, charming his way to the best table without a reservation, and, by dessert, he'd be best friends with the people seated next to us.

It didn't matter to me that he was ten years older or, if I was honest, so self-absorbed. It was a way out and I took it. I climbed into that lifeboat and didn't look back.

Wedding bells rang the following spring. We married at the house of his friend in New Jersey, a man thrice divorced. Burgundy flocked wallpaper surrounded us, and the dining room was castle-themed with dark, ornate, medieval-styled furniture. Don thought it looked great, so I kept my mouth shut.

His parents, who flew in from Ohio, were friendly and chatty. A handful of his friends and some colleagues showed up. Martin Blanchet and a few other people from my office came, and Vickie, who had been with us when we met, stood by my side as my maid of honor. My mother came wearing the pretend smile she trotted out in public. My brother, beside her, looked uncomfortable, not sure whom to talk to or what to say. My sister, who had moved to Texas, didn't come, call, or send a card.

Like all of my big life decisions, this one, too, was made in a vacuum. Don had charmed my mother, playing to her narcissistic streak that he understood so well. My brother, who barely knew him, offered no opinion. My family's indifference was all that held us together. The threads that connected us were tentative, as flimsy as lace.

I smiled as the camera clicked and pretended this was what happiness felt like.

The next morning, snow fell as we boarded our flight to Hawaii—a rare April blizzard. It wiped the tarmac like a clean slate—*like my life,* I thought, gazing out the airplane window.

The trip felt like the beginning of something new, but on the return, reality hit. Don unlocked the door to a small house perched above a pond the locals called a lake. It wasn't much, but it was his. "Welcome to my home," he said as I stepped inside, giving me pause. *Not "our" home? Was I just a bit player in his life?*

I moved in, with my few boxes of possessions and a fragile container full of hope. But when I looked around that first night—at the wood paneling, the pond, and my new husband—I felt it. A flicker of doubt.

Had I escaped anything? Or had I just traded one kind of loneliness for another?

Chapter 58

Pleasantville, New York, 1982

A few months after the wedding, Thomas called me out of the blue. "I'm thinking about moving to Texas," he said, his voice unsure. *Texas?*

He had never left my mother's apartment. Never cleaned a toilet, never even washed a dish. He'd tried to make a fresh start at Long Island University in downtown Brooklyn, but despite being very smart, he floundered. There were too many ghosts from his drug-dealing days that he couldn't escape.

"Peggy and Roy are down there. Terry, too. At least I'll know some people," he added.

Peggy and her husband, Roy, had settled in San Antonio a few years earlier, trading a stoop for a porch, thinking life might be easier. Our only cousin, Terry—Uncle John's son—was a criminal attorney there. So it seemed like the best place to go. And I guess if Thomas got caught dealing drugs in Texas, at least he had a friend in high places.

He landed in San Antonio with a duffel bag and a college brochure. He enrolled at the University of Texas a week later and rented a place near Peggy and Roy. I wanted it to work for him. I really did. But starting over isn't easy, and I'm sure he kept looking over his shoulder.

Thomas was extremely intelligent, great at math. But high school was a disaster. Kicked out of Brooklyn Tech, he was only able to graduate from Fort Hamilton because of the attendance letters I forged for him.

In Texas, he tried. He did. But the pull of the old life still had a grip on him. He had been a dealer for so long, he struggled, not knowing how to be anything else.

Back in New York, I was learning how to be married. Don and I would arrive home from work separately and eat takeout at our dinette set like we were in some sitcom. Once in a while Thomas would call. He was trying—I could hear it in his eager voice as he emphasized the good parts about his new life in Texas. From time to time, he asked for money. Knowing his history, I only wrote checks to the university or to buy equipment or pay for licensing for businesses he wanted to start.

The space between us remained. The distance wasn't just geographic, it was also the layers of memory and silence we learned from Ma. I didn't feel close to him. I didn't feel close to anyone.

I learned that escape wasn't a destination, but a muscle to be built one step at a time. I was doing everything I could to walk not just away from something, but toward something else entirely. Work, at least, gave me a compass and structured my days.

Chapter 59

Stamford, Connecticut, 1982

For the first few years, the job at Neyrpic felt full of possibility. Martin Blanchet, my boss, was generous, encouraging, confident, and supportive. His energy was contagious, and I was doing great things.

But then the merger happened. Our little office was swallowed up by a large, old-school New England–based engineering firm, Combustion Engineering—a name all too fitting for what I was about to endure.

Walking into the offices in Connecticut that first day, I adjusted my silk J.Crew dress and matching cardigan, looking as polished as I could muster. But as soon as I entered that cavernous office, the air hit me—stale and suffocating. The space was just outside the city, yet it felt like another world.

In the conference room, I laid out my proposal, detailing innovative ideas for an upcoming project. I felt a shift in the energy; it was slower, heavier. The middle-aged men with their brown suits and Brylcreemed hair wouldn't meet my gaze. They huddled in clusters, pushing stale ideas. I felt like I was being dragged through mud, back in time.

Their subtle dismissals became routine, and then less subtle. My suggestions met with sighs or sidelong glances. The engineers under my supervision barely acknowledged my presence inside their smoke-filled rooms and bloated egos. They weren't going to let me in—a woman, barely twenty-three, with too much ambition and not enough space to move.

I'd gone from being the number two person at our small firm in Manhattan, respected and responsible for much, to being a nameless cog in the gears of a massive corporation. Now, I was just . . . there. Lunchtime came and went. I always ate alone. And the break room fell silent whenever I entered.

Determined to get the hell out of there, I enrolled in night classes at NYU Stern School of Business, with my boss's support. The MBA program became my beacon, a tangible path out of the stifling environment. I immersed myself in coursework, taking classes in the evening when I wasn't traveling, my textbooks a refuge from the daily grind.

Then I earned an invitation to give a speech at an alternative energy conference in Beijing. It was my first trip to China, and I addressed an audience of hundreds of engineers in a massive auditorium on the future of alternative energy. I was also invited to a private meeting with the minister of energy—who, remarkably, was a woman too. I thought this might be a chance to make my mark, to show the old men back at the office what I was capable of.

But I was wrong. Instead, it amped up the tension and their insecurity. The space that already felt too small was now closing in on me. I was sick of wasting away in endless meetings with sallow-skinned men in saggy suits, their voices flat with regret. They had climbed the corporate ladder, I imagined, rung by painful rung, only to realize, too late, that their lives had passed them by.

I didn't want to be one of them. I wanted more.

Two years of enduring their bitterness was enough. Mornings

were the hardest; I often pulled over on my way to work, battling waves of nausea and sometimes vomiting on the side of the road. One particularly grueling day, after yet another meeting where my ideas were overlooked, I sat in my car, hands gripping the steering wheel, and made the decision. I couldn't do it anymore.

I said *no* to Combustion Engineering and *yes* to myself.

Chapter 60

Patchogue, New York, 1985

It seems that many decisions get made when people are sitting in cars. Sometimes in the back seat, by two women who hadn't spoken in over a decade.

A few years into our marriage, Don and I drove to Brooklyn from time to time to see my mother and my aunt Joan—separately. Two women bound by blood and silences, they hadn't spoken in more than a decade since the fallout over my grandmother's will. Still, I kept in touch with both of them.

A relative had died. Their mother's sister, Edna, with whom we were never close, had lost her husband. I only remembered them from one visit after Da died decades earlier. I missed him fiercely as I walked the beach that day, wishing he could chase the waves with me, my grief so raw.

Now, Edna's husband was gone, and both my mother and aunt wanted to pay respects—but not together. I offered to take them. I made them both sit in the back, the hump between them, in the same red VW I bought years before. I thought of the cross-country trip Bernard and I took in another VW Beetle. I smiled, thinking of the affection Bernard and I still had for each other. We remained in touch. Turning the radio dial to an AM station, we hit the road for a very quiet two-hour drive. Despite the eighty-degree temperature outside, the back seat was frosty.

Less than a week later, Edna went to bed and didn't wake up. When we visited her the week before, she'd shown us old family photos and talked about her late husband with a soft, aching kind of love. I wasn't surprised that she followed him so soon.

Once again, Ma and Joan sat in the back as I chauffeured them to Patchogue. But on this day, the weight of death loosened something between these two women. Somewhere around Exit 49 on the Long Island Expressway, the ice began to thaw, with help from Gloria Gaynor and then Blondie.

"I like this song," Joan said, tapping her foot to the beat.

"Me, too," my mother chimed in.

No "I'm sorry" from either one of them. No acknowledgment of a decade of silence. No hug. But memories and laughter began to tumble out.

By the time I dropped them back in Brooklyn, the two of them had made plans to meet again without me. They brokered a quiet truce, on their own terms. No grand apologies, no dramatic reconciliations. Just a nod, a shift, an opening, and then the hatchet was buried. The sharp elbows and bitter words were quietly put aside.

Chapter 61

New York, New York, 1986

Wall Street didn't operate with such grace. If the back seat of the car was about unspoken wounds and delicate negotiations, the trading floor was a chicken coop full of roosters, each one strutting more forcefully than the next, jockeying to be the biggest "cock." I had front-row seats to a constant barrage of dares and bravado. The traders seemed to be motivated by a relentless need to prove dominance, even when the market stood still. When the market was slow, they invented other kinds of bets, no matter how trivial or idiotic, to fill the gap—how many Big Macs or spicy chicken wings could someone inhale, or who could bench-press the most; anything was fair game.

Someone once overheard me say that I was five-five. I said it without thinking; I had rounded up, like everyone does. I was actually five-four-and-a-half. Maybe.

"No way you're five-five," someone barked across the desk. "Prove it."

In a nanosecond, money was flying. A few grand thrown down on both sides of the bet. A tape measure miraculously appeared—of course it did—from some assistant's desk drawer. Suddenly I was standing tall in the middle of the trading floor, heels off, arms outstretched, while someone crouched down and called it out.

"Five-four-and-a-quarter."

A few weeks later, it was sit-ups. Sick of hearing about the guys' gym routines, I made the mistake of belittling the difficulty of doing two hundred crunches.

"Bet you couldn't do it," he challenged. And that was it.

For two weeks I trained every night, no matter how tired I was. Feet wedged under a door, I got carpet burns on my tailbone. I strengthened my core, in every way.

Then, on a quiet Wednesday morning, I lay down on the filthy carpet in the middle of the trading floor and cranked out two hundred crunches. A mortgage-backed trader counted while everyone watched. I won.

Nicknames were dispensed on the desk like M&Ms on Halloween. You got one whether you wanted one or not. Spidey, Ronzoid, Stickman—skinny as a toothpick. Moon Eyes, a salesman who couldn't hide his disapproval when trades didn't go his way.

Me? I got Jojo. Sometimes Roxanne, thanks to Sting and the guys who loved the fantasy of a hooker with heart.

If you didn't make it home after too many drinks or whatever else, you wore a "Xerox" the next day to work—with shame doled out for wearing the same outfit. Someone would announce it over the loudspeaker like it was the morning news.

"Nice Xerox, Jojo."

I wore my nickname like armor, laughed off each Xerox walk of shame, and learned to survive in a world where bravado was currency. Power, even in its most ridiculous forms, stuck. But beneath the nicknames and noise, a quieter truth was waiting—the realization that I'd entered a world I was never meant to understand, let alone belong to.

The truth was, I'd entered a world I hadn't even known existed.

Growing up, my parents didn't have investments, let alone a clue what a bond trader did. Now I was surrounded by people who seemed to believe abundance was their birthright. The best colleges, jobs, bonuses, and corner offices—it was all preordained.

I felt incredibly lucky just to be there. And I always felt like any day I might be found out and asked to leave. I waited for the tap on the shoulder. *Sorry, you're not really supposed to be here.*

After two years at Citibank, I was tapped to be on the recruiting committee, where I was the only woman in the room. Conversations often devolved into frat stories, high fives, and raves about someone's sports ability or shared connections. I often found it painful to listen to.

I lobbied heavily for candidates who reminded me of me: kids who hadn't grown up with summer houses and trust funds, but who knew how to fight for an opportunity and would work like their life depended on it. Because it did.

But I was always ignored. I might have earned a seat at the table, but I wasn't supposed to actually talk. Although I was accustomed to this dynamic in my family, it stung to encounter it yet again at work—and I was starting to feel it echo in my marriage as well.

Because of these experiences, I was beginning to understand power—not just how to earn a seat at the table, but how it could be withheld even when you'd earned it. I was learning to push back, to speak up, even when it cost me.

Chapter 62

New York, New York, 1987

Just as I was starting to find my footing, my brother came home, still searching for his. After a few years in Texas, Thomas flew back one winter day, hoping to start over in New York. He was awkward and still struggled to find the right words. He asked our mother if he could move back in with her while he got his feet on the ground. She didn't even hesitate; she just said no, which must have shocked him after all the years when she'd cooked and cleaned for him without question. Winter's chill was in the air.

Texas hadn't offered the new start he'd hoped for. During his years there, he'd called me periodically as he bounced from job to job, taking classes from time to time. Sadly, through all these years he kept self-medicating, chasing a fix he couldn't find.

Meanwhile, my sister had rewritten her own story. Having met someone new at work, she left Roy, and San Antonio. The soon-to-be second husband came to her office to resolve a computer issue and resolved her life as well. They fell in love and came back to New York together, staying at the house on the pond with me and Don for a few weeks while they found themselves a home and a second chance.

And then there was Don.

He walked through life like he owned the stage—the life of the party, the center of attention, the master of ceremonies. Funny. Loud.

Always on. He loved his jokes. But over time, the punchlines started landing on me, the jabs sharpened, and even the smiles began to sting.

At first, I laughed. Of course I did. I'd been trained to keep the peace. *Maybe this was how it was supposed to be?* I wondered. After all, I grew up with my mother, playing the same game. So I smiled and stood beside him, often confused as to what I was doing there but unsure of what else to do.

As my life improved—as I outearned him, outpaced him, outgrew him—his jokes took on a nastier edge. Like most bullies, his behavior toward me reflected his own insecurities. I felt like an extra on *The Don Show.*

But I didn't want to be an extra. So I stepped back and took a hard look at my life. Something began to click. I realized that I'd been the main character all along.

Sure, I still caught myself trying to earn love like it was a reward for good behavior—staying small, playing along. But the old insecurities were losing their grip. I finally realized I didn't need to beg to be chosen. I could choose myself.

One night, I had dinner with a dozen colleagues, all men. As the night wore on and wine was served, I was touched by the kind, complimentary things they had to say about me. As I listened, I thought about Don and how he used to express and show those same sentiments. But I knew things had changed between us. As I grew up and became the person I wanted to be, he mimicked my mother's behavior, becoming jealous and unsupportive. And insulting. By the time dessert was served, I realized I had to do something. I knew I'd had enough. That wasn't what I wanted in a relationship.

I'd been carrying those voices for years—my mother's, Don's, my own—mistaking them for truth. But they were just noise. Echoes of what had been said or never said.

And one day, in the quiet, I stopped listening to them.

Growth wasn't a switch that flipped overnight. It was a slow shift. I had left Brooklyn, gone to New Paltz. I went to France. I left Alitalia and Combustion Engineering. I went to business school. I earned respect on an incredibly competitive trading floor. With each step, I was rewriting the story I'd been told about who I should be. It was like peeling away layers, finding the parts of me that had been buried under what I thought I should be. Trying to turn my wounds into strength. And with each new discovery, I began to feel stronger and more certain.

Still, on top of all of that, I wanted to feel loved. I wanted Don to be the one who'd hold me up, not tear me down. I wanted to believe we were a forever story. But I came to understand that I was just a prop in his spotlight, an accessory.

I really didn't know what love was. I thought being noticed was enough. I thought love meant doing whatever it took to keep the person I loved from leaving, the way I wished I could have done with my father.

Don wanted kids. But the truth was I was a kid myself. And he acted like one. I wouldn't do it. I stood my ground.

I wasn't going to let someone else define me. I had earned my place—in the world, in my work, in my own skin. But even as I rose in my career, I was still coming home to a man who resented the very thing he claimed to admire.

So I gave him a hand: I got him a job as a broker. But instead of gratitude, I got grief. The jabs and jokes continued at my expense, and I didn't find it funny anymore. They felt familiar, like something I'd grown up around—my mother's insecurities showing up as jealousy and sardonic humor. Only now, I had the confidence to call it what it was.

One rainy Saturday afternoon, when neither of us had an excuse to avoid being together, I finally sat down with him and said it out loud.

"I'm not happy."

"What are you talking about?" He looked away from the television, still clutching the remote.

"I'm not happy with how you treat me. You mock me. You belittle me. Men who aren't my husband treat me better than you do. I don't like being the brunt of your jokes."

"The jokes are funny. You just need to lighten up," he shot back, dismissively.

"No. I don't need to lighten up. You need to grow up. I'm a good person and I want to be treated like one. I'm sick of this."

He shrugged it off, the way he did with anything he didn't want to deal with. But I meant what I said. Discussions were had, ultimatums given. I gathered the courage to tell him exactly what I needed to make things work. Then I gave him six months.

Six months later, I told him I was leaving.

"I found an apartment. I'm moving out," I let him know on a Thursday night in September, after we both got home from work. His hand hovered, a chip full of guac suspended midair. Clearly shocked, he dropped to the kitchen floor. "No, no. Don't go," he begged. "I promise I will change. I didn't think you'd really leave. But I will now. I promise."

I snorted, a bitter chuckle escaping. "You didn't change because you thought I wouldn't have the guts to leave? Wow." That was the problem. It was okay to keep me miserable, as long as he was comfortable. He didn't think I'd have the courage to leave. But I did.

But there was the gun. The one he'd joked about shooting me with if I ever tried to leave him. It didn't feel like a joke now.

One Sunday morning, when he was out, I took the gun from the drawer in his nightstand and drove to the police station in town. I told them I was leaving him. I told them what he'd threatened. They wouldn't take it. It wasn't "mine." Apparently, my life wasn't worth protecting.

So I took it to the one place I knew he'd never find it: my mother's apartment. I slid it under her mattress, telling her what was happening. I didn't know what else to do. A few weeks later it was gone. My mother had mentioned it to my brother, who was still in Texas. He must have told one of his old drug dealer friends, and then it disappeared. I reported the theft to the precinct in Brooklyn.

Ironically, the cop I reported the theft to called to follow up—but not about the weapon. Instead, he wanted to ask me out on a date. I felt unsafe all over again.

A week later, a muscular young guy from my office helped me move while Don was at work. We didn't breathe easy until the last bag was in the truck. I left a note on the kitchen counter: *You weren't robbed. I left.*

The morning after I moved out, Don emptied our joint account. All of it. Every last penny. As if he thought it would hurt me. But it wasn't money I was after. It was to be free of *him*.

Don didn't want the divorce. He realized, too late, the mistake he had made. He wasn't going to let go easily. He apparently wanted to make this as painful as possible. Enter the lawyers.

I got the letter—he was suing me for alimony.

I called my lawyer. "One check. A lump sum. That's it. I'm done. I do not want a monthly reminder of him. I will not write him a check every month."

A few minutes later, my blood was boiling as I dialed the lawyer again. "He better pray I never see him on the street," I snapped into the phone, my voice tight with fury. "If I do, I'll run him over, back up, and do it again, hoping there's a missing manhole cover he falls into. I'll be on the front page of *The New York Post* before I'll write him a check every month!"

There was silence on the other end of the phone. I could almost hear the lawyer's fingers tapping on his desk, unsure if I was joking or not. It didn't matter. Don had pushed me past the point of civility. Eighteen months of bullshit. Eighteen months of roadblocks, frivolous demands, and mounting bills went into getting out of this marriage. Every step I took to get out of this mess felt like wading through thick, foul-smelling mud, and now Don was slinging it at me.

"Give him whatever number he wants," I told the lawyer, my voice flat, as if I was already over it. "One lump sum. I just want to move on with my life. I'm done with his back-and-forth bullshit."

Later, my lawyer thought he was accompanying me to the divorce proceeding, but I said no. "All I need to do is sign papers, right?" I asked. It wasn't rocket science.

"Yes, that's correct," he responded, unsurprised. He knew me well by then.

"I can do that by myself," I said, not wanting to incur his $500-an-hour fee. I didn't want to pay him to sit and watch me sign away the last vestiges of a failed marriage. There were no kids, no reason for this to drag on any longer than it had.

My heels clicked on the marble floors, the sound echoing in the hushed space, as I entered the polished Westchester law office. I was dressed to make a statement: Armani pinstripe suit, with a pencil skirt sharp enough to cut glass. I opened the door to the conference room to see a dozen or so men seated around a polished walnut table, stacks of documents in front of each of them. Their heads all lifted in unison and their eyes scanned me—some looking surprised and some bored, some smirking.

"Who's in charge?" I asked, my voice cool but loud enough to fill the room. My gaze swept over the table, challenging someone to step forward. Don and his lawyer stood up together, their voices overlapping as they tried to outmaneuver each other. I didn't care. I didn't have time for their jockeying. "Fine," I said, cutting them off, my tone blunt and dismissive. I wasn't there to make friends or engage in any more of their childish theatrics. "Just pass me the documents I need to sign."

The silence that followed was thick with tension. The men at the table exchanged glances, but this was *my* moment. I didn't care what they thought. This was the end of the road. And for once, I wasn't going to let anyone—least of all any of them—have control over me.

As I slid the final document across the polished table, watching it glide smoothly past the potted orchid until it stopped just short of the attorney's outstretched hand, for the first time in many months, I felt a strange sense of peace wash over me. "Thank you, gentlemen," I said, my voice calm but firm. "Good luck, Don." The words felt almost empty, but they were all I could muster in the moment.

I stood, stretching my neck and lifting my shoulders, the weight of all that had led to this point rolling off my back. It was done. The worst was over. And then, out of the corner of my eye, I saw him—Don, standing up. *What now?* I thought, already tired of the circus. "Hey, Joanne," he said, his voice unreasonably calm, like we hadn't just finalized a divorce. I turned to face him, countering every muscle in my body, all of which were screaming at me, telling me to walk out the door without engaging. But I couldn't help myself. The absurdity of what was happening pulled me in.

"Listen, I have tickets for a show Friday night," he said, a hopeful smile sliding across his face. "You wanna come?"

I blinked, not sure if I had heard him right. *A date? After everything?* Unbelievable. The heads around the table lifted like puppets being snapped up simultaneously.

"Don," I said, my voice low but steady, "What don't you understand? I just divorced you. I don't want to date you." I shook my head in disbelief. "And I am out of here," I muttered under my breath, turning on my heel and heading for the door. The sound of my heels was the only thing that followed me. This time, I didn't look back. I didn't need to. I was free.

I settled into an apartment in Battery Park City, on the tip of Manhattan, across from the World Trade Center. It was my new beginning. Twenty-five stories up, facing the Hudson, with just enough space to breathe and be. A tiny galley kitchen. A terrace that caught the wind. It wasn't just a new apartment. It was a clean break.

That first night, I kicked my feet up on the railing, looked out at the water, and felt it—freedom. Real, actual freedom. Two months later, I threw a kick-ass divorce party to celebrate.

And I knew, finally, there was no going back. I was in charge of my life. And I was moving forward.

Chapter 63

New York, New York, 1988

I'd left a husband who mocked me for sport. I'd walked out of a job that rewarded the men who ignored me in meetings and then moved on from one where bonuses rewarded the boys' club. That should have felt like freedom. And for a while, it did.

I had a new job at Chicago Research and Trading, a new apartment high above the city, and a new sense of who I was. I wasn't waiting around for anyone to validate me anymore.

Then one night, the phone rang.

I was deep in sleep after a long, exhausting day on the desk. The sound startled me awake. It was the '80s, so this was no soft buzz or text vibration. It was a landline, sharp and urgent, ringing through a dark apartment.

I ran into the kitchen, heart pounding. My first thought: Someone had died.

No one had died. But something did die that night: my sense of safety.

The silence stretched out, static crackling like a storm. Then a voice, creepy and high-pitched. "I want you. I'm going to get you." Heavy breathing followed, like a slobbering dog in heat.

I slammed the phone down hard, repulsed. I checked the locks on the door. Told myself it was a prank. It wouldn't happen again.

The next morning at work, I tried to fake it. To act normal. But after an hour of silence, the guy next to me—an Irish guy in his thirties—sensed something wasn't right. "Hey. You okay?" He was concerned. I told him about the call, the voice, and my fear.

They kept coming. Always in the dead of night. Always that same grotesque voice, like a child reciting something obscene.

On this trading desk at CRT, I was the only woman. I worked surrounded by men, moving in sync with their bets and bluffs and their energy. I matched it. I thought I was one of them. But this? This cracked that illusion. No man on that desk had ever felt this kind of vulnerability. Not like this.

I knew I couldn't keep it quiet. After work, at the bar where we usually traded war stories over cocktails, I raised my voice above the noise.

"Guys—I need to say something."

They kept talking.

"Hey. I need to talk," I said, an edge in my voice.

That got their attention. The bar went quiet. "What's going on, Jojo?"

I told them. About the calls. The voice. The fear. They were stunned. Angry. Protective.

"Whoa, someone's stalking you," a colleague said, eyes wide. The guys were shocked into silence. "That's fucked up. How long has this been happening?"

"It's been a few weeks. I'm really scared, and I don't know who it is."

"What can we do?" Another colleague approached me, stopping before getting too close, sensing my unease.

"I'm not sure. But since I don't know who it is, I can't be alone with any of you. I'm just so scared."

"Okay. That sucks, but we get it." There was murmuring around the bar. The bartender approached and discreetly laid a platter of appetizers down on the bar. Aromas of toasted crostini and roasted peppers filled the air.

"We've got you. We will keep you safe. Once we figure out who this bastard is, we'll take care of him! He'll never do this shit again."

And they meant it. That night, and every night after, they circled around me like brothers. In elevators. In cabs. Walking me home. Calling to check in.

It was the first time I had felt truly safe since I was a kid—since Da held onto the back of my bike, steadying me while I learned how to ride.

Kenny, someone I had worked with at Citibank, had a guy—a childhood friend from the Bronx who now worked in the phone company's investigative unit. His friend advised me to log the calls. With each call, one by one, the bastard revealed himself. He slipped up and called from his apartment. The investigator told me who it was: Tim Johnson, the assistant to a trader I knew. Polite, forgettable. I'd been kind to him, even gone out of my way to make him feel seen because I knew what it was like to feel invisible.

And still he chose to terrorize me. To make it worse, I knew that if I pressed charges, some people would say I overreacted. That I made a big deal out of nothing. That I ruined a man's career. So instead, I let the investigator scare the hell out of him—with his badge visible, he made an office visit, in front of a full audience. Tim was forbidden to come within 150 feet of me. If he saw me on the street, he needed to turn around. If he entered an event and I was there, he had to leave.

He never called again. Our paths never crossed again. But the damage stayed with me. What gutted me most wasn't just the fear. It was that I had to choose silence over justice to protect myself. Because even then—even after everything—I knew how easy it would be to lose everything just for speaking out.

But I did gain something: the absolute clarity that I would never let anyone make me feel small again. Not a husband. Not a job. Not a man hiding behind a phone.

I had survived too much. I had fought too hard.

And now, I was done being afraid.

Chapter 64

New York, New York, 1988

Refusing to be a victim was a turning point—but turning points aren't finish lines. I had declared I was done being afraid, but the truth was, fear had been living in me for years. It would take more than a vow to silence it. To truly reclaim my power, I had to look back at the beliefs that had shaped me: the ones I'd buried deep, the ones that still whispered *you're not enough.*

I'd been in an emotionally abusive marriage, and I stayed far too long. Somehow, I thought it must have been my fault. I believed that my father's suicide was my fault—if only I had been somehow more captivating, he wouldn't have jumped. It still haunted me that he took the time to unlace his shoes and place them neatly next to the car. And I felt that my mother's indifference, her coldness, must be my fault as well—I didn't deserve to be loved.

My father abandoned me by jumping, and my mother did so in a quieter but equally devastating way by ignoring me. She was often physically absent and *always* emotionally absent. I wondered whether the other adults who had crossed my childhood path didn't notice the cracks in my life or simply didn't care. I was struck by a quote from Elie Wiesel—"the opposite of love is not hate, it's indifference"—and how it described my mother. She offered us the opposite of love. There were moments when the resulting loneliness crippled me—when my heart felt as empty and crushed as the beer cans in her kitchen garbage.

Still battling shame and fear, I kept that part of myself shut off. Already feeling rejected, I couldn't risk showing my true self. No one would want to see the messiness and darkness inside. *Who would accept me then?*

It often felt like I was living two lives, with two separate selves. One I showed to the world: polished, practiced, saying the right things, mimicking the right moves. Just like I'd been trained to do as a child. The other, hidden beneath the surface, never quite belonged in the world I'd learned to pretend was mine. I'd been pretending for a long time. I laughed along when friends joked about how "crazy" their mothers were or how "fucked up" their families were, secretly wishing mine were that kind of crazy and fucked up. Once I was out in the world dining in restaurants, I never picked up a glass or silverware first. I watched and learned the new things I needed to pretend to know.

A week after the investigator told Tim Johnson never to come near me again, on a stormy Tuesday evening, I braved the wind gusting off the Hudson to meet up with a few other Wall Street women. A handful of female traders and brokers were already at the table when I arrived at the Italian place in the Village. We gathered, as we did from time to time, for a meal to compare notes and laugh about the daily grind. I slipped into my usual role, keeping my distance from anything too deep and sticking to surface conversations, the ones that didn't expose the mess underneath.

I excused myself, heading to the restroom to wash my hands. As the liquid I pumped onto my palms began to work into a lather, the scent of the Ivory soap transported me back to the apartment where I grew up. To that awful day—the day my mother set me afloat in the world. The day she cut me loose. The day she told me I'd forever have to take care of myself. I returned to the table unable to shake the feeling of rejection.

As the wine flowed, someone mentioned a childhood memory, and without thinking, I shared something I'd never spoken aloud before—the loneliness that had wrapped itself around me as a kid, creating the shame I then carried into my marriage. I didn't expect to feel anything when I said it, but when the words were out, I felt something strange. A small release. Like I had dropped a stone I didn't know I was carrying.

The table fell quiet for a moment. My heart thudded, expecting judgment, expecting distance. But then something shifted. One of the women spoke up, her voice small but steady. She shared a story about her own shame, something she had never told anyone. Her ex-husband beat her, and he used to make her cower under the coffee table until he released her, like a dog. Another colleague joined in, talking about the abortion she had, and how she had never spoken of it before. Soon, one by one, we were all opening doors that had been locked for years. Each of us revealed something we'd been hiding—whether it was fear, a mistake, or a shameful secret. The weight of those stories, once buried and now released, suddenly felt lighter.

I finally saw that it was only when I braved cracking open the door to my true self that others opened their doors as well. Friends showed me that we are all afraid of something. We are all hiding something. We are all ashamed of something. I realized we were all carrying things, and the longer we kept them buried, the heavier they became. But as we shared them, even in their messiness, I saw something I hadn't expected: The vulnerability we were all so afraid of was what connected us. It was like we had been walking around with invisible walls between us, but now those walls were crumbling, piece by piece.

It wasn't an instant change. I didn't magically become someone who could open up without hesitation. But that evening, I caught a glimpse of what it felt like to let someone else see the real me.

However, the shame ran deep. Even flipping through magazines with quizzes about the number of sexual partners I'd had brought it rushing back. I'd always pretended that sex was all I wanted, that I wasn't searching for something deeper, something meaningful. But the truth was that I was lonely and didn't know how to ask for more. I was afraid to reach for a real relationship, convinced that no one would think me deserving. And so the pattern continued for a long time. I found myself with men who offered me nothing more than a warm body, the emptiness of it all gnawing at me.

Chapter 65

Westhampton, New York, 1988

That's why Greg took me by surprise. The connection was immediate; it happened the moment our eyes met across the trading floor. The air was crackling, and something shifted in the space between us. Every muscle in my body suddenly seemed on alert and exquisitely alive, like I'd stepped into a current, an invisible electric charge that hummed beneath my skin.

After I left Don and Citibank, I joined CRT, the firm where Greg worked. We sat only a few feet apart, separated from each other by towers of computer screens flashing numbers like mini Times Square billboards. When I'd lift my eyes from my phone bank, they'd find his behind the screens. He was unexpected, an anomaly in the world of traders. He had a calmness to him, and a modesty that was out of place in this hypercompetitive world of enormous egos. I felt something palpable between us, and it stunned me.

We let it sit. We didn't go near it. We didn't touch it. For a long time.

And then we did. And it slayed me.

I had many lovers before I met him. Some were kind and said they loved me. Some were adventurous and they excited me. Some were attractive and they bored me. But Greg, he was different.

He was tall with a few extra pounds around his waist, a body that spoke of weekend pickup basketball games and evenings with cocktails. He liked to gamble, football, mostly. He was smart and a really good trader. His face was framed by thick brown hair holding hints of auburn. When he looked at me, he made me feel like I had his full attention. Like I was privy to some secret. Like I was the only person who mattered.

We both happened to be on Long Island one weekend in July, the year I left my husband, each of us alone. I was staying at a friend's house in Sag Harbor. I went there for some time to relax. Greg had rented a house in Westhampton to play some golf. He and his wife were giving each other some space. But here we were together, feeling as though we'd known each other forever.

We met in Westhampton, at a golf course where one of his brokers was a member. We played nine holes, batting the ball through thirsty blades of grass and across ponds of sand circled by sedge and fescue that danced and bowed in the breeze.

He bought food and flowers from a roadside stand and made dinner for us, back at his beachfront shack. He threw the fish, fresh from the nearby surf, on the grill out back, and cut the sunflowers, placing them, one by one, in a mason jar found in the old faded teal cupboard. I felt at peace, comfortable in the best sense of the word.

We ate, cross-legged on the deep-pile tan rug, sitting across from each other at a low glass table, eating off thick, exquisite plates that looked like they were bought in Portugal on a vacation long forgotten. The spattering of color in the ceramic enhanced the pale green asparagus spears drizzled with olive oil, and the swordfish glistened with drops of lemon juice. We laughed, we talked—about everything and nothing. I was at ease. We sipped wine; it was red and smooth and seductive.

We abandoned the dishes and walked, side by side, along the

beach as the sun slowly slipped toward the horizon, finally dipping beneath the water's edge. Our feet made imprints, impermanent, in the still warm grains of sand, and our toes curled into the cooler parts, kissed by the water. Time slowed as each word, each glance, became a quiet invitation.

Every molecule within me tingled with energy. My body was charged and restless like a sprinter at the gate. Our skin had not yet touched.

He led the way up the wooden steps to the deck and slid the door open, then turned immediately to envelop me in his arms. The space between us vanished. With his arms encircling my waist, we kissed deeply. I was aware that I was trying to quench a voracious thirst, like a parched desert soaking up each precious drop.

We made love on the floor in the living room. The voice of Jesse Jackson punctuated the pauses, the 1988 Democratic National Convention droning on in the background, an absurd soundtrack to our passion.

I savored the taste of his lips, salty and sweet, and noted the scattering of freckles across his fingers, fingers that grazed my skin like a cool breeze kissing the bark of a jasmine tree. The wind moaned outside like a hungry animal, while he softly whispered as he nibbled my ear. His tongue on my body traced unseen currents, lingering at times to quench his thirst, which seemed to match my own in ferocity. Eventually, the graceful rhythms of our satisfied breath echoed the lapping of the waves as we lay twisted and sticky like licorice.

The rain started, playing music on the corrugated tin roof, the lyrics seemingly written for me. The wooden blades of the ceiling fan stretched out, lazily circling overhead. Scents of coconut oil and briny seashells enshrouded our bodies. The passion we let loose, thunder and tenderness in equal measure, startled us both. Every part of my body was alive, and I knew, without a doubt, that nothing would ever be the same.

I used his toothbrush the next morning. Bristles bent by his teeth. We went into town and sat at the counter at the local diner and ate bacon and eggs. We balanced on the stools lined up along the chipped counter flecked with green, mirroring his eyes. Eyes that saw me. We shared the newspaper. Black ink smudged our fingers as we passed sections back and forth, like a couple comfortable in their connection.

His right hand found my left under the counter. Our fingers intertwined. "How do you like your eggs?" he asked in a soft voice. The first data point collected.

"Bacon or sausage?" His eyes twinkled, enjoying learning these little details. I felt shy but not at all nervous. Although everything was new, it was as though we had been here a thousand times before.

This is what love tastes like.

Startled by the passion discovered in each other, we continued to explore it. He came to my apartment, near our office. We left work separately so no one would know—or so we thought. I had never felt so at ease, so safe. I had never felt so completely loved. I soaked him in like a sponge. He swaddled me, offering safety and warmth I had not known before. For so long, I had thought myself too damaged, too broken, for someone to love me completely. In the warmth of his embrace, I realized that maybe I was wrong. Maybe I could be loved. Maybe this could last. But we didn't talk about his marriage. Having walked out on my husband, I knew leaving was possible. I didn't know what he was thinking. I kept blinders on, not wanting to break this spell.

He was gentle and delicate with me, as though he sensed how fragile I really was, how easy it would be to shatter me. He handled both my body and heart with such tenderness, in sharp contrast to what I had known. He called just to talk, for hours, on the phone at night, his voice soft. He brought me gifts and held me tight. I felt like a lifetime of emotion had finally arrived. I dared to allow myself to feel safe, to believe it was real and that this could be my life, forever. I treaded carefully.

He told me he loved me, not just when we made love, but in the comfortable silences that followed. He spoke of a future, of children—our children—and I let myself imagine it.

We spent hours together, making things up as we went along. We rode the ferry to Hoboken and back again, leaning into each other, his fingers running through my hair. We took drives to nowhere, him struggling with the stick shift of my old Porsche, grinding gears as he pulled out of the tunnel toll booths.

One night, we headed to an old beachside motel in Long Island, but the place felt too sad for me, too cheap. So we turned around and returned to my apartment, where I felt safe.

We met as often as we could, several times a week. We shared dinners out, where he pretended we were married whenever people would chat with us. He made up names for our children. He held my hand, and he held my heart. I dared to believe that maybe, just maybe, this—we—could last forever.

That fall he ran the New York City Marathon. I stood outside my mother's apartment building on Fourth Avenue in Brooklyn, watching him run by with quiet pride. My mother was next to me. She asked no questions, and I didn't offer information about who he was to me. Nothing had changed between us.

I was still working hard at trying to chip away her walls, trying to temper the coldness she wrapped herself in. I still held onto the hope that one day, somehow, she'd change. That she'd become the mother I had always hoped for, the one who'd laugh with me in the kitchen, the one I could share my secrets with, the kind of mother I had always read about. But, deep down, I knew it was a losing battle.

The only time I have ever seen her look truly happy was when I got us tickets to a Giants game, with seats on the fifty-yard line, and a limo ride to the Meadowlands, provided by brokers. She was a huge Giants fan. When we sat down, we were greeted with skeptical groans and taunts from the guys in our section, their eyes rolling. But then it all shifted. My mother came alive, cheering for Phil Simms with a joy I'd never seen from her. "Go Giants!" Her face lit up in a way I had always longed to see, her emotions raw and unfiltered, and for a moment, nothing else existed. The stadium buzzed with energy, but all I could focus on was her—unselfconscious, unguarded, happy.

Riding that high, I thought we were finally having a moment, the kind I had always wished for. I leaned in, the roar of the crowd fading, and told her about Greg, whom we had watched run the marathon the week before. I wanted to share something personal, something real, hoping for a flicker of connection.

But her response was sharp, cutting like the cold wind that was kicking up. "Shhh! I'm trying to hear the ref's call." And that was it. The moment was gone, leaving me alone with the silence between us.

Greg called me every night and on weekends, without fail, from a pay phone near his place. The sound of his voice, steady and warm, caressed me like a soft blanket. I was consumed by my love for him. It wasn't just the passion, the heady fog, the longing—it was deeper than that. It was the feeling of being completely seen, of someone knowing me—not just the polished version I showed the world, but the messy, broken parts that no one ever seemed to notice. With him, I felt safe. For the first time in my life, I felt loved by someone. I could not imagine that going away. To hold on to that feeling, I ignored the fact that he had a wife he went home to, and told myself our love was too strong to rupture.

Which made what happened with my boss, Jim— the offer he'd made me in front of the Odeon—seem all the more disturbing. Finally feeling comfortable and secure in the world, thanks to Greg's love and support, I had let my guard down, just a little, only to have Jim's crazy, entitled proposition shake me to my core.

Chapter 66

New York, New York, 1989

What Greg and I shared was quiet and hidden. I believed we were protecting something real in a world that often felt unreal. He made me feel seen and wanted for who I was. In a stark and wretched contrast, Jim's offer landed like a slap in the face. He would give me a million dollars—not for my mind, or my heart, but for my body to produce a baby.

I woke up the day after Jim's proposition with his words going round and round in my head. "Well, I've really been thinking about this for a while now and I wanted to talk to you about it. I've got a proposal for you. A really good one," he had said, and I knew immediately that it would be bad. Really bad. "It's very important to me and I've given this a lot of thought." He had paused and run his tongue over his bottom lip. "I'd love for you to have my baby. I know it sounds crazy, but I think it would be perfect. I'll pay you a million dollars cash to do it. Please. This is really important to me. It would mean a lot."

I couldn't imagine anything more revolting.

Nauseated and terrified or not, I had to show up: It was a workday. When I arrived, the trading floor was in its usual chaotic state, dominated by the long trading desk lined with stacks of back-to-back screens running down its center, flashing with relentless data. Behind it, the sales force sat at their bank of tiered desks, shouting above the din, digesting the daily economic releases.

I showed up a little earlier than usual to deal with the actual elephant, Jim, as well as the other elephant in the room before the markets opened. My disgust was overshadowed by the tight knot of dread in my stomach. All night long, I had rehearsed little speeches in my head, refining them in the bathroom mirror before dawn—speeches that, God forbid, wouldn't offend his delicate ego, but would let him know in no uncertain terms that there was no way in hell that would ever happen. Speeches that might cushion his fragile self so he wouldn't be embarrassed and/or pissed every time he looked at me, so he wouldn't know how revolting I found him. Speeches that might help postpone my now inevitable firing, for who wants to be reminded of rejection on a daily basis. *Fuck!*

In one corner, along the perimeter of the floor, was Jim's expansive office, a fishbowl of glass exposing it completely to the trading floor. I knocked, then pushed open the door. He was seated behind his desk, feet up. I tried to tamp down my disgust, praying not to vomit.

"Hey, got a minute?" I ventured a small smile that felt like a grimace. "Listen, um, I was thinking about what you asked last night. You know I'm flattered," I said as I screamed at myself inside my head not to retch, howl at him, or claw his face. The words tasted like acid on my tongue. "Really. It's so nice of you to think of me. What an offer! Really, amazing. But honestly, you don't really know me that well. I don't think I'm the right person for you. I've got a lot of shit I'm dealing with right now. Um, but I really, really appreciate it though. I hope you understand. I really am flattered. I think you're a great guy."

There I was, *actually apologizing and thanking this bastard.* This man who made an incredibly inappropriate overture to a subordinate, at least a decade younger than him, and forced me to come into work today and grovel, trying not to offend *him* because my life, professionally speaking, was in his hands. I was groveling at his feet so that he did not destroy my career. The one I had worked so hard to build. Because of what *he* did.

He gazed at me from behind his desk, feet still up, unembarrassed. "Sure. No problem," he muttered, looking me up and down. He didn't even have the decency to apologize, or to act as though he didn't really mean it. He could have blamed it on too much alcohol, a moment of weakness. But he didn't bother. He knew he didn't have to. He either had no clue how out of line he was, which was hard to believe, or he just didn't give a shit. I was doomed.

Chapter 67

New York, New York, 1989

One man made me feel like nothing more than a body with a price tag. The other had made me feel like the only woman in the world for over a year now. Neither story would end the way I wanted.

Greg and I carried on through the winter months, each contact more intense than the last. On Christmas Eve, we found ourselves together, his eyes soft as he called me "Jolie Joanne" a name that felt intimate and tender. "This is for you, my love. You'll have them forever," he whispered in my ear, handing me a small gift, so elegantly wrapped it made me think of Christmas at Joan's house. I tugged on the ribbon and lifted the lid to see a gorgeous strand of pearls with matching earrings. It was the most beautiful gift I had ever been given. He also shared a list with me, a wild, almost impossible list, of one hundred places where he wanted to make love to me. Paris, the city I adored, was on it, and he promised we'd experience it together.

I had never imagined that love could feel this raw, intense, and primal. I had never believed something so consuming could exist outside the bound pages of a book. My body was electrified with every touch, every whisper, while my mind was soothed and my heart calmed.

The sun rose on the new day of the new year.

And then his wife was pregnant. He called me, his voice ragged, raw with emotion. He was crying, looking for something, but I wasn't sure what. Did he want comfort? Did he want me to beg? Did he want an ultimatum? I didn't know, but I was *terrified* that if I pushed too hard, he'd walk away. Show too much emotion, and he'd shut me down, like my mother always had. So I donned my protective shell and kept calm. No tears. No demands. No ultimatums. I told myself I was being rational, mature—but the truth was, I didn't believe I was worthy of being chosen.

His wife must have known about us for a while. The signs were there for a long time. There were too many trips to the store that took forever, and coming home, the scent of me was still on him, my long blond hairs on his clothes. He spent hours on the pay phone, calling me, like he couldn't breathe unless he spoke to me. She had to have noticed and had no doubt been wishing it all away.

After the call he reached out to a friend, a colleague who knew all three of us, seeking advice. This friend told Greg that he had stayed in his own marriage longer than he should have because of his kids and regretted it. He was facing cancer now and realized how short life was. This friend told him not to deny his happiness for duty. That leaving his wife wouldn't prevent him from being there for his children.

"Go to her. Stay with her. I see how much you love her," he told Greg. "That's the love you deserve."

Greg was not that person, though. Although he let this—caused this—all to happen, his sense of duty, or perhaps cowardice, overrode all else.

Yes, I too let this happen. I found myself in a situation I swore I would never be in—the other woman. Guilty as charged. Finding myself walking in those shoes made me understand the gray areas of life. Who was I to have dared judge anyone else? I knew he was married when I let him in. But then I loved him so much, so deeply, I convinced myself we were truly meant to be. And for a time, I didn't regret it.

Greg was the golden boy, who couldn't disappoint his family. He came from an intact, well-to-do family, with several siblings, all of whom went to private schools. He needed to do "the right thing," but by then, it was far too late for that. Of course he'd stay with her. How could I have deluded myself into thinking otherwise? "My parents will be broken. They'd be so disappointed in me," he choked out, hoping I'd understand. Sad that he didn't think of that before. The part of me that still loved him, that part of me that was broken, couldn't help but admire him in a way. He had a family that cared about him, and he them. It was a tragic, bittersweet admiration.

We spoke one Sunday night in late January. He called from the phone booth, the same one that was witness to his unending love, to tell me about his choice. He was staying with his wife.

I told him, my voice thick with the weight of everything I couldn't say, "One day, when you're sixty, you'll find yourself sitting on your porch, in a rocking chair, thinking of me."

The next morning, we went back to work, separately. We sat at our desks, with our friend Rob between us, trying to act normal. Yet we could barely breathe. We both looked like we had suffered a terrible death in our lives. We had, yet we were still alive. We couldn't touch. We couldn't look. No one dared come near us. The people around us, sensing the implosion that had happened, were frightened for us. We were paper-thin, fragile, ready to shred in an instant. Misery engulfed us like a shroud.

Chapter 68

New York, New York, 1990

For a time, I slid down into a black vat of despair, so deep I feared for my life. My mind clouded, lost in an inky, suffocating fog. There were no handles to grasp, no lifelines with which to haul myself out.

My body was paralyzed, as though the weight of distress pinned me to the bed. I couldn't get up. There was no reason to. I missed work. I missed life. The love I had finally found was gone. The hollow ache of my loss seemed immeasurable.

One night, my friend Marianne came into my apartment, determined.

"Come on. I'm getting you out of here," she said firmly, as she helped me out of my bed, her arm around my shoulders. She ran the shower, testing it with her fingers, and handed me a fresh bath towel. "A few of us are meeting for dinner and you're coming with me. I'm worried about you."

I tried to protest, mumbling, "I'm tired, I really don't want to see anyone."

She wasn't having it. Minutes later, she had me dressed and in a cab. The ride felt surreal; I was there, but I wasn't. I sat down at the round table, surrounded by the chatter of people whose lives were still intact. When the waitress came to take my order, I beckoned her lower with a crooked finger and whispered, "Bring me anything. It doesn't matter. I don't care." She didn't blink, apparently unfazed by my helplessness. It seemed she had faced her own demons at some point in her life.

Months later, I read Styron's *Darkness Visible* and felt naked. It was as if my skin was transparent and he was describing my insides, the hollow pit I'd been living in. A small voice echoed in my head, calling out for help, a voice no one else could hear. I was alone and afraid. *I needed help.* I thought about my father, how his depression had consumed him. How he disappeared into it and launched himself off that bridge.

Growing up, a gnawing ache had settled inside me. I longed for someone to guide me through life's bewildering maze. Someone to offer advice about boyfriends, jobs, and first apartments. Someone to cheer my triumphs, to catch me when I stumbled. Mostly, I just wanted someone to listen.

I always had a secret tucked deep within me, coiled tight—the secret of how unbearably alone I felt. My friends seemed to move through life with an easy lightness, as if acceptance and safety were their birthrights. I watched them, wondering what I had done wrong. Was there some invisible ledger where I'd been marked unworthy? If so, how could I make it right? How could I become lovable?

That nagging doubt had clung to me like a shadow for two decades, whispering the same cruel question over and over. *How do you become worthy of love when you've never been shown what it looks like?* I thought what I had with Greg was what it looked like.

I had always thought that if my father had just given life some more time, things could have been so different. I kept that in mind and thought maybe I could hold on too.

So I tried. I really tried. I called a friend and got a number for someone I could talk to. It took me a moment to realize that not everyone has felt like they were extraneous, that they didn't matter—that shoving their head into the oven like Sylvia Plath might not be something they'd ever considered. And for the first time, I wondered if I had been skirting that edge, closer than I'd ever admitted.

I made a phone call. I reached out and made an appointment to meet the doctor who might grab my hands and help pull me out of my despair. I was frightened, but I did it.

I had been loved and discarded. Again.

It was a pain I couldn't bear.

Chapter 69

New York, New York, 1990

Winter turned into spring, and spring into summer. Deep down I knew I had to try to put myself out there, to get on with life.

The men who asked me out, the ones I encountered, were like the more obnoxious guys on my desk. Like the prep school and Ivy League–educated pompous prick who'd pontificate about his perfect life, while shoving his hand down his pants to scratch his balls. The hand that, when not jiggling his testicles, was picking his nose.

He once sent me a hotel lobby–sized floral arrangement with a dinner invitation. He was completely baffled when I turned him down—I, who came from nothing and nowhere, turning down him, who believed himself the crème de la crème? I suspect people like him rarely got turned down.

So I settled for a few "friends with benefits" pairings, telling myself it was the perfect compromise, meeting everyone's needs without any complications. No harm, no foul, or so I thought.

Looking back, I see it clearly for the first time. All the men I chose were inaccessible. They were already involved with someone else, or they were strangers to whom I'd give a fake number as I slipped out of bed. At the time, I told myself it was easier this way, that at least I couldn't be rejected. Someone had wrapped their arms around me and held me close—that's what I craved. I convinced myself I had the power, that I was making the choices. No one could abandon me if I never went all in.

When men stroked my skin and kissed my lips, I hoped this meant they cared. My body responded, aroused by desire, but my soul craved more. Sometimes, I felt soothed and stayed in these quasi-relationships way past the expiration date, but they were never more than a small Band-Aid, pathetically inadequate to patch my gaping wounds. The men I latched onto were always older than me. A therapist might say I had "daddy issues," but I just always felt too old for my skin. Too old for my life. Too familiar was the sting of being ignored, the feeling that I was invisible. I didn't seem to matter. I knew too well the cruelty of circumstance and the harshness of hearts. These crumbs of compassion, these scraps of affection, were more than I was used to. And, for a time, they pacified me. For a very long time, I was like a dog at the dinner table, happy to accept scraps.

In spite of my outward success—my job, the apartment, and cars—I was still alone. I had opened up to Greg and ended up gutted.

That summer, I met Rick through a mutual friend in Battery Park City. Our friend thought Rick and I might hit it off, so I gave him my number, cautiously testing the waters.

He called and invited me for a drink at the South Street Seaport. I wore something unremarkable, my mind still thoroughly tangled up in Greg. But Rick didn't seem to notice. We talked easily, nodding along to Van Morrison, who filled the pauses. "Can I see you again? Maybe dinner this weekend?" he asked as he walked me home. Calm. At ease. Maybe he sensed my skittishness, but he kept at it. He wasn't pushy, but persistent, checking in once or twice a week. Then he introduced me to his friends. He was all in.

Rick appeared at a time when I felt scraped clean, emptied by everything that came before. He had a quiet warmth, a steadiness that felt like a gentle hand on my shoulder when everything else felt like it was slipping through my fingers.

He was impressed by my accomplishments, not intimidated. And he had his own. He was sharp, working as a banking analyst at Goldman Sachs. He was very smart, but it wasn't just that which appealed to me. It was his soft-spoken nature; he radiated a sense of calm that was rare in the world of Wall Street. He was an authentically good guy—kind and modest, he never spoke unkindly about anyone. He was easy to trust.

Being around him felt safe, like coming in after a storm. And I was tired of the rain. I let down my guard. I leaned in. And for the first time in a while, I remembered what it felt like to matter.

Chapter 70

New York, New York, 1990

After I turned down the million-dollar-baby offer and watched my hopes of a future with Greg be blown apart, I tried to reboot my life. I needed to get out of the office, away from the whispers and sideways glances, away from Greg and Jim, whose ogling had become a constant source of discomfort. Happily, that's when CRT sent me to Paris.

JPMorgan had started trading French zero-coupon bonds, and CRT wanted to get in on the action. Stripped of interest payments, zero-coupons sold at a deeply discounted price, with big tax advantages. A few guys on the desk lobbied for the spot, but I fought for it. Hard. I spoke fluent French, had lived there, and already was an arbitrage trader.

Besides, Paris was my escape. My sanctuary.

By then, Rick had begun showing up in small but steady ways. He wasn't part of the chaos. He didn't ask for anything. He was just . . . there. A calm voice. A safe place to land. As everything else cracked and shifted, he was the one thing that didn't.

The stories I shared about my family didn't scare Rick off. If anything, they seemed to bring him closer. His own family's past had horrors that were crushing—his father, just seventeen, was sent to Auschwitz, a Catholic Pole lost in an unimaginable nightmare. His mother's family, exiled to Siberia, carried their own scars. Maybe it was our shared proximity to pain and suffering that became the foundation to our relationship.

The more I got to know him, the more I knew he would never abandon me. That realization was like a lifeline thrown into the stormy sea of my past. I latched on like a New York rat to a pizza crust.

At that moment in my life, having spent decades living in my carefully crafted shell, tamping down the thoughts of being unworthy of love, to have someone I believed truly loved me, someone with whom I could see my life unfolding, was irresistible. So I caved. I believed I had now found someone who wouldn't abandon me. In my mind, that was the best thing I could hope for.

Before I left for Paris, I introduced him to my mother. I watched her perform the dance she saved for the outside world, the Dorothy who didn't let you peek behind the curtain. She charmed Rick with the ease of someone who'd spent decades working on the role. She smiled with that practiced warmth, the smile that never quite reached her eyes. And, of course, he charmed her back.

Still living at her place in Brooklyn, she had recently retired from teaching and filled her time by volunteering at Lutheran Hospital and keeping up with some old friends. She lived on the surface, keeping her world neatly contained, and the rest—her bitterness, her loneliness—remained carefully hidden.

I boarded the plane to France without much of a plan, just a sense of empowerment. Given my credentials, it would have reeked of sexual discrimination *not* to send me. Before leaving, I overheard several colleagues muttering, "Well, they had to send her after *that* mess," thinking the issue was the affair. What they didn't know about was the million-dollar offer. But it didn't matter to me what they thought. I was on my way to Paris.

For the first month, CRT put me up at the Grand Hotel—all marble, silk, and champagne. Checking out the gym, I came upon NBA legends Scottie Pippen and Dave Robinson, fresh off the Bulls' Eastern Conference loss to the Pistons. I refrained from dropping to the floor and showing them my sit-ups.

Eventually, I found an apartment across from the Jardin de Luxembourg. The croissants, the courtyards, and the cafés were intoxicating. Bernard and I picked up as old friends—a familiar rhythm. We had seen each other a few times since we broke up, when he visited New York and when I was in Paris on business. "Tu resembles encore plus fort qu'avant. C'est remarquable," he observed, noting my personal growth. Our friendship was a steady, safe haven. It felt great to be back, catching up with old friends and making new ones at Banque d'Escompte, where I had a seat on the trading desk.

Back in New York, my colleagues dubbed me "the French stripper," referring to how zero-coupon bonds were stripped of their coupon payments. They were grown men *still* acting like frat boys.

I didn't care. I wasn't just surviving now—I was thriving.

Chapter 71

Paris, France, 1990

Even with an ocean between us, Rick and I kept our relationship alive. He visited me in Europe twice, and I flew home every third weekend—it was part of my work package, a tether to a life that still felt in flux.

We spent Thanksgiving together in Venice. The city with its labyrinth of narrow streets and winding canals was magical, and we got blissfully lost together. The air was rich with history, and the music of footsteps echoed on old stone. We watched glassblowers swirl molten liquid into works of art, and rode gondolas, listening to the gentle slap of the oar against the water. As the sun tossed gold speckles on the canals, we drank Bellinis at Cipriani's, the haze of the late afternoon blurring the edges of it all.

While in Europe, I kept up my weekly calls with Ma, never quite sure which version of her I'd get. Sometimes she was light, discussing the news of the day. But most days, she was cold, the distance in her voice wide. I still, naively, hoped for something more, something real. But it was always just out of reach.

As the Christmas markets started coming to life, with the twinkling lights and scent of mulled wine hanging in the air, I got the call. The New York office summoned me back. They were shutting down the Paris operation. It wasn't a surprise. Trading French bonds had been profitable, but not enough to justify the expense. The life I was carving out, the tentative happiness I was feeling, was slipping through my fingers. I was heading back to the same world, the same people I seemed unable to escape.

Back in New York, it was no surprise when the would-be million-dollar daddy, Jim, informed me there was "no longer a seat at the desk" for me. I smirked, chuckling to myself, the irony thick. Of course there wasn't.

"No problem," I said, my head held high. Greg's wife had insisted we couldn't work in the same office. We couldn't be in the same city. So, they moved him to Connecticut, and me? Well, I was out.

So I took care of myself. Reaching out to colleagues around the street, I landed a job on the futures and options sales desk at Morgan Stanley.

But I had a score to settle, a loose end to tie up. I had been a limited partner at CRT with a financial investment in the firm. I'd put my money in, trusted the promise of growth, and bought into their vision. When I was pushed out, my initial investment was returned to me. Then two months later CRT was bought by NationsBank, and the investment was worth much more. I felt I deserved the gain I would have received if I hadn't been forced to leave. It wasn't just about the money; it was about the principle.

I reached out to a lawyer and got names of a few litigators. I met several of them for drinks at a midtown bar, the kind with dark wood and low lighting, where conversations were private. I laid it all out for them. The investment. The million-dollar baby offer. The day I was let go. The buyout by NationsBank. As the words tumbled out, I watched the lawyers' expressions shift. Their eyes widened, shining with the realization of what this could be: a major lawsuit. Discrimination. Harassment. I saw the gears turning in their heads. This wasn't just my story; it was a case. A big, meaty, profitable case. The kind that makes the headlines of *The New York Post.*

As their excitement mounted, I shook my head. "No," I said, my voice low but firm. "If I sued for that, for the million-dollar-baby proposal, I'd never work again. Not on Wall Street. No one would hire me. Because they're all men. And the firms are all guilty of it in some way," I said, the truth heavy in my voice. I was sad that this was the reality. "I'm only asking for the increased value of my investment. That's all."

They didn't get it at first. They thought I was crazy. I had a clear path to a major lawsuit. Didn't I want to fight? Didn't I want justice? But I wasn't interested in being part of a public circus. I couldn't imagine my life, my background, and my behavior being dragged through the mud, my many sins aired, my professional reputation being torn apart in public.

One letter was sent to the firm's owners in Chicago. Just one. Then an envelope arrived at my door, sent overnight. It was thick with paperwork and a check.

They thought I was giving up. That I was letting them win. But they didn't understand. I wasn't afraid of the fight—I just knew the cost. I wasn't willing to set fire to everything I'd built just to watch it all burn.

So I took the check. And I moved on—because survival, in their world, meant knowing when to walk away.

Chapter 72

New York, New York, 1991

It turns out, walking away was the easy part. Starting over meant stepping right back into the fire—only this time, I knew how to keep from getting burned.

I took the job at Morgan Stanley just after the New Year. Despite its polished reputation, this trading floor was like a frat house too. My desk mates—married, white, conservative men—routinely called me a "lefty, liberal, lesbo, pinko commie." I didn't care. I was happy not fitting into their little mold. They reminded me of the mothers on Seventy-Second Street, the ones who judged my open blazer, their eyes and world views narrowed by blinders.

The reality of a woman being a woman as well as a successful trader or salesperson on Wall Street seemed impossible for many to wrap their brains around. There were a few male clients who wouldn't even speak to a woman.

My first week at Morgan Stanley, the transition from a very laid-back trading desk at Chicago Research and Trading to this uptight, blue-blooded environment felt uncomfortable. But that feeling quickly faded when just behind me, Becky, a very seasoned top producer—elegant, impeccably dressed in a Chanel suit and Louboutin shoes—answered a line for a colleague.

"Yes?" she said into the phone, ready to take a trade order or handle a research query. But that didn't happen; apparently there was a pause on the other end. Then she held the phone aloft, Cartier bracelets jingling, and in her soft southern accent shouted "Hey! This asshole wants to talk to someone with a penis."

That was the moment I knew I would be fine.

After having worked there a few months, having moved to the sales desk to cover hedge fund accounts like Soros Fund Management, Tiger Management, and Omega Advisors, I was among a group of women invited to golf at one of the president's private clubs in Westchester. It was a huge honor, a privilege we'd earned. We were some of the top-producing women at the firm, and it was the kind of acknowledgment we craved. The air was fresh and crisp; it was the kind of day that made you feel alive.

We arrived in limousines and were led through the stone gates and down a winding driveway, the manicured lawns sprawling before us. Stepping out, golf outfits and clubs in hand, we approached the clubhouse, anticipation filling the air.

We passed the ornate ceramic planters dripping with ivy, full of pansies and forest grasses. "Where should we change?" we asked, as we were greeted by the manager, erect in his tailored navy suit.

The response was almost too absurd to process. "There's no ladies' locker room," the man responded, his voice awkward, his feet shifting like he couldn't find balance. He couldn't look at us as he gestured vaguely down a hallway. "Women normally aren't allowed to golf here."

Silence stretched among us, each of us staring at one another in disbelief. There was nothing to do but blink and let the reality settle in. We exchanged looks of shock, frustration, and even amusement.

How could this be happening? How could we be standing in a hallway, holding our golf outfits, in a place we weren't welcome?

The fact that the head of the firm had invited women employees to a club that didn't allow women was so astounding it was almost comical. Had it not occurred to anyone how unwelcome this would make us feel, or did the thought cross their minds and they just didn't care? The invitation suddenly felt more like a gesture to check off a box, an empty token, rather than an acknowledgment of who we were or what we brought to the table. As we stood there, the awkwardness crawled up my neck like a slow burn. How did the president not see the absurdity of this?

But I knew the answer. It was how the firm—and Wall Street in general—viewed women: as an afterthought, as a side issue, as something peripheral to the real players. We didn't matter enough to even be seen, let alone considered.

So, we made the best of it. There was no locker room, no place to change—so we did what women like us had done for years: We adapted. We took the insult, the ridiculousness, and turned it into a moment we could laugh about, even if the joke was bitter. But deep down, the sting lingered. We were here because we were good at what we did, but the world still couldn't quite figure out how to let us in. And it wasn't just here, at this club—it was everywhere.

We were invisible, even when we were standing right in front of them.

Chapter 73

Washington, DC, 1991

We were invisible in plain sight—successful, sharp, impossible to ignore, and still somehow unseen. But invisibility wasn't new to me. I'd grown up in it.

Through lies, omissions, and half-truths, my mother had written her own version of our history. And I was finally ready to read between the lines. On an unremarkable day in May, I found myself on the steps of the Library of Congress with an hour to kill before a meeting at the World Bank.

When we were growing up, Ma told us that the letters her father had written while serving in World War I were here. Of course, we never believed her. For so many years, she had proven herself to be a master of misinformation, starting with lying about my father's death and continuing with her campaign to pit Peggy, Thomas, and me against each other. She was the queen of bullshit.

I pulled open the massive doors, and the familiar scent of old paper and wood wrapped itself around me. Approaching the research desk, I felt a bit foolish. I handed the clerk a slip of paper on which I had written John Frances Callahan, and I watched as she typed it into the computer. "I'll be back in a moment," she said, and briskly walked down a corridor. I was stunned when she returned with a thick stack of my grandfather's correspondence. My mother hadn't been lying after all.

Chapter 74

New York, New York, 1992

As I eased into my new role in sales at Morgan Stanley, life began to take on a steadier rhythm: Rick and I grew closer in the quiet year after Paris. We married late on a lovely Tuesday afternoon on the slightly sloped grounds of the Trail Creek Cabin in Sun Valley, Idaho. Soft light, the color of daffodils, threw a dappled diamond pattern on the freshly mowed lawn, a breeze tossing around the sweet scent of the cuttings. It was just the two of us with our witnesses—the woman who had been our fly-fishing guide the previous day and the photographer's husband—silent partners in our intimate event. The mayor of Ketchum roared up on his motorcycle and dismounted, adjusting his leather jacket. He officiated, standing between two baskets of wildflowers, as we spoke our vows. Our heartfelt words formed a balloon of hope held aloft by a gentle wind.

Rick had proposed a few months earlier over dinner at the 211 Restaurant in Tribeca. He looked terrified as he popped the question. Unsure of what I'd like, he didn't have a ring, so he was empty-handed, and his voice cracked as he asked, "Joanne, will you marry me?" I thought I saw a flicker of terror in his eyes.

"Yes!" had barely left my mouth when he waved the waiter over and ordered a large tumbler of whiskey for himself. I was taken aback, expecting champagne to celebrate. *Where was the celebration?* The whiskey felt more like a crutch to hold him up than a celebratory sip.

But I knew this was what I was supposed to do. It had been ten years since I tried it the first time. At thirty-three, I figured it was now or never.

Having decided to marry, we thought it best to do it on our own. Ma still lived close by in Brooklyn but remained distant in every way that mattered. Peggy and Thomas were both in Texas, and I knew they wouldn't come up. Sadly, Rick's family wasn't much different. They weren't big on rituals or celebrations either, and his relationship with his brother was particularly strained. So we decided to keep it simple, go somewhere beautiful, and stay for a week.

A few months later, we threw a party in New York. Friends came, but no family. They celebrated with us, but Sun Valley was ours alone.

Chapter 75

New York, New York, 1995

Sun Valley felt like a pause in time, a moment that belonged only to us. We managed to sustain that boundary around our family issues for several years—until the call came. My mother never called me on the trading desk; no one did. My friends knew if they did, they'd be met with a curt "Morgan Stanley" and inevitably be abruptly cut off with a short "Gotta go!"

So it startled me to hear her voice. "Joanne?"

A shudder ran through my body.

"Your brother is dead," she told me in a flat monotone.

My breath caught. "What? What happened?" I gasped, trying to ignore the flashing lights screaming for my attention.

"Joanne, the Merc for you!" someone yelled.

"Hey, Duquesne is ringing!"

"Swaps desk!"

"Pick 'em up," I barked, focusing on my mother. "Ma, what happened? Talk to me."

"They say he killed himself," she told me in a voice devoid of emotion. As if she were delivering the weather report.

"No, no, no, no, no," I moaned, slumping over. The guy next to me realized something was wrong and began picking up my lines. He grabbed my trade tickets.

“I got a call from the Sheriff’s Department in San Antonio,” she said. “Here’s the name and number. You call them.” And she hung up.

I had been standing; my knees gave way, and I dropped down into my seat. The phone in my right ear fell to the desk as I reached for the left phone, pushed another button, and dialed the Texas number.

I can’t say I was surprised. I’d always known this call might come. My brother never recovered from my father’s death. How could he? He was quiet, sensitive, and shy. None of us ever recovered. We were never given the chance to mourn, to talk about it. We just kept moving forward, putting one foot in front of the other. And now, he had stopped.

We three kids handled life after my father’s death in very different ways. It seemed like my sister locked her heart away, retreating into herself like a turtle, allowing in only one person at a time. I threw my love out all over the place, hoping someone would catch it and send some back to me. And my brother? He hid, wishing someone would find him, and tried to medicate away the ache.

The day before this call, I’d been joking with a client, comparing families, trying to decide whose was most dysfunctional. We laughed, one-upping each other with tales of incredibly appalling behavior. That night was his annual Christmas party. I had to tell him I couldn’t make it. Looks like I had won.

The detective answered the line gruffly, identifying himself. I gave him my brother’s name and case number. “What happened?” I asked. Thomas had been arrested for cocaine possession a month earlier and was told it wouldn’t be a big deal. But maybe that put him over the edge.

He had checked into a seedy motel on the ragged edges of San

Antonio, unwrapped the cellophane from the square piece of soap, and scrawled a farewell message on the bathroom mirror. He wrote that he was sorry and that he loved us. Then he wrapped his lips around the barrel of a rifle and pulled the trigger. He was thirty-nine.

After his death, the police found every window of his apartment covered in foil, blocking out the world. My brother, the man my sweet brother had become, had been treading water for years until he couldn't keep himself afloat anymore.

But he had made an effort: He had recently begun speaking with a therapist, trying to sort through the demons in his head.

A few months earlier, he had called me to apologize for what he did when I was a kid—the abuse. "There's something I need to say," he began.

"You don't have to," I said quickly. I didn't want to hear him put words to what he had done, to say it out loud.

"I have to. For me." The line went silent for a bit. "I'm so sorry for what I did."

I squeezed my eyes shut. "I know. I forgive you." And I meant it. I told him I loved him.

Not long after, he reached out for a life raft from our mother, asking her if she'd get on the phone for a session with his therapist. He told her he needed her. He told me, "She said no. Just no."

A few months later, on that clear warm Thursday in December, he killed himself.

The pain and horror, the self-loathing and sadness, the fear and disappointment, were splattered across the walls of the shower, mixed with pieces of his brain and his face. Tears of burgundy blood dripped down the tiles. His dreams, hopes, future, his sweetness, kindness, goodness were all gone. Down the drain. Gone forever.

Hanging up on the detective, I slumped down and called Rick. We met at our apartment, grabbed a few things, and drove to Brooklyn to pick up my mother and Aunt Joan. We drove to the house we rented near the beach in Southampton.

My sister was living in Florida when Thomas died and didn't make it up to New York. We were still not the family that rallied together. Still not big on ceremonies or celebrations. Nor support or love. We didn't do anything that involved putting emotions on display. We kept it all inside.

For a week, my mother, aunt, husband, and I sat by the fire with Rick putting out bits of food and filling glasses with Scotch. I took long walks in the sand, hoping my brother had found peace.

Chapter 76

New York, New York, 1995

We mourned in our own quiet, fractured way, each of us in separate corners, as we always had. The silence between us wasn't new; it was inherited. So when the phone rang weeks later and I heard my mother's voice—needy, demanding, irrational—I wasn't surprised. Just tired.

She continued to maintain an emotional distance as wide as the Grand Canyon. Then out of the blue, there she was whining that she hadn't heard from me. "I could be lying in a pool of blood, and no one would know." It was a game of push and pull. She wanted nothing to do with me, lacked any curiosity about my life, but would then slip into the role of the martyred mother forgotten by her beloved children. It was exhausting and confusing.

As much as I hated to admit it, I saw parts of my mother in me. Dorothy came off as engaged, even charming. She was witty in conversation when she thought the world was watching. But at home, she was cold and disinterested. As children we were left to fend for ourselves. She never asked about our friends, our lives, our dreams, hopes, or fears. As a young teenager I could stumble in just before sunrise to find her snoring, unawake, unconcerned. She was our mother in name only.

And yet, somewhere along the way, I learned to do the same

thing—put on a version of myself for the world. Strong. Confident. Untouchable. Letting anyone see the hurt, loss, and shame that lurked underneath felt like weakness. I perfected that image, and working on Wall Street rewarded it.

People thought I didn't need anything. The truth was, I didn't know how to ask.

With my father gone, my mother trapped in the chaos of her own mental health issues, and my brother's suicide, I lived braced for impact—always waiting for the next shoe to drop. My mother seemed unable to help herself but perennially refused help. So, finally, I stopped trying to save her and turned to saving myself.

Chapter 77

New York, New York, 1996

Letting go of the fantasy that I could fix my mother gave me space to focus on what I could hold, what I could heal. And part of that meant finding a resting place for Thomas.

Grief was not something any of us wanted to deal with. Painful and unpredictable, it stalks you, sliding into your consciousness, making you seethe or stagger depending on how the wind is blowing.

My mother buried it so deeply, it never bubbled to the surface. She'd done it with my father, and now with my brother. Her call to me that December day was the only time she acknowledged his death, and the end of her involvement. She threw my brother into the same dumpster of dysfunction she had tossed my father into decades earlier.

A few years after Thomas died, when Peggy moved back up north, on a dull gray summer day with an unwashed sheet hanging over the sun, the two of us interred his ashes at a cemetery—a place in Queens, where relatives I never knew were buried. Joan accompanied us. Standing at the foot of his grave, I spoke words I needed to say and played a few of his favorite songs on my phone—"Castles Made of Sand" by Jimi Hendrix and "Wild Horses" by the Rolling Stones. In my eulogy, heard by only us three, I lamented how there was "no one to throw a baseball with you, no one to show you how to tie your tie, no one to tell you that mistakes are okay." I wished, "If only you had a harder heart, or thicker skin. If only you could've toughed your way out of that dark place we all were trapped in." I told him, "I'm sorry I couldn't save you. I'm sorry I couldn't change things." Peggy and Joan stood by quietly, listening, indulging me. The sky above hung heavy with clouds the color of bruises.

The gravedigger watched at a distance, head bowed, leaning on the handle of his shovel. I'm sure he'd witnessed a full range of graveside emotions. With a few shovels of dirt tossed, we crossed the road to an old German restaurant my aunt loved. Feasting on heavy food, we toasted my brother's life with tumblers of whiskey.

Through the Central Park Conservancy, I bought a bench in his honor, which sits in a quiet spot along the edge of the lake near the gazebo. A plaque reads: IN LOVING MEMORY OF THOMAS J. REDDING 1956–1995, MAY GOD TAKE YOU IN HIS ARMS AND LET YOU REST IN PEACE. He would have loved it. My mother and sister have never visited it.

For a decade, Ma cut me off whenever I tried to speak of Thomas's death. When she finally asked what became of his ashes, I told her I'd taken care of it, and she threw a fit. "I wanted his ashes to be mixed with mine when I die," she raged. The thought made me gag. She'd never once asked where they were. Shut me down when I tried to talk about it with her. But now she wanted him back.

Chapter 78

New York, New York, 1996

Thomas had reached out to her before he died. He wanted help convincing himself life was worth living. Thomas was trying to rid his mind of the demons that had held him captive for so long, but my mother refused to speak with his therapist. Ferocious in her obsession to keep her heart locked up, she said no.

I wondered what my mother had done to help my father. Joan told me my father had spoken to her about his depression—how it gripped him like a vise, squeezing tighter until he couldn't breathe. He needed help and knew it, but the walls kept rising higher. My aunt's advice to "buck up" didn't offer much comfort. As for my mother? I know what he must have faced. I lived with it.

I had been running from this trauma my whole life, and I realized I had to walk through it to get to the other side. I couldn't bury the past any longer. I couldn't ignore the pain and pretend it wasn't continuing to make me behave as I was. Dodging and weaving to avoid the blows wasn't working. I realized I had to step right into the middle of the ring.

I had just given birth to my first child, a daughter. I needed to break this cycle.

I had to go back and try to find peace with the past. My mother had buried everything under a rug, and I realized I needed to pull that rug up or I would keep tripping over it. The questions I had about my father, the negligence of my mother, the grief over my brother, and the shame surrounding it all were killing me. I wasn't dredging it all up to relive the pain; no, I had to understand what it had made me into so I could move on.

When my mother called about my brother's ashes all those years later, it triggered something within me. It wasn't about the ashes, or even about her. She remained twisted with her bitterness and the lies she told herself. I didn't want to be like that. I needed to figure out how I had gotten to where I was. It was the only way I'd be able to get out of there. In spite of all my growth, I realized the past still held me by its tentacles. I needed to face it head on in order to fully move on.

So I took a hard look back. My father's past was a shadowy blur. He had been an MP in the Army, stationed in Redding, California, before moving to New York, where he studied at St. John's University. He'd lost nearly his whole family to various illnesses—three siblings and his parents—before he met my mother. The only one left was his sister, Honor. Da was nine years older than Ma, soft-spoken, kind, and funny. A good man with a soft spot for hockey, boxing, and a good cigar with a cocktail.

They met on a blind date, set up by a work friend of Ma's at the phone company.

Ma was bright, articulate, the first in her family to go to college, a great debater of politics, and a lover of both opera and Elvis Presley. After a string of successful dates, she had a loving husband.

But under the surface lurked more complicated dynamics. Their world appeared neat and secure. They had food, shelter, and jobs. Then three little kids, with all their needs and wants, came into their lives. There were bills to pay, mouths to feed. Da was a gentle man but at some point started a slow drift into depression. Was it his job? His health? I'd never know. He seemed to be searching for help, but asking that of my mother was like trying to open a locked door without a key.

What had happened to my mother? I wondered yet again. She had her own wounds, tucked away like secrets—the sting of not being the favorite child in her family, and grief over losing her brother Charlie, as well as her father, who was her anchor. The hollow ache of abandoning her dream of leaving Brooklyn for college. Was she too tired? Had her compassion already shriveled up before she had children? Or was she now drowning in her own regrets?

The mother I knew was a woman who had encased her heart in a hardened shell, and over time layers and layers of lacquer smothered any evidence of that heart. Seeking help for herself would have meant admitting she had a problem, something she'd never do. She lived in a house of quiet losses, crushed by the weight of a life that hadn't turned out how she'd expected. I'm sure my father's death amplified these feelings, but I believe they existed long before he showed up.

When I was sick as a child—curled up on the bathroom floor, feverish, and throwing up—she'd step over me, telling me "You're not sick," dismissing me with a wave of her hand. Her moods could swing from dismissive to volcanic in a flash, and when they did, we were scorched by the lava, then buried in ash. The outbursts, like jagged glass, would leave us bleeding.

Even decades later, when I showed her the scar on my face where skin cancer had been removed, she smirked. "Oh, please. You don't have cancer." That was my mother—denial, manipulation, and gaslighting wrapped in one neat package. And she played us all—Peggy, Thomas, and me—by twisting the truth and pitting us against each other like pawns in some cruel game, her own version of *The Hunger*

Games. Maybe she was doing her best. But her "best" was destroying us. And for years, I was her victim.

But here I was, the eternal optimist, still holding on to hope. I kept dreaming of the day when she would come around, when we would have the kind of family with white picket fences and laughter echoing through the rooms. My sister thought I was crazy, but I couldn't help it. I believed in that impossible dream.

When my poor brother reached out to her, hoping she had changed, she shut him down. And then erased him from the family, refusing to talk about his life, his death, or even his ashes until she called me out of the blue a decade later. She played the same role then that she had assumed when I confronted her about my father's death. He, too, had been erased from our family. And because I dared to question her about him, she tried to paint me as the bad guy—and maybe she actually believed it. Her impenetrable barricade, so well fortified over many years, stood firm.

She could hold on to her bitterness, but I didn't have to. This was my life. It was my time to break free. I was determined—I would never be her.

Chapter 79

New York, New York, 1996

I was pregnant when Thomas died, though I didn't know it yet. My pregnancy was a surprise in a way. For most of my life, I didn't think I would have children. I was not the girl who fantasized about marriage and kids. I was too focused on surviving and figuring out how to get out of where I was. The idea of family was so distant, it was something I couldn't really fathom.

The thought of having enough love to bring a child into the world seemed so foreign to me. My greatest fear was that if I had children, I'd realize I was ignorant about how to love or be loved—and they would feel the same about me as I had felt about my mother. However, after being married a few years, as I was approaching forty, I thought Rick and I should throw caution to the wind and roll the dice. I didn't want it to be just the two of us alone forever. I figured, at the very least, if I became a mother, I would know what *not* to do.

After my first trimester, I figured I better tell the people I worked with at Morgan Stanley before anyone noticed my escalating appetite and expanding waistline. I could still squeeze into my suits and pull on my stockings, but that wasn't going to last.

I waddled into the office of the head of Fixed Income, Keith Burns, after enlisting someone to keep an eye on my phone lines. The office was huge, with floor-to-ceiling windows offering a bird's-eye view of Times Square, and interior glass walls allowing Keith Burns to oversee everything. He was one of the few men at the firm who I thought actually supported women—a nice guy, someone with a family of his own of whom he spoke fondly, one of the rare non-assholes. I felt excited to share my good news with him.

I knocked softly on the glass door. He waved me in. "Hey, Keith, I have to talk to you about something," I began.

He looked up and smiled. "Sure, Joanne. What's up?"

"I'm pregnant."

Instead of the hoped-for congratulations, he shot up from behind his massive walnut desk like a coiled spring and barked, "How the fuck did that happen?"

To which I, never one to be at a loss for words, responded, "How the fuck do you think?"

He blanched, and sputtered, "Shit. I guess I shouldn't have said that," backtracking, of course, because, God forbid, I might sue him.

But suing was still not an option for a woman on Wall Street. No man, and it was men who did the hiring, would hire a woman they saw as a "troublemaker." Even the "non-assholes" couldn't help themselves.

When I was very visibly pregnant a few months later, the head of one of the trading desks, who later would be promoted even higher, gave birth to her fourth child. Earlier in my pregnancy, I'd been conferring with her at her desk one day when her son called to ask if she was making it to a school event that morning. Barking a sharp "No!" and hanging up, she turned to me and muttered, "This is exactly why I have nannies. So I don't have to do that kind of shit."

This particular day, the trading floor was abuzz with chatter. This woman was back at her desk four days after giving birth. The young women on the floor, mostly sales assistants and clerks, looked stricken. If a managing director didn't avail herself of maternity leave, how could they? I was appalled. I took a deep breath and hoisted my body up out of my chair.

"Excuse me!" I bellowed to get the attention of the three hundred or so bodies on the Fixed Income floor. Usually an announcement is made due to a surprise change in interest rates or some other major news event that would impact the markets.

I just wanted to make a statement.

"In case anyone is wondering," I said, very loudly, "I, as you all can see, am pregnant, and I plan on taking *every single day* of maternity leave when I give birth to my baby. Every single day to which I am legally entitled."

I lowered my body back into my seat.

Don't mess with a woman whose hormones are raging. I could almost hear the oxygen being sucked out of the room. Activity was suspended, the floor went silent, and all eyes were on me, undoubtedly waiting to see if I'd disappear in a puff of smoke. Mere moments later, my internal line lit up, and I was summoned into the bigwig's office to explain myself.

That I would get pregnant at this point in my career was shocking. When I resigned a little over two years later, after my second child was born, the powers that be were apoplectic. Who in their right mind would walk away from a job like that to spend time with babies? These men were fathers, but many of them would stop every night for drinks at the bar across the street, staying long enough to catch the train that would get them home after their kids had been put to bed. It felt like an updated version of the men from the bar of my childhood.

These were the heady days of the nineties when visits to the Pink Pussycat Lounge and the Platinum Dolls Gentlemen's Club were still acceptable on expense accounts. A client ski trip with a "masseuse" dead in a hot tub after a night of partying was swept under the table. Those involved got bonuses and promotions. It was just the good old boys having fun.

We endured HR's mandatory chats on "sexual conduct," in rooms full of coworkers—most married, many in relationships with each other. Everyone avoided eye contact in perfect, awkward silence.

Between the indoor smoking ban, which put the kibosh on the pervasive, obnoxious cigar smoking, and the presence of women on the desk, my male colleagues confessed to me that they felt persecuted. Apparently, we women were ruining their fun. We interfered with their boorish behavior.

My daughter was born when I was in my late thirties. I needed help to get pregnant, and it was a difficult pregnancy. I hosted the First (and only) Annual Fixed Income Women's Golf Outing while six months pregnant. When I proposed the idea for the event, the men on the desk dismissed it, adamant that their female clients didn't golf, as they had never accepted their invitations. Clearly that wasn't the case. The event, which featured female pros, was a huge success. The event was, unfortunately, also the catalyst for my being put on bed rest for the remaining three months of my pregnancy.

The previous fall I had hosted the Million Women Cocktail Party on the coattails of the Million Man March in Washington. More than a hundred women came from around the country to compare stories and consume canapés and cocktails. Upon hearing of the number of RSVPs, the president of the firm offered up the executive dining room. A hundred stories above Times Square, in a wraparound venue replete with mahogany paneling, cushioned carpeting, and panoramic views, wait staff clad in tuxedos and white gloves, who were used to serving the titans of industry, were at our disposal, offering truffled tidbits and perfumed prawns to the women of finance.

I felt on top of the world. I felt fierce.

Chapter 80

New York, New York, 1997

Three months after Hannah was born, I returned to work, having made good on my promise to take every single one of the days allowed for maternity leave. I came back on a Wednesday, having read somewhere that it would feel less traumatic than starting back on a Monday. The truth was, no matter how carefully I planned it, that first day was still a punch to the gut.

Thursday evening, the day after I started back at the office, I checked the footage from my nanny cam. It wasn't that I didn't trust our baby nurse, whom I hired to be our nanny, but I needed to be sure. I wasn't fully convinced that Pat was just low-key as opposed to lazy, so I'd installed a camera in the living room to put my mind at ease.

The instructions I'd given Pat were few and straightforward. The swing was only to be used for a few minutes at a time for fun, not for my baby, Hannah, to be rocked into oblivion. And there should be no stuffed animals in the bassinet so she wouldn't accidentally suffocate. Simple, or so I thought.

As the tape rolled, my stomach sank. Hannah, my baby with the soft golden hair and blue eyes that missed nothing, was strapped into the swing, and Pat left the room. Hannah was left swinging while Pat snored away in the other room. Over four hours passed before Pat reappeared.

A tsunami of doubt, guilt, and fear crashed over me. Then, the rage. My head was on the verge of exploding. I was apoplectic. My sweet, sweet little baby was being ignored, neglected, and put in danger. This was not what I wanted.

I called my office, fighting to keep the rage in my voice down. "I've got a problem with my nanny. I've got to fire her. Not sure what I'm going to do. I need some time."

I wasn't sure if I'd be going back. My heart pounded with anger. How could I have let this happen?

I didn't know if I could ever trust another nanny or if I needed to resign. Then, after a slew of painful interviews with incompetent candidates, the universe graced us with Placida. She was everything I had hoped for—kind, soft-spoken, responsible, loving. She was a sweet, incredible human being. A modern-day Mary Poppins, a solid anchor in the storm. I felt blessed. She was what I'd always hoped my mother could have been.

As much as I tried to leave the damage from my childhood behind, the trauma of it, like the scars of an old wound, was still deep within me.

Science says that trauma stays in our body, takes up residence in our bones, and it's true. I carried it with me. Trauma grasps our insides, not easily relinquishing its grip. In ways I didn't even understand, it shaped how I parented, how I reacted to my babies' cries.

I couldn't do it. I couldn't Ferberize my babies—the "cry it out" technique, gradually lengthening the time between going in to calm them. The idea of it twisted something inside me. My pediatrician tried to reassure me, but I couldn't shake the fear that my babies would think I'd abandoned them. He and I both realized this was my problem.

When Cole, my son, a beautiful ball of love and light with thick dark hair and perfect, bowed lips, was born two years after Hannah, he was like a tiny old soul wrapped in a baby's body. His spirit was gentle, but when it came to sleep, he fought with a desperation I couldn't ignore. At eighteen months, I watched my son rail against the crib, clinging to the bars, his little fingers so tight his knuckles turned white, his face contorted in distress. He rocked the crib back and forth, wailing with desperation. I felt his pain deep inside me. It was almost as though he had been a prisoner in a past life. His loathing of the crib was raw and visceral.

I asked the pediatrician about moving Cole to a toddler bed and was advised he was too young. But I trusted my gut and bought a toddler bed with a mesh railing on the side. That first night, something miraculous happened. Cole slept for eight hours straight. And I let out a breath I hadn't realized I was holding. I was learning to trust myself in a way I had never been able to before.

Chapter 81

Callian, France, 2001

The following summer, Hannah was four and a half when we flew to France to visit a friend of mine and her daughters. We left on a Thursday from JFK, while Cole stayed behind in New York with his dad. My friend Monica's parents had been renting a castle in the little town of Callian for the past five years. The massive stone edifice sat on top of the highest hill in town, at the end of a narrow, twisting cobblestone road.

The walls were made of plaster, thick with centuries of blood and sweat absorbed from those who had passed through. The floors were laid with huge hunks of stone and tile, covered in parts by immense oriental rugs whose fringe had long deteriorated, like a dog needing to be groomed. There was an authentic dungeon in the basement, the dark underground prison bearing scars of horrors past. The kids were alternately fascinated and frightened by it.

The day after we arrived was Saturday, market day. The sun shone with no clouds around to mask it. The girls skipped down cobblestones, still damp and shiny from the shopkeepers' hoses, to the plaza below. Stalls with plump purple aubergines, fat juicy tomatoes in shades of red, orange, and yellow, and lettuces tinged with greens and purples, edges ruffled and spikey, spilled out of wooden crates lining the paths. Dozens of different cheeses, runny and hard, pale yellow and creamy white, were displayed on wooden pallets. Vats of black and green olives of varying sizes bobbed in briny baths. The perfume of the flower stall, with its riotous colors, drenched the air, stirred by the gentle breeze from the sea. And canisters brimming with all sorts of fresh nuts lined up in rows, beckoning.

It was late afternoon; the kids came out of the pool and snacked on a few nuts. My daughter tried a pistachio—she had never tasted one before. I was pleased since I'd been encouraging her to try new foods, even though she said she didn't like it and spit it out right away, into the garbage can in the kitchen, as we headed up to our room to clean up before dinner. Upstairs she kept saying "I don't like how this tastes," and rinsed out her mouth a few times in the bathroom sink.

We went back downstairs where bowls of penne pasta drizzled with marinara and sprinkled with freshly shaved Parmesan cheese had been set on the table for the children. Hannah sat but didn't pick up her fork. She had a faraway look in her eyes, a blank stare, and her skin was beginning to break out in red blotches.

"Hannah? Hannah? What are you feeling, hon?"

"My mouth is itchy, and my tongue feels big," she answered, her voice tiny and distant.

"Monica, we need to call an ambulance. She is having a reaction to the pistachio. Run upstairs and get the Zyrtec from my room. It's on the dresser."

Her pediatrician had suggested bringing Zyrtec, an allergy medicine, to help her sleep on the long flight over. It didn't help for the flight, but now I had her drink as much of it as she could. A month before, I had read a book in which a character died on the kitchen floor after an allergic reaction to a nut. I knew what was happening.

We didn't know what number to call for help. It's not 911 in France. Thankfully, my fluency in French, which I had been told for years was useless, allowed me to call a neighbor to get the right number—*dix-huit*—and call for the ambulance.

Firefighters arrived with an ambulance, and a doctor came separately. The doctor hustled in carrying a beat-up brown leather bag, like the ones you see in old movies when doctors used to make house calls. He took one look at my daughter, who was curled in a fetal position, her body beginning to methodically shut down in full-blown anaphylaxis, and sat on the couch. He clucked his tongue, shaking his head from side to side, unable or unwilling to meet my eyes, and said the hospital was too far away.

Hannah needed the epinephrine soon or her body would give out. When I called, I had told them she needed epinephrine, that she was having a severe allergic reaction, but he didn't have any in his medicine bag. The doctor told me before we left in the ambulance that my little girl would not make it to the hospital alive. We were too far away. He calmly informed me, "She will die in the ambulance."

"No!" I barked. "No! She will make it! She is going to be okay."

In my head I tried to rewind what was happening, to undo this nightmare in front of me. To make it go away. A piece of my consciousness retreated in disbelief, not permitting the possibility of losing her to enter my brain. If I refused to let it in, if I barricaded that thought with all my might, it could not happen. I lost my father, I lost my brother, I refused to lose my daughter.

The firemen looked stricken as they loaded her little body onto the stretcher and into the ambulance. I climbed in the back and held Hannah's face in my hands. They gently tucked a little teddy bear near her side. There was a supply of them in the corner of the vehicle for comforting the smallest of their patients.

"Plus vite, plus vite!" I yelled at the firemen. Not wanting to annoy them, as Hannah's life was in their hands, I pleaded, "S'il vous plait, je sais que vous allez aussi vite que possible mais il faut aller encore plus vite!" I begged them to get us there in time.

I spent the forty-five-minute drive lashing out, begging them to force the ambulance to go even faster. I kept smacking Hannah's little cheeks firmly to keep her from submerging into shock. I dissociated from what was happening. Part of me was watching my own desperation, telling myself that there was no way she was going to die. I would not permit it. It was just not possible. My brain could not allow any of what the doctor had told me to be processed as truth.

Finally, we swung into the ambulance bay at the hospital, the doors on the rear of it whipped open, and out went the stretcher. We banged through the swinging doors into the emergency room, where someone garbed in scrubs jabbed Hannah's thigh with an EpiPen and slapped a mask over her mouth and nose. We had made it to the hospital in Grasse in record time, despite the thoughtless bastard on a motorcycle who had cut in front of us and kept weaving in and out, trying to slow us down.

Monica arrived at the hospital, breathless with fear in her eyes, and rushed to the gurney Hannah lay on. She had followed us from the castle. "She's okay," I said, grabbing her hand. "We got here just in time. We are so lucky."

I relaxed into her hug, so grateful Hannah was okay. My heartbeats slowed with relief. The epinephrine injection had restarted her organs, and the albuterol mask stabilized her breathing. I sat for a few hours observing her with a nurse by my side, making sure the anaphylaxis episode had passed. I watched her little lips purse with every breath she took.

A gorgeous sun, the color of an egg's yolk, was climbing over the horizon when the doctor came to discharge Hannah. "I am so happy we were able to save your little girl's life. There are some very great doctors in France," he told me proudly in his nearly perfect English, smiling. The staff sent us on our way with a week's worth of prednisone to suppress her immune system from reacting to anything more. Monica drove us back to the castle where I snuggled Hannah in my arms as she bounced off the walls for hours, coming down off the adrenaline that was still in her body.

We nestled under the covers, and I read *The Family Under the Bridge* by Natalie Savage Carlson aloud, the story of a kind man who offers shelter to a mom and her children under a Parisian bridge. I read it over and over and over until Hannah's body finally unclenched and embraced rest.

Months had passed when an invoice came from the hospital in Grasse. The ambulance had driven us over thirty miles, the doctor had saved my daughter's life, the hospital had given us a week's supply of prednisone, and they charged us $12.65.

Chapter 82

New York, New York, 2001

I almost lost her. My daughter. The one for whom I'd give up everything, anything, without a second thought. I felt the kind of love that is in your bones, deep and urgent. Now a mother myself, I couldn't wrap my head around a parent not feeling this way. I couldn't fathom it.

Looking back at my own childhood, I was appalled by the indifference shown to me. No bedtime stories. No snuggling or sitting on someone's lap. No kisses on foreheads or lullabies sung. Growing up I knew our family was different, but it wasn't until I had children of my own that I understood just how different we really were. How neglected and abused we were.

When I began my own family, I didn't have a parenting guide. I had one rule: Do not do what my mother did to me. I wouldn't flinch when my children tried to hug me. I wouldn't turn away when they wanted to simply be near me. And I'd never walk out the door with a suitcase in hand, dragging one of their sobbing little bodies behind me. No disappearing on them, physically or emotionally.

I never believed my mother loved me. She never said it to me. She never showed it to me. But my children? My children would feel my love every single day. They'd know it in the way I looked at them, in the way I held them close, in the way I never let them go. My children were sunlight, warmth against my skin—drops of golden honey that kissed my soul. When I looked at them, I saw everything I never had.

When I watched my little girl's life slipping away, when I watched her fade before me, it wasn't just horrifying. It was unimaginable. Despite all the deprivations of my childhood, I had never before known terror like that.

Chapter 83

New York, New York, 2001

It was different between my mother and her grandkids. I witnessed the moments of tenderness she offered them. My mother seemed somehow able to accept my children's uncomplicated affection with a softness that was never directed at us.

Ma didn't come to the hospital when Hannah was born; it was just me and Rick. But a short while after her birth, she asked to spend Friday mornings with her.

Once we got settled in, she paid us a visit. She undid her kerchief as I hung her coat in the closet. Placing her pocketbook on the big table in the living room that served as the place to eat, craft, and gather, she hustled over to the bassinet.

"Ma, could you please wash your hands first before you touch her? You've just come off the subway."

Clucking, she went into the kitchen and sighed. "A few germs won't hurt anyone. You're such a pest."

Biting my tongue, I watched as she sat on the couch, cradling Hannah in her arms, oohing and aahing to each drool and gurgle.

As Hannah grew, and Cole came along, she played the role of indulgent grandparent. She let them entertain her with their antics—styling her hair with tiny plastic clasps and mini clip-on bows, putting on puppet shows, running make-believe restaurants, and performing plays, all directed by Hannah, with Cole as her sidekick. Their joy seemed to soothe my mother's spirit. Their light reflected on her.

I loved that she took an interest in them. It was good for them, and for her. And for me.

But I put boundaries on her. She seemed fragile. By that point, she had Ménière's disease, which caused unpredictable bouts of vertigo. She had fallen a few times without warning, so I never left her alone with the kids. She resented that and threw a fit.

"I don't need to be babysat when I spend time with my grandkids," she snapped one Friday. "I raised three children myself, so I don't need to be watched," she spat when I refused to let her take them to the park by herself. "I just won't come anymore!" she threatened.

"Your gait is off, and you have vertigo attacks with no warning," I responded, holding firm. "Your walking is unsteady, and I'm not risking something happening when you're with my kids. *Period.* What if you fell? Their safety is more important than your hurt feelings." When I pushed back at her, she relented. She fumed but had no choice.

But she hadn't really changed. Hannah, an early and big talker with her soft little-girl voice, was showing my mother something in the living room on one of her visits. Coming out of my bedroom, I saw her pulling Hannah close, lips curling into an approximation of a smile. In a stage whisper, she was telling Hannah conspiratorially, "Mommy is such a pain. She's no fun at all," as though letting Hannah in on a secret.

It was the same pattern of her diminishing me, and it was not okay. An image of Don, husband number one, popped into mind. He used to do the same thing.

I didn't have to put up with it—not in my house. I no longer felt compelled to contort myself in hopes of receiving a morsel of affection from her or anyone else.

I pulled my mother aside, looked her straight in the eyes, and told her, "If you ever utter a disparaging word about me or anyone else in my home again, you will no longer be welcome."

She stopped. I was in charge now. I was taking care of my family.

Chapter 84

New York, New York, 2001

A few months later, on a gorgeous Tuesday in September, summer still lingered in the air. The sky was bright and clear, the air sweet, and the trees, still sporting leaves in all shades of green, stood at attention, a column separating brownstones from asphalt as we walked down West Seventy-Fourth Street in Manhattan. It was Hannah's first day of kindergarten at Calhoun, and we were both excited and apprehensive at the thought of it.

We signed in at the welcome desk where the nice lady peered over the bifocals perched on her nose and asked my daughter her name so she could check it off the list with her pencil.

"Can you say your name, sweetie?" I coaxed gently.

Hannah was too shy to respond, despite the fact this same woman had greeted her with the same question every school day for the previous two years. She shook her head, her eyes glued to the ground. My heart hurt a bit for her. Her pediatrician had told me her shyness would serve her well when she grew up.

We gripped the banister as we climbed the wide oak stairs to Lil's room to meet the dozen or so children in her class. Hannah, just shy of five, stood in the doorway assessing the situation before she went in. I believed the pediatrician as I watched her surveying the sea of unfamiliar faces, getting the lay of the land. She took a deep breath and stepped inside.

I watched her, a little sad and a little proud. The kids mingled, laughing and talking, their voices loud and high. The parents drifted out after a quick catch-up, some rushing to offices, others looking to make use of the freedom that came with the half-day kindergarten.

Outside, I ran into my friend Laurie, and we crossed the street to Levain Bakery for coffee. As we sat on the teak bench out front, her cell phone rang.

"Hey, Eric. What's going on, hon?" she asked, her forehead creasing as she listened. It was her husband saying the television was reporting a small plane had crashed into one of the Twin Towers downtown, the North Tower.

"What," she muttered, shaking her head no. We were puzzled and unsettled, wondering how that could possibly happen. The Twin Towers loomed large in the sky, impossible to miss. As we tried to make sense of it, Eric, still on the phone, told us the news was now saying it was a large passenger jet, not a small plane.

"What? Now they're saying it was a passenger jet? How is that possible?" she asked, her voice thin. She hung up the phone, her hands unsteady.

We headed quickly back across the street, confused. We told the principal what we'd just heard. Her face fell as she searched for the remote under the cluttered mess on her desk. Turning on the small television in the corner of her office, fear and disbelief filled the room as we looked and listened to the frantic reporting.

Smoke. Flames. Chaos. As we watched, the South Tower was struck by another jet. Debris and bodies were falling like confetti. None of us was capable of grasping what was going on. The principal made the decision to keep the children in class until more was known.

I don't remember walking back home. Rick, who was between

jobs, was there with Cole, who was two. The joy of the morning, the excitement of Hannah and her first day of kindergarten, was a distant memory. The world had shifted in an instant.

Picking Hannah up later that morning, my hand clutched hers a little tighter than it had when I dropped her off. The group of parents were joined together by a collective fear. Walking up to Columbus Avenue, the city felt vastly different than it did that morning. When a car backfired as it passed us, I flinched and ducked, pulling Hannah under my chest. Crouched over, I thrust my free hand out, as though I could ward off the threat. *What was happening? What was this nightmare we were in the middle of?*

I looked around and steadied myself, realizing what my daughter needed was strength. I ached to scoop Hannah up and wrap her in my arms, to hold her close and make it all go away, but I knew I had to try to be calm and act normal for her.

"Mommy, what's going on? You seem scared?" she said, her voice small, unsure.

I felt the fear in the air. She could feel it too. It was everywhere.

I paused, taking a shaky breath before answering her with what was, at that moment, the truth as I knew it. My voice steady, I said quietly, "A plane crashed into a building this morning." Wishing I didn't have to say any of this, I added, "It was an accident, but it really scared me." At that point, I couldn't imagine it being anything but an accident. My mind could not accept the idea that a human being would do something so horrific intentionally.

The streets of the Upper West Side seemed paralyzed, stuck, frozen in fright. People moved in slow motion, their faces pale with fear, their eyes darting. I kept walking, but the images of horror I had seen on the television kept replaying in a loop, like a broken record. I could not unsee the unthinkable.

The next dawn, the sun garishly rose to offer another gorgeous day. It seemed wrong. The air was tarnished by the smoke and ash blowing up from downtown. The city felt as if it were holding its breath. Everything was closed. Storefronts shuttered, metal grates rolled down and padlocked to the sidewalk. Colorful graffiti splashed across their fronts. Offices were shut and schools were closed.

As evening fell, candles began to appear, dotting the windows on the Upper West Side, lit to offer hope, to show solidarity. The people of New York, who normally seemed hurried and brusque, were kind and delicate with each other. As though we were made of porcelain, afraid we might break.

My little family walked the few blocks to Laurie's apartment that night, trying to maintain some sense of normalcy in this world we no longer recognized. Her husband, Eric, had roasted a chicken, the comforting smell enveloping us as they opened the door for us. They welcomed us in, offering comfort amid the chaos. My heart felt as fragile as the paper lanterns sold in Chinatown, ready to be torn apart with one breath.

The city strove for normalcy. Schools reopened that Thursday, just two days after the horror. The world was still trying to figure it all out, but life trudged on. When I picked Hannah up from kindergarten, she was very angry with me. "You lied to me," she declared, her cheeks flushed with anger. She'd learned the truth that I hadn't been ready to share with her—the truth that it wasn't an accident, as I had told her that day. That it was something bad men had done on purpose.

"Bad men," she repeated, her tiny voice sounding fierce. "Bad men did it."

In her eyes, red and puffy, I could see the outrage. The loss. The betrayal. The anger that I would *lie* to her. I knew that feeling all too well, thinking back to the anger I'd felt about the lies my mother had told me. I hated that I had made Hannah feel this way.

I laced my hand in hers and walked with her to the park, slowly, a weight settling in my chest. As we sat on a bench, I felt my sweet little girl's innocence seep out of her. Gone forever. I tried to explain, my voice cracking, "When I told you it was an accident, I believed it was. I couldn't imagine someone would do something so terrible on purpose. I couldn't believe it."

That day, the world stripped us all of something precious. Our innocence. And there was no going back. I did not want to lie to my daughter. Not like my mother did to me.

A few weeks later, Lil, Hannah's kindergarten teacher, pulled me aside. Her fingers fidgeted and her eyes didn't quite meet mine. "Joanne, I'm sorry to ask you this, but could you not wear your black dress to school anymore when you drop Hannah off?" she requested, haltingly. "The other parents find it too upsetting."

By then I had been to over a dozen funerals. Memorials for colleagues from my years on Wall Street—one had sat next to me, a few were brokers of mine. They were friends. My grief had become too much for others to bear. My black dress was a reminder of things they wished to forget.

It was hard to move on. I was drowning in anguish. The rhythmic cadence of the hymns and prayers at the funerals that initially offered some solace over time began to haunt me. I attended too many services and missed many more, no longer able to bear the searing pain of grief. Rick, too, was swimming in his own sea of sorrow. One of his closest friends had gone to work that morning on the eighty-ninth floor of Tower 2.

Chapter 85

New York, New York, 2001

Greg tracked me down about a decade after he walked away. September 11 had just happened, and we were both reeling from the loss of so many people we had known.

I had accomplished much since I had last seen him, professionally and personally. I had weathered many storms and had come out the other side, wet and windblown, battered a bit, but still in one piece. I had married again, and I was blessed with two of the most fascinating people in my life, my children. I was so profoundly grateful for what life had offered me.

We met across the park on the East Side at a hotel bar: The Regency, I think. He was there when I arrived, seated on a barstool. I had spent a long time trying to decide what to wear. It didn't matter.

I slid in next to him. The nearness of him caused my body to tremble and my heart to pound. Warmth coursed down my limbs. My bones seemed to soften at the sight of him. I steadied myself on the seat of the stool with both my hands.

I could see his fingers, the ones that had played symphonies on my skin, tremble slightly as he traced the drops of condensation on his glass of beer. We tiptoed around what we were feeling, words skipping on hot coals. We spoke of 9/11. We whispered of our friends who were no longer.

"I can't believe we lost so many," he said in that low, soft voice I knew so well, with his head bowed. His eyes looked up at me through his lashes, always too long for a man, and made me feel like I could drown in them all over again.

"I know. It's hard to wrap my head around it. And their kids, they're all so little. It's awful they'll never know who their kids will become."

"What about you?" he asked. "How are your kids?" I didn't want to talk about my kids. It felt like I was betraying them just by being there. That was too hard.

"They're amazing. I never imagined how much I could love them." I left it at that. He didn't deserve to know anymore. And I didn't want to hear about his.

He told me that, back then, he didn't think it could last. "It was so intense it seemed as though we'd go up in flames." He exhaled slowly, his hand still exuding heat as he reached for mine. He said he was in love with me but had thought such intense passion couldn't possibly last. He sat on the barstool, his eyes soft and damp, and looked at me. He said, "I stayed where I was because I didn't think it possible to sustain the depth of what we had."

"Ha," I chuckled, retrieving my hand before he could take my heart again. It was a bitter chuckle. I told him, in a voice that was barely a whisper, how he had ripped out my heart and shredded it into a million little pieces and then tossed it aside. How he had altered the trajectory of my life.

And I explained how that experience allowed me to know—when I was honest with myself—that finding your person, your soulmate, the one love that will never be transcended, is indeed possible. But that love might also ruin your life.

Sitting up a bit taller, I told him, "I realize now that we accept the love we think we deserve. And I know now I deserve better. It's taken a very long time to get here." What I did not tell him and could not admit to myself is that I still carried him with me.

Chapter 86

New York, New York, 2003

We left the city when Hannah was six and Cole four. The yellow cloth tape measure in my junk drawer had grown frayed, the numbers faded, from the constant search for a few extra inches in closets and my quest to rearrange furniture in a desperate bid to create an illusion of more space.

Our life in the city had been wonderful in so many ways. There were trips to H&H Bagel, where we'd open the door, our mouths watering as we'd get hit with a blast of steam that carried the scent of the delicious puffy circles of dough. Taking the bag of bagels, we'd head a few blocks north to Barnes & Noble to sit on the floor in an aisle of the children's section and read for a while. There were our daily walks to Central Park—our backyard—with the double stroller loaded up with balls and a blanket. We lived in a beautiful corner apartment with lots of light and a fantastic view.

But the city had its drawbacks too. There was the stench of urine in the summer when the mercury hit ninety and the asphalt would sweat, matching the sticky rivulets that trickled down my back. There were the staggering five-digit tuition bills for first grade, and the logistics and expenses involved in escaping the city's confines when summer came and the concrete canyons of oppressive heat crushed down on us.

"Hon, the kids are getting bigger, and our apartment isn't," Rick said one night after the kids had been tucked in. "I think it's time we look for a house." We embarked on an investigative journey, spreading out a map on our big pine table. We drew a circle around Manhattan, marking the boundary of how far we were willing to go—close enough for convenience, far away enough for space.

We made lists of what we wanted. For me it was simple: stairs, a window seat (inspired by *Nancy Drew* books), a fireplace, a flat backyard, and a barbecue. Things I never had and always wanted. Rick wanted great outdoor space, a yard where he could play sports with the kids. Hannah added her wish for a laboratory, like in the television show *Jimmy Neutron*, so she could do experiments in the basement. With each house we toured, she carried a little black notebook, checking off items on her list.

After months of traipsing around Westchester on the hunt for our next home, moving day arrived. With the air thick with July heat, the movers packed, wrapping our life in bubble wrap and cardboard. We said goodbye to our two-bedroom apartment across from the Museum of Natural History. A place we loved, where every year we watched the enormous balloons getting blown up for the Macy's Thanksgiving Day Parade. Watching the men empty the apartment, I missed it already. But I was also excited for the adventure ahead.

I had resigned from Morgan Stanley a few years earlier, after Cole was born. I made the decision, to the shock of everyone I worked with, because I wanted to soak up every moment with my kids while they were still little. After waiting so long to have them, I was determined to savor it all—while they still needed me, and while I was still theirs. After years of building a career, I found the courage to step away from it all. After a lifetime of taking care of myself, I took a leap of faith, making myself dependent on Rick.

There was an ache inside of me, an understanding that this chapter of our life in the city was closing and a new one was about to begin. And with that, I made a promise to myself—to give my children the kind of childhood I had always dreamed of, to create memories not in the hustle of city streets, but in the quiet, open spaces of our new home.

The moving van rumbled to a stop in the driveway, tires crunching against the gravel. The back door creaked open, and out they came—boxes, bags, furniture—one piece at a time, each item carrying with it the weight of a new beginning. The men, their biceps bulging under the strain, grunted and swore as they heaved our world into our new home. Sweat dripped down their foreheads, a steady stream trickling into their eyes as they shuffled past the front door, each step taking us closer to this life we had dreamed of.

The house was everything we had imagined and more. Stairs that creaked underfoot, a fireplace for winter nights, a window seat where I could lose myself in books and daydreams. And the backyard—the kind of backyard you only saw in movies—with lush grass that spilled out toward a sparkling pool, its surface glinting in the afternoon sun. I couldn't help but stand there, taking it all in, as the movers passed by, the rhythmic thump of furniture being carried upstairs somehow making it feel real. It was perfect.

I directed the men around the living room, their muscles straining under the weight of our life. The couch went along one wall, with chairs placed carefully in the corners, as the house seemed to sigh around us, settling into the idea of becoming our home. Books were stacked by the shelves flanking the bay window, the smell of fresh paint still lingering in the air. The place had already started to feel like ours. Almost.

But one thing was missing. Something I had dreamed about for years to make our home feel complete. I stood near the sliding glass doors, watching the movers as they broke down the boxes and gathered up the rolls of tape. They looked confused, unsure of how to arrange the last few pieces in that empty corner of the living room. I didn't blame them. How could they possibly know what I needed next?

When the door clicked shut behind them, I picked up the phone and dialed Steinway. My finger tapped the receiver anxiously, the weight of my decision pressing on me. When the call connected, I said the words out loud. I ordered a piano. It would be the finishing touch, the sound of life filling every room.

In my mind the piano had always seemed an artifact of another world. An instrument of the rich whose children took lessons from stiff-lipped teachers with accented speech. The instructors were virtuosos who had fled their home countries under the cloak of darkness. Piano music filled the spaces of stately homes, playing in the background of dinner parties where beautiful people sipped cocktails and debated politics. I had longed to have one from the moment I laid eyes on the one in the living room of my Aunt Honor. I hung up, and for a moment, the house stood still around me. The movers were gone, the place was quiet. But soon, it would be alive—with the sound of music echoing through the halls. Just as I had always imagined.

When the kids started school that September, there were two options for afternoon pickup. Parents could stay in their cars, and the kids would search for them in the line of vehicles that snaked down the street, or we could park and stand in front of the school.

Just before the bell rang, I pulled into a spot, scanning the crowd of women gathered by the school's entrance. The moms were clustered in groups, as if the invisible threads of some unspoken hierarchy wove them into tight circles. A few stood alone, eyeing the front door, awaiting the onslaught of children. Others chatted loudly, gesturing with hands as polished as their appearances. I approached, feeling a cool breeze tug at my jacket, button undone, and a familiar knot settled in my stomach.

Having read a lot, I thought I understood the social dynamics in groups of women. But having missed out on my own high school scene, and working in predominantly male jobs, I hadn't really ever experienced it myself. And today I didn't feel like I was one of them. They appeared to have it all figured out.

As I took my place on the sidewalk, a part of me hoped someone would notice me and invite me into their group. I wished—quietly, achingly—to be seen, to be welcomed. But I remained on the edge, watching the other mothers exchanging pleasantries, their laughter a language I hadn't yet mastered.

I kept getting out of my car and showing up, day after day, hoping to be let in. And slowly, with time and patience, I found my place—and with it, a few lifelong friends.

Chapter 87

Newfane, Vermont, 2005

Learning how to belong hadn't come naturally to me—it was something I had to work at. Over time, I found my footing among the mothers on the sidewalk, and I began to build the kinds of friendships I'd longed for. But connection can take many forms. Sometimes it's forged slowly in the day-to-day, and other times, it comes rushing back in the form of someone from your past.

It was a crisp, perfect fall Saturday when a friend and I decided to take our kids—on the edge of becoming preteens—on a road trip. We loaded them into her SUV, the smell of coffee caressing our nostrils from the thermos stashed between us, and headed north. The kids settled into the back seat, plugged into their worlds of headphones and games, while my friend and I caught up on all the little things in each other's lives.

We were headed to Vermont to visit a friend: Rob, a friend from my past. In one of life's many strange coincidences, he had once dated my friend's sister. Rob was the one who sat between Greg and me on the trading desk at CRT. The three of us spent years trading arbitrage, all under the watchful eye of our boss, Jim—million-dollar Jim. We lived in the chaos, each day a race, each minute a test of whether we could outsmart, outlast, or outpace the competition. It was a world of extremes—one minute your stomach dropped from a bad trade, the next you were riding high on a big win. The only constant was the pressure.

Rob and I had reconnected in this quiet, leafy place, far from the buzzing streets of the Wall Street. After years on Wall Street, he retired to a farm he bought with the spoils of his success. Horses, dogs, cats—a life far removed from the madness of securities and risk. It was strange—this calm, this stillness. The contrast between the chaos of the markets and the peace of his farm felt surreal.

It had been almost fifteen years since I'd last seen him, but here we were catching up as if no time had passed. We traded stories, laughing about the old days. Traders, by nature, act tough. Most fall into three camps: the phone-throwing, foul-mouthed types who are the most prevalent, the jittery types who don't last too long, and the quiet ones—the ones whose calm demeanor belies the blustery tornado that often lurks beneath the surface.

Rob had always been one of the rare ones who didn't hide behind bravado. He didn't throw phones across the room or shuffle around nervously between trades. He was sharp and steady—the kind of trader who weathered huge market volatility and made it look effortless. He remembered me the same way. "I always admired how you handled that desk," he said. "It was a mess—testosterone everywhere. You made it look easy. And it was anything but. I admired you for it."

I simply smiled in acknowledgment, but his words affected me more than he could have known. The trading floor was a battlefield, and at that time, I was the only woman on the desk. Back then, I was just trying to hold my ground. I never thought I was making it look easy.

He paused, and then added hesitantly, "I always thought you were tougher and smarter than I was. I know it wasn't easy, especially after Greg and I left. And then Jim punishing you for not accepting his baby offer. But you never let on. You were always in control." I hadn't realized he'd seen it. I hadn't shown it, I couldn't. There was no time to be vulnerable in that world. He continued, "When no one knew yet about you and Greg, the other guys were all too scared to ask you out. They thought you didn't need anyone. You were intimidating."

In the silence of Rob's farm, with horses grazing in the background and the air tasting of pine and earth, I thought about what he said. He was right. I had made myself impenetrable—harder than I probably needed to be. It wasn't a conscious decision, but somewhere along the way, I had learned to bury my fear beneath layers of strength. I had fought to prove myself in a world that didn't make space for women like me. And I told myself I didn't need anyone—that I could take it all on alone.

But what if one of those men had seen beyond the tough exterior, like Greg had? What if one of those men had dared to scratch the surface? They'd have found the scared little girl underneath, just trying to keep up, trying to belong. That girl had always been there, hidden beneath the sharp edges I'd so carefully crafted.

Rob's voice broke through my thoughts. "I always thought you were untouchable," he said. His words hit harder than I expected. "But I think I know better now."

For a moment, I didn't know what to say. The gap between that hardened version of the woman I had been and the person I'd become felt so vast. We sat there in silence, the sound of birds calling softly in the distance, the weight of our shared history hanging in the air between us. Rob had seen me at my toughest, but he had no idea what it cost to be that tough. I wondered if anyone did.

And then he mentioned Greg again.

"Why Greg?" he asked. "I never quite understood why you were with him. You were too good for him."

"Ah." I sighed, still unable to shake the seductiveness of those memories. "It was complicated. I really believed he loved me—like no one else ever had," I answered, rattled, not having spoken about Greg in a very long while.

"He was a coward," Rob said tenderly. "He did love you. He should have left for you. Like I said, you were too good for him."

I turned my head, not wanting him to see the pain that was still within me.

Chapter 88

Rye, New York, 2005

Some pain doesn't fade. It just festers beneath the surface. Rob's words remained with me long after the visit. He saw me more clearly than I'd seen myself. Back home, life continued its steady rhythm—school pickups, grocery shopping, and hosting holiday dinners. But somehow amid the soothing rituals of daily life, the ache of the past found its way in.

It was Christmas Day, and everyone was coming to my house to celebrate. I had taken over hosting holidays—first in our apartment in Manhattan, and now at our house in Rye. I tried to re-create the joy I felt as a child at my aunt Joan's house with a gorgeous fir tree and decorations galore. Cooking was my thing—an attempt to make up for years of being subjected to my mother's uninspired meals. This year, we were a small group: my sister with her husband and two kids, and my mother. My aunt Joan didn't make it.

Even though Peggy and I had hired a driver to pick up my mother in Brooklyn, Ma was grouchy when she arrived.

"Hey, Merry Christmas, Ma! How was the ride up?"

"Fine. Don't know why you couldn't come get me," she said with an edge.

"Sorry! We're busy getting everything ready here, and Peggy's coming from Jersey. It doesn't make sense," I responded, putting up my boundary to deflect her negativity. Now, having my own family and our challenges, I could imagine how difficult my mother's life must have been. But she made it more difficult by refusing to discuss it or deal with her feelings at all. It was still buried under the rug.

"I don't know about all that." She kept at it.

"Well, having a car bring you up is a lot nicer than if you had to take the subway and then a train, right?" I tried to coax some reason from her, however begrudgingly.

It seemed that getting through these family events called for lots of wine, and this Christmas was no exception. But with four happy kids at the table, we shared good food and lots of laughs—and managed to pacify my mother.

After dinner, when the moon was suspended in the ink-black sky like a thin wafer of alabaster and dessert had disappeared, we gathered by the fireplace in our approximation of the American dream and exchanged gifts. We unloaded the presents and carried them in from my sister's car, arms full of holiday cheer. Hannah, Cole, and my sister's children, who were ten years older than mine, had lots of boxes to open. The gifts ran the gamut from Legos to videos, fake makeup sets to the real thing. The adults joined in as well, unwrapping scarves, gloves, puzzles, and sweaters.

I admit that since my da died, I've dreaded Christmas. As a kid, after his death, it seemed as though the joy had vanished. Christmas Eve at Grandma and Joan's was never the same. We'd go through the motions, handing out gifts, but it felt more like a chore than a treat. I always wished we could skip the entire week—my birthday, Christmas, and New Year's. I thought that would be less painful. The days that were meant to be filled with happiness and celebration were always shadowed by what was missing.

I always dreaded the inevitable disappointments—something on the Christmas list that was sold out, the gift that didn't come in time, the wrapping that wasn't flawless, the cards that were late, the snow that never fell, or a nice Christmas that was over too soon. I struggled with it all.

Maybe that was why I hosted. I could control most of it: the timing, the menu, the seating, the guest list, the entertainment. And when I felt like my head was going to explode, I could always escape to the kitchen, where I could breathe.

But what I couldn't control was other people's behavior. Snide comments muttered, criticisms flung, egos bruised, dreams shattered, hopes dashed. And with my mother, we were lucky if we made it through appetizers before her pointed words pierced the balloons that held our emotions aloft.

It was getting late when the car showed up to bring Dorothy back to her apartment. The driver graciously took a bag loaded with the gifts she'd received and offered his bent arm for her to grasp. "I don't need your help," she sneered, always a font of holiday cheer.

Brushing him aside, she strode ahead, then stumbled down the brick path, veering right and landing in the boxwood hedge. Her face pinched, skin slack like dingy underwear clasped in a clothespin, she reached for the railing, picked herself up, and clutching her handbag to her bosom, slid into the back seat without so much as a glance back toward us. The only thing bruised, apparently, was her ego.

I got busy. I cleared the plates and stacked them in the dishwasher. I stashed the few leftovers in the fridge. I took a cloth and rubbed the dining room table to a soft shine. Gathering the scraps of wrapping paper and loops of ribbon, I shoved them into large garbage bags and crushed the boxes flat. Another Christmas, come and gone. *Phew, another holiday survived*, I thought.

About an hour later, my phone rang. My mother's driver, being a gentleman, had insisted on escorting Dorothy safely inside her building. But when she got inside, she couldn't find the keys to her apartment—not in her handbag, not in her coat pockets. He searched his car without any luck. They had fallen out somewhere, maybe in the boxwood hedge.

I ran outside to check the hedge where she had fallen, but they weren't there either. As I was letting the driver know that my search was unsuccessful, my mother grabbed the phone, screeching "This is all your fucking fault!" Bad things were *never* her fault. They were *always* someone else's.

Rummaging in my junk drawer, wading through the sea of paper clips, sticky pads, and rubber bands, I found my old address book with the name and number of one of her neighbors, a woman my mother had been friendly with at one point, until my mother cut the woman out of her life for some perceived slight.

It was late on Christmas Day, but I didn't know what else to do. The driver needed to leave, taking his phone with him, which would leave me with no way to get a hold of my mother. I was an hour's drive away.

Carol answered on the second ring. I introduced myself, apologized, and explained the situation. Carol was kind, and embracing the spirit of the season, she said, "No problem. My brother is here, and we were just having some dessert. I'll send him down to get her, and she can join us. Merry Christmas!" Having experienced the wrong end of my mother's wrath, Carol knew how difficult Ma could be. I let Carol know the emergency locksmith would be there within the hour.

I called the driver to thank him and told my mother about the locksmith and Carol's generous offer. Thanks to the kindness of others and a call from the locksmith letting me know the job was done, I went to bed that night, happy my mother was safe and sound.

Carol called the next morning. She told me how the night before, her brother, a priest, had left his tumbler of brandy and slice of apple pie on the table to escort Dorothy up into the warmth of Carol's apartment and await the day's true savior, the locksmith. And my mother, instead of embracing the offer and the generosity with which it was made, insisted she needed no one and wanted no help. She raged at the priest, cursing and spitting like a trapped rat, telling him to "mind his fucking business."

I believe her fierce impulse to refuse help stemmed from her narcissistic inability to handle any criticism. A narcissist can never be seen as weak or wrong. Losing her keys and being locked out showed weakness. She couldn't allow that.

And Carol's brother, a genuinely gentle soul—a priest, for God's sake—someone who dedicated his life to others, on the day celebrating the birth of his Lord, offered loving kindness but got rebuffed by Dorothy.

Carol called to let me know that she and her brother were praying for us—for my sister and me. After all that had happened, it felt oddly tender. It made me wonder what it was about our family that made us wary of kindness, that made love feel like something to be resisted rather than received. We had worked so hard, for so long, to project the image of self-sufficiency that it was very hard for all of us to let our guard down and trust.

Maybe this was another sign of the fabric of our family wearing thin. The threads that held us all together were coming loose. Maybe the rest of us had been unraveling too, quietly, for years. I just hadn't wanted to see it.

Chapter 89

Rye, New York, 2006

The threads of our own family—the one Rick and I had created—so carefully woven together with strands of silk, had always been delicate but strong. But now, they hung limp, tenuous, frayed at the edges, like a hammock stretched too thin under the weight of life.

Rick was the anchor we all needed, but now he seemed adrift, sinking. Anxiety and depression, buried for so long, had begun to make themselves seen in ways that I couldn't ignore. The man I loved—the man so full of energy, laughter, and kindness—was drowning in alcohol to bury his pain, as if it were the only thing that could fill the empty spaces within him.

He still loved us. I knew that. It was obvious in the way he coached the kids' soccer teams, in the way he cheered them on as their biggest fan. I could see it in the way he played monster in the pool, lifting them high and laughing as they squealed with joy, begging for more. He loved us with everything he had, but the bottle had become a wedge between us, sliding in and, like a chisel, slowly chipping away at our family.

On a clear Tuesday evening, the sky sprayed with stripes of pink and orange, we sat for dinner at the kitchen table—the same one we'd hauled up from the city a few years earlier, when Hannah was just starting second grade. Its surface, marked with fork tine indents and faded splashes of paint, held the history of our children's early years: scars from their toddler days, worn into the wood like a memory you can touch.

Dinner was our usual ritual—kids eager to fill their bellies and share highlights of their day. It was a ritual I loved. As I put food on the table, I heard the buzz of their voices getting louder and louder as they raced in from the backyard. Our Lab, Blue, scooted in behind them just before the door slammed shut. Hannah and Cole, their faces a blur of energy, were just on the far edge of childhood, their limbs stretching into adolescence. They had stories to tell, and laughter spilled as they fought to get the words out, their voices rising with excitement.

We took our usual seats, and passed around the platters of chicken cutlets, mashed potatoes, and roasted broccoli. I filled glasses with milk and ice water.

"The funniest thing happened today. I've got the best story! You should've seen it!" Hannah said, jockeying to tell her story first. She launched into the tale, her eyes wide. "We were practicing our speeches about the presidents for next week's presentation and, in the middle of it, one of the boys let out a huge fart! A huge one! Then—get this—the teacher started laughing so hard, she farted too!"

The kids cracked up and so did I. Cole, doubled over, fell off his chair, giggling uncontrollably. Rick sat with us, but he seemed elsewhere. His smile didn't quite reach his eyes, and his features blurred, as if he were fading into the background.

Cole chimed in, his voice full of pride. "We had a soccer game during recess. We were the best! We destroyed the others!" He detailed their winning strategy, replaying it blow by blow, his arms gesturing wildly.

Minutes passed and their dad looked over at them, his mouth moving slowly as if the words came from far away. "Anything fun happen at school today?"

I looked at him—the man who had been our rock. Their coach, their buddy. Their dad. Rick loved us all with his big heart, but somewhere along the way, that love became tangled with something else. The smile ran away from my face.

The kids' laughter faded, swallowed by the space between us. And in that moment, though nothing was said aloud, I could feel the room shift. The silence in him stretched like an invisible thread, pulling at everything we had tried to build.

On the way home from work, he'd stop at the bar by the train station. Arriving home, he fortified himself with his hidden stash of bottles in the garage. He sought numbness from them before climbing upstairs to be with his family.

Rick had always liked to drink, but the pull of the bottle had become dark, something that got between us now. He wasn't present anymore, not really. He was chasing shadows in his mind. But I didn't know then that his drinking was going to blanket us all with ugliness and darkness.

I'd made many bad choices when it came to love. I married two men who were both inaccessible to themselves and, therefore, inaccessible to me. Don, my first husband, was a narcissist. Just as I did with my mother, I spent years trying desperately to get his attention, his approval—chasing something he never intended to give.

Rick was different, but equally unavailable. I didn't see it at first, but he was a deeply troubled man, haunted by demons he refused to face. I made it my mission to keep Rick afloat even though he was sinking.

In the end, I had married my parents. I built my life on a foundation filled with holes and cracks, that crumbled as the years went by.

One afternoon, I felt it give way beneath me.

Chapter 90

Rye, New York, 2007

The collapse came on a Tuesday afternoon in the quiet of my kitchen. I stood there, my hand shaking as I dialed the number I'd been avoiding for months: my doctor. The house felt unnervingly still. Carpool duties were done for the moment. Cooking hadn't started. The calm only seemed to deepen the weight in my chest, the crushing realization of everything that was slipping through my fingers.

Rick—my husband, my partner, the father of my children—was slowly disappearing into a fog of alcohol. No matter how I pleaded, bargained, or cried, I couldn't reach him. I invoked everything I knew mattered to him: our family, his job, and the future we were supposed to have together. But it was like talking to a wall. Every attempt to get him help was a battle with someone I no longer recognized, someone who didn't want to be helped. By this point, he'd sat in therapy a few times, nodding at all the right places but never opening up and letting anyone in. He was drowning but wouldn't admit it, and I was standing on the shore watching him sink.

I couldn't breathe.

When the call finally connected, I almost couldn't speak. The words were tangled in my throat, a knot I couldn't untie. But I tried, pleading for a lifeline. I was desperate. My voice cracked as the words spilled out, a flood I had been holding back for far too long.

"I don't know what to do," I gasped, not even recognizing the sound of my own voice. "I can't keep doing this. I don't know what's next. I don't know what's going to happen to us."

Tears, hot and relentless, began to pour from me. The dam I had spent years building around my grief finally broke. I was always the one to hold it together, to keep the family running, to be strong for everyone. But not today.

"I'm so scared," I sobbed, my face buried in my hands, my chest tight, as if the grief itself was physically crushing me. "I'm losing him. I'm losing everything. Please . . . please, is there something—anything—you can give me to make it stop? To make the tears stop?" I was truly afraid I might never stop crying. There were decades of tears inside me that had never been let out. I pleaded desperately, begging for a cure. I didn't know how much more I could take.

The voice on the other end of the line was calm and understanding, which only made the pain sharper. "I'm so sorry," the doctor said softly. "There's no prescription for this. There's no quick fix. I can't stop your tears."

The heavy silence that filled the space between us was broken only by my choppy breaths now mixing with a quiet realization. There was no magic pill. There was no cure for the kind of pain I was feeling. And yet, somehow, it was this truth—this stark, awful truth—that made me understand. I had no choice but to hold on. I hoped I had the strength to do it.

Hope, I realized through the chaos and the heartbreak, was the only thing left. It felt fragile, like a wisp of smoke in the wind, but it was all I had. And that's how it had always been.

As I wiped the tears from my face, I made a vow. I didn't know what the future would hold, or how much longer I could go on like this, but I knew one thing. I had to hang on. For me. For us. For him, even if he couldn't make it back. I had to keep hoping.

Chapter 91

Rye, New York, 2007

Hope is a quiet thing. It doesn't shout or promise. It lingers. And sometimes, when the present feels too heavy to hold, memory becomes a kind of anchor, pulling you back to where it all began, offering hope. I had just found an old photo of Da—one I thought was lovely.

With Peggy's birthday approaching I gave her what I thought was a great gift, one I would have loved to receive. It was the photo of Da smiling, happy, standing in the surf in a swimsuit, the sunlight bright on his face. In the few photos of him that existed, ones that were secreted away after his death by my mother, he was usually hidden behind dark sunglasses. I had this happy photo matted and framed and gave it to my sister.

A few weeks later, I asked her about it, hoping to hear she loved it as much as I did. Instead, she shrugged and told me she had hung it up with his face to the wall. "I hate him," she told me, her words sharp with pain. "He jumped off that bridge knowing we'd be left with her, and that's unforgivable."

Her words hit me like a smack across the face, my head yanked backward. I had never thought of it that way. When my father died, I was too young to realize how mentally ill my mother was. To me, my father's death had always felt like a tragedy of missed opportunities. I always felt sad for him, thinking that if he had only gotten on a plane to California and started a new life somewhere else, he might have been happy. But Peggy was older, and she had seen it all too clearly for too long. She had already known how things would play out. And I couldn't ask what my brother thought; he was dead by then.

That night, after hearing Peggy's reaction to the photo of Da, I went to bed down the hall from my kids. Before falling asleep I thought about my sister's words and prayed to whatever universal power might be listening. I felt empathy for my mother and prayed that she felt okay and that she would know I was thinking of her.

And that night I had a dream. In the dream, my mother was flying a small two-seater plane with me as her passenger. High above the Hudson River, we flew by Battery Park City, where I used to live. Suddenly, she turned the plane toward the water, attempting to crash it. Ma was trying to kill herself, and me with her.

But in the dream, as in life, she didn't succeed. We hit the water, but both of us bobbed up to the surface of the Hudson. We swam to safety, but we were rescued separately, as we were heading in different directions. That part was certainly true.

Chapter 92

New York, New York, 2009

In real life, we'd survived too. And so had our complicated tangle of relationships—which is how Peggy and I found ourselves in Chinatown for lunch with our aunt Joan.

We sat reminiscing as we speared dumplings with our chopsticks. The relationship between Joan and my mother was complicated to say the least, fraught with resentments. We were coming up on a decade since they'd spoken; it was the second time they'd severed ties, the first being over Grandma's will. I can't remember what perceived slight caused this rupture.

For their entire lives, even through the silent periods, they both attended the same Lutheran church, sitting a few feet from each other on opposite ends of their family pew, which was built when their grandfather helped found the church at the turn of the last century.

At this stage in their lives, they were alike in many ways. Both bitter, viewing the world as conspiring against them, intolerant of those they deemed fools, and filterless with their speech.

My mother usually kept everything locked behind her eyes—her real thoughts, her pain, her humanness. I imagined all that silence rotting her from the inside out, slowly, painfully, quietly. When she did erupt, it was ugly.

My aunt, on the other hand, vented regularly. She'd exhaust

every thought, every opinion, every complaint, expelling them loudly from her smokestack of a mouth. Her comments were always peppered with expletives and the kind of blunt honesty that could empty a room.

Over the chicken, broccoli, and cheap white wine, Peggy and I regaled Joan with stories of our chaotic childhood growing up inside our old apartment. We spoke of our mother coming home, cracking open a six-pack of Schlitz, and trying to cook. Or how she'd just not come home at all, which was usually better for us. We grew up like street urchins left to fend for ourselves. We cracked up, letting loose a few belly laughs reminiscing about those days, something we hadn't done before. I looked up from my plate, glancing across the booth, and saw Joan, normally loud and brash, sitting stock still in silence.

"Joan, you okay?" I asked, concerned.

"I never knew," she said, her voice barely a whisper. "I never knew. I never knew how bad it was." She shook her head. "You'd come for Sunday dinners with Grandma and you children were clean and dressed. I had no idea."

"I should have," she continued, her voice cracking. "I knew who Dorothy was. I knew how she was. I should have done something. I am so sorry. I am so sorry that you had to live like that. That your father left you with her. We should have taken you kids in. We offered her the downstairs floor. To come live with us. She refused. I didn't know it was that bad. I'm so sorry." The words poured out of her.

The words sat heavy like fog on the Scottish coast. Someone had finally acknowledged what we'd lived through. No one had ever told me before that if they had known they would have helped us. This was the first time I heard that someone cared. Like a wave in slow motion, it hit me—the realization that all this time, the damage we'd carried had never been seen by anyone outside our family.

I cocked my head to the side, gazing at my sister. For so long, I'd tucked our story into neat compartments, buried it under the label of *not abuse*—because that's what I needed to believe. I always knew our life wasn't like other people's, but it was the only one we had. We'd been good at pretending. Better than I realized. We'd perfected the house of pretend. But now, in this moment, the illusion cracked. The truth was cold and undeniable. It *had* been abuse. All of it.

Peggy had only mentioned a tiny bit of what our life was like, a fairly innocuous example in the vast ocean of disaster and disappointment that was our childhood. My mind drifted back to Grandma's backyard, with her roses and mint, imagining what it would have been like to have someone home after school. We could have lived downstairs from Grandma and Joan, and Ma had refused. She could never admit she needed help. She could never show any weakness.

We three kids were permanently scarred by shrapnel sent flying by the implosion of our family.

I swallowed hard, shoving my feelings down, something I had perfected over the years. "Hey, Joan. It's okay," I said, clearing my throat. "It wasn't that bad. Not your fault."

We ordered another round, like that might somehow soften the edge of the past. But the truth lingered, heavy and unresolved. Eventually, it caught up with us.

Chapter 93

Brooklyn, New York, 2009

Life trudged ahead, with our family dynamics as fractured as ever. My sister and I hadn't heard from my mother for six months—not since Veterans Day—so we decided to pay her a visit. We went down for an "intervention." We arrived at her apartment building, a six-story relic on Fourth Avenue in Bay Ridge, the name *Royal Poinciana* etched in stone above the front entrance.

The glory days that caused it to be named the Royal Poinciana were long gone. My mother had moved in years ago, when my sister got married and I was away in college. It had been just big enough for her and my brother.

We rang several of the buzzers in the vestibule, just not hers.

Peggy had asked me to come with her. My mother had summoned her down to talk. The reason was a letter my sister sent her a few months before, in which Peggy railed against her, laying bare the details of our broken childhood. My mother was offering her a $20,000 check, a bribe to shut her up and get her back into her life.

For years, my mother bragged about her savings, her great returns on investments due to her incredible financial acumen. She lived like a pauper, but she'd tell anyone within earshot how she planned on paying for her grandkids' college tuition. She'd puff up her chest and boast, "I'm thrilled to be in a position to help my grandkids with college, so they won't be encumbered by debt." Her lips pulled into something like a smile, but they lacked the muscle memory to finish the job. She'd dart her eyes around to gauge how others were looking at her, seeking admiration.

"My funds are doing very nicely," she'd say to me. "I really have a knack for investing. I guess having an MBA isn't everything," she added, making a snide dig at the degree I had earned. Instead of my education being a source of pride for her, it seemed she viewed it as an affront. The fact that the person managing her funds also had an MBA never crossed her mind. Her "knack" was putting her money in the fund recommended by the NYC Teachers Retirement System during a massive bull market.

As she droned on about her "astute" investments, I wondered if she really would do such a nice thing. Was she trying to compensate for all she failed to do for us, her children? But there was always a voice in the back of my head telling me not to trust her. Not to count on her generosity. Given Ma's propensity for bullshit, it was difficult to believe any of this, but my mother remained adamant. Sensing skepticism, she went so far as to flash her financial account statements to back up her claim.

My kids were nine and seven when my mother's promises were put to the test. My niece, the oldest grandchild, had just graduated from high school and, with my mother's repeated promises to cover any and all tuition costs, she turned down a full scholarship at a state school to go to a private college with a high price tag.

The day of my niece's graduation ceremony, my mother joined Peggy and her family to celebrate. With limited tickets available, my family didn't attend.

The sun refused to light up the sky. Instead, slate gray clouds hung overhead, threatening to dampen the celebration. The rows of white folding chairs were moved indoors where families would sit to clap and cheer for the graduates.

My mother had always loathed physical touch, recoiling in horror if we tried to hug her. So, my sister tried to steer her safely to a seat by placing just two fingers on her elbow. As they settled in, Peggy mentioned the upcoming tuition payment, thanking my mother in advance for her help.

And then everything shifted. The earth tilted. If there had been a barometer nearby, it would have shattered. The energy in the atmosphere plummeted, as oxygen was sucked out of the air. A storm was about to roll in.

The day of reckoning was upon us. Dorothy's head snapped sideways, her bony back rearing up like a rankled hyena. Her eyebrows drew together like a wishbone, and she snarled, "What are you talking about? Ha!" She cackled, her mouth curling up into a sneer. "I never said I'd pay for college. How the hell would you think I'd do that?!"

Denial and venom spewed from her lips, red hot lava decimating everything in its wake.

Using all the strength she could summon, my sister held it together, biting her tongue through the ceremony. It was only when my niece left to celebrate with her fellow graduates, and my mother was being dropped off at a motel, that my sister let loose years of hurt. "You were an awful mother to me and Joanne and Thomas," Peggy spat, shaking from years of repressed pain. "But how dare you do this to my daughter? I thought you were actually trying to make amends. This is *my child*. You are liar, a sick, sick person. She turned down scholarships because you said you'd happily pay for college. Get out of my car and out of my life! This is low. Even for you!"

The words were a tidal wave, spilling out all that had, for so long, been unsaid.

The next day, my mother called me, having found her way back to Brooklyn on her own. She tried to get me to commiserate over what she described as the audacity and absurdity of my sister. "She's fucking crazy," she said to me. "I never said I'd pay for her daughter's tuition. Why would I do that? They've got their own money!"

For as long as I could remember, my mother was always trying to pit us against one another. She'd call me with nasty comments, ones that she created, and attribute them to Peggy or Thomas. She'd disparage Peggy and denigrate Thomas and tell them I had made the cruel remarks. She lied about each one of us to the other, working hard to drive a wedge between us, trying to sever the already tenuous ties we had. What she didn't realize was that we learned to call each other and compare notes, exposing her manipulations and neutralizing her attempts at gaslighting. At times, her cruelty seemed to be our only bond.

On one of her Friday visits when my kids were small, I watched her read to them and I racked my brain for a memory. "I don't ever remember you reading to me when I was little."

"Hah! Of course, I read to you. What are you talking about?" she snapped, as if I were the one with a faulty memory. As soon as she left, I dialed Peggy, wondering if I had just forgotten.

But thankfully, now that we were older, I remember Peggy helping me validate my memories, always reminding me how mentally unstable Dorothy was. That none of this was my fault.

We might not ever have been the closest siblings, but I wasn't letting my mother make it worse. Not this time. I called her out.

"No, Ma. It's you. *You're* the crazy one," I told her in no uncertain terms. "You promised to pay for the kids' college tuition. You even showed us statements. You're the liar here, not Peggy."

I held the truth, steady and unshakable.

A few weeks after the graduation debacle, my sister confided in me that she was having trouble sleeping. I suggested writing a letter to Dorothy. Sometimes putting things down on paper helps. So, she did.

Years before, while wrestling with my own demons, I had spilled my soul and written my own letter to her. Ink bleeding onto paper, I detailed horrific things she visited upon us growing up, snippets of the neglect and abuse she doled out. The lack of empathy and just plain kindness. Things she did, and things she didn't do. Countless wounds she never bothered to help heal.

My letter read like a list torn from a textbook of emotional abuse: lying to us about our father's death, erasing him from our lives forever, dismissing things that felt important to us (everything from thoughts of the future to tokens of the past), randomly throwing out favorite toys without warning, belittling us for wanting emotional support, dismissing illnesses as imagined, trivializing our accomplishments, pervasive sarcasm, feigning helplessness, walking out, gaslighting, guilting us, mocking our feelings, being jealous of us as we grew apart from her, being indifferent, and, worst of all, withholding affection. She never tried; she gave up. She'd made us feel invisible.

I felt purged having written it. I ripped it up and threw it out. It felt like cleaning up my own vomit.

My sister mailed hers.

So there we were on a sunny day in early fall when the leaves were just starting to put on their show, pressing buttons that were not my mother's. We were buzzed in by some unknowing neighbor. We pushed open the heavy glass doors with their black metal latticework overlay and strode past the elevator down the hallway to her apartment in the back, our footsteps echoing off the marble floor and walls.

My sister banged loudly on the brown steel door. My mother was a little hard of hearing. I stood off to the left side, where she wouldn't see me right away. We wanted to be able to get a foot in the door before she could shut it on us, like on *Law and Order.*

She opened the door, and in we went, with her protesting, "What is she doing here?" as she pointed at me. "Get out of here. Go away!"

My sister had to go to the bathroom, of course, after the drive down from my place. She had a bladder the size of a gnat. I stayed in the living room, the one with an air conditioner that was never turned on, even in ninety-degree weather with 90 percent humidity. My mother had sworn, "This room has good cross-ventilation," as if she were an expert in air currents.

Ma screeched loudly, index finger jabbing the air, "I don't want you in here, get out! Where is she going?"

"She's gone to pee," I said.

Ma asked, "She's got the key?"

I said, "No, she's gone to pee."

"What key?"

"Ma, she's gone to pee." A quick one, I hoped.

Being the eternal optimist, and always clinging to the possibility of a miracle, I was convinced that now in her eighties, Dorothy would finally realize the value of family. She'd see how nice it would be to straighten things out with us and live the years she had left with the semblance of a normal family. We'd laugh, make memories with her grandkids, and be the kind of family that other people had, that I'd read about. For forty years, I had been holding on to this fantasy of a white-picket-fence, loving family, keeping it alive, no matter how many times she tore it down.

Peggy reappeared from the bathroom, the pink tiled one with steel bars on the window, where the water bugs amassed at night like an invading black-helmeted army, and the conversation began. Well, not quite a conversation. My sister tried to discuss things logically with my mother while my mother interrupted and rambled.

"Listen. I don't know why you did what you did, why you told us this story about paying for college for all these years, but you need to admit that you did it," I said.

Dorothy denied, digressed, disagreed, and deflected.

"No. I never said that. Why is she here?" she asked repeatedly, again pointing at me. "No, I don't know what you're talking about." Her words tried to drown out Peggy's. She stood in the hallway just outside the living room gesturing wildly, her finger poking back and forth between the two of us.

I sat on the couch, the one with the broken springs and fraying upholstery, watching the scene unfold like a particularly bad episode of the talk show from the '80s hosted by Geraldo Rivera. My mother's head spun like a whirling dervish. She screamed, "I don't need either of you! I don't want you here! Get the hell out!"

Peggy stayed calm, trying to make sense, to talk things through. Neither of us wanted her money. Her acknowledgment of what she'd done would have been nice. I'd always been the one who maintained a relationship with my mother. But this day, I stood up abruptly, looked at Peggy, and said, "Let's go. We're done here."

Peggy, surprised, nodded and followed me out. We crossed to the other side of Seventy-Ninth Street, stopping on the corner. My sister expressed concern for me. She was fully aware of my ongoing family fantasy and my desperate craving to hear the words "I love you" come out of my mother's mouth someday.

"Yes, I am just fine. I finally get it." I paused. "She doesn't love me. She never will. But it's got nothing to do with me. She is just not capable of loving anyone."

Although profoundly sad, it was such a relief to admit it. I exhaled decades of yearning. All those years spent fantasizing, an entire lifetime hoping for a real family and a mother who would say she loved me—I finally realized this was never going to happen. I got it. I understood.

My sister and I decided to head up the block to lunch at the neighborhood pub. As we turned, there she was—my mother, coming out of her building and spryly sprinting across the four lanes of traffic on Fourth Avenue. We were dumbfounded. For years she had complained about her walking being unsteady, her balance being off. She'd regularly bitch and moan about it, while crouching over and taking little steps. To help, we'd drive down, or send a driver, to bring her back and forth from family gatherings. There she was moving like someone half her age, dodging cars as she ran.

"Wow! Did you see that?" I gasped between laughs. "She's running across the street."

It seemed like the final punchline to this twisted comedy, the last laugh I'd have at her expense. I laughed so hard I cried. But this time it was tears of relief, not sorrow. As Churchill once described Russia, our mother was a riddle, wrapped in a mystery, inside an enigma, but I was done trying to solve it. That day, I stopped chasing answers and started making peace with not knowing. But just when I thought one chapter had closed, another loss crept in.

Chapter 94

Rye, New York, 2009

It was a few days before Thanksgiving in 2009 when the phone rang. I felt a small wave of relief when I saw Aunt Joan's number light up; I'd been trying to reach her for days to finalize holiday plans. She still had a landline and no answering machine, so I'd left nothing but unanswered rings.

"Joanne Redding?" a voice said. "This is Officer O'Connor."

My heart sank. I already knew.

She'd had a heart attack alone in her living room, the television still tuned to her favorite soap opera. As I'd been calling, the phone rang through the silence—while she was already gone, slumped on the couch. I sank to the floor, devastated.

"You need to get down here," the officer said gently.

My kids were thirteen and almost eleven. In recent years, my aunt and my mother—after a long estrangement—had found their way back to each other. They even took a few trips together. But now Joan was gone, and it felt too soon.

Peggy and I arrived on a cloudy, gray morning, the air stinging our faces. The police were gone. The body had been taken to the morgue. The hazmat crew had cleaned up and left. All that remained was the house—and the stillness she left behind.

Stacks of life's debris accumulated over the course of a century needed to be sorted through—piles of linens with intricate needlework, crates of delicate china brought over from Germany, old-fashioned glass Christmas ornaments, including the requisite German pickle. All stuffed high on shelves in deep closets.

I stood in the middle of the living room and shut my eyes, trying to summon Christmas Eve. The last best one, when the lights were shiny and bright, when Da was still with us. I inhaled deeply and could almost smell the roast pork. I pictured Grandma in her armchair, her gnarled fingers on the armrest, and Ma leaning back on the couch, her face relaxed into a smile. Thomas, out of breath as he ripped paper off his presents, Joan and Peggy grinning by his side. And Da coming out of the back room with my new bike.

My sister and I divided up the heirlooms, vowing to use them every day. It was sad to see that the finest pieces had been stowed away, missing out on their chance for glory, saved for a special day that never came. Like so much in our lives.

Joan would be missed. I loved how she had always been provocative, emotional, intense, opinionated. Never boring, never dull, never middle-of-the-road. Sitting next to her at a holiday dinner meant being on your toes, prepared to do battle. Her conversation was lively and passionate, especially as wine was poured and the evening wore on.

In many ways she was a paradox. She loved to travel to far-off lands yet lived her whole life in the house where she was born. She complained about the teaching job that she took up when she left publishing, but she kept in touch with students long after they graduated.

She was a collector—Hummel statues, old porcelain dolls, needlepoint linens, photographs, costume jewelry—each item carefully amassed and loved, even the creepy dolls. She adored her daily dose of *The Young and The Restless*. She loved her sweets, and she loved us too.

I can't imagine her entry into the hereafter was easy. She had plans, things she wanted to do. She'd just scheduled another knee replacement surgery. I'm sure she raged on her way out, making it clear to whoever was manning the pearly gates that she was not pleased.

Months later, when the ground had thawed with the dawn of spring, and daffodils poked their heads up through remnant patches of blackened snow, my sister and I went back to Queens, to the plot where we'd buried my brother's ashes years before. I enlisted a minister to say a few prayers; Joan would have wanted that. Peggy and I stood side by side at the edge of the grave, missing Joan. The grave-digger waited, standing off to the right under a massive oak tree, a silent witness to our pain.

The sky opened, as if the heavens couldn't hold back their tears. Rain beat down hard, the steel gray clouds wringing out the tattered rag of our grief. I read the eulogy I'd given at the service we'd had a few weeks before at her church. "Amazing Grace" played on my iPhone—every verse—followed by a New Orleans funeral dirge. Peggy generously indulged me, knowing I needed the ritual to try to soothe my own soul.

With our clothes drenched, Peggy and I crossed the street, once again, to the German restaurant Joan so loved. We ordered sauerbraten and raised a glass of whiskey to her.

Chapter 95

Rye, New York, 2011

Years passed, and I kept trying to be there for my mother. Even though the "white-picket-fence" family fantasy had long unraveled, I held on to what little connection we still had, especially for my kids' sake. Peggy, Ma, and I were all that remained.

My mother seemed to have shrunk. She looked hollowed out, fragile like a bird who could no longer fly. More a buzzard or bird of prey than a dainty, melodic swallow. Her toenails and fingernails curled around her digits, as if nature was overtaking her. Left unchecked, the nails were encasing her, like the chitin-protein fibers of an exoskeleton reclaiming its crab.

Her shoulders, a question mark on a frame that was once tall and strong, seemed to be inquiring whether this was all that was left. Her mind, thinking itself lucid, spun tales of conversations with souls long gone. The bitterness inside of her, enriched with time, still cut through.

I couldn't toss my mother aside. After years of facing mental health struggles in myself and others, that wasn't an option. I could see her differently. I recognized that being as she was wasn't really her choice. Her mind was trapped in swirling thoughts of paranoia that regrettably translated into meanness. She lived in the hell of someone gripped by mental illness, and her narcissism compounded it. Convinced her problems were the fault of others, Ma believed it wasn't she who needed the help—it was everyone else. I read a lot of books about borderline personality disorder to try to understand her better, in particular *Stop Walking on Eggshells* by Paul Mason and Randi Kreger. It helped a bit. But all that new knowledge didn't make it hurt any less.

Now in her eighties, my mother was losing her grip on reality, on herself. The woman who'd once commanded the room now couldn't remember if she'd turned off her oven in her Brooklyn apartment. With no one left to help her but me, a voice inside of her told her to trust me.

"I know I can't stay here anymore," she said, finally agreeing with me, the realization settling between us like a heavy stone.

My mother and I arrived at Willow Towers, an assisted living facility, on a clear, crisp autumn morning—my heart full of hope, her battered suitcase in my hand. What she felt was harder to know, but I suspect she was scared. This was a huge change, and we both knew it.

We set up her room, placing photos on the dresser and her old needlepoint pillow on the rocker I lugged up from Brooklyn. The walls were a pale peach with a large bay window overlooking the courtyard, pretty with its planters and benches. In the distance the Long Island Sound shimmered. With the window cracked open, we heard the seagulls squawking.

Lunch in the dining room felt like a scene from a different world, filled with people all in the same season of their lives. As we slurped soup and sucked down soft foods, her head spun, eyeing those around us, confused. "What am I doing here?" she asked, her voice rising. "These people are all so old." Perplexed, she continued to look around, surveying the sea of bluish-white hair.

Later that evening, when she appeared in the lobby, suitcase in hand, saying she had a train to catch to go to her brother's house—her brother who had been dead for over two decades—they called me.

I rode in the ambulance with her to the ER in the hospital nearby. A few days later, the doctors declared her a danger to herself and signed commitment papers. They transferred her to Payne Whitney Psychiatric Hospital in White Plains, New York, having determined that she'd be better off in a locked ward where her delusions could safely play themselves out in her head. The train she had been riding through the snow-capped Ural Mountains when she was attacked by hordes of fur-clad, armed men existed only in her mind.

The solid oak door, with remnants of a sheen long gone, had a tiny peephole in the center, and to the left of that a black buzzer in a chrome mount, dulled from nearly a century of use. The brass doorknob was merely ornamental with so many deadbolts to be undone. The place was a fortress. I was intimidated and shocked, yet not surprised, that this was where I found myself. I buzzed, held the pass issued at the main entrance up to the peephole, and waited to be admitted.

The door opened and my escort, a male nurse in head-to-toe white, reminded me of the rules and led me down the hall, sneakers squeaking on the tattered gray speckled linoleum. The low drone of the television could be heard in the distance, its canned laughter sounding inappropriate.

Lining both sides of the passageway were double rooms outfitted with unadorned wooden twin beds and dressers without knobs. The walls were painted the color of weak pea soup. My nostrils flared at the biting scent of Pine-Sol that lingered in the air. Names of the patients were written on thin chalkboard slats outside the doorways.

Metal bars and shades without cords obscured the view of the lushly landscaped grounds, varying shades of green dotted with spots of soft muted colors.

I was led to a room with a small conference table surrounded by a half-dozen chairs. On a counter in the rear sat a Mr. Coffee machine with an inch of dark sludge clinging to the bottom of the glass carafe. Next to it sat a stack of Styrofoam cups, one chipped mug stuffed with colored packets of sugar—real and fake—and another mug that read "Have a Nice Day!" jammed with red plastic stirrers. Under the counter was stowed a small refrigerator and a white plastic lidless garbage can. A faint odor of burnt coffee hung in the air. The windows were bolted shut.

In walked the psychiatrist, Dr. Kalayam, a handsome man in his early sixties, who warmly shook my hand and welcomed me to sit. His eyes soft and kind, he explained in layman's terms how a psychotic break is described as a "break from reality." "Suffering one, the person experiences reality in a different way from other people. The sufferer often experiences strong and inappropriate emotions or no emotions at all."

I almost laughed. Unbeknownst to him, my mother, Dorothy, could have been described this way for most of her life.

Each visit to the hospital felt like walking into a scene from *One Flew Over the Cuckoo's Nest*. The television blared as patients grunted back and forth over whether to watch a soap opera or a show about guessing the price of groceries—neither of which had relevance to their lives. Around them, board games were scattered on tables, along with paper and crayons. There was a lack of sharp objects and a lack of privacy.

In front of the meds room, I could hear the shuffle of slippers on the linoleum as patients lined up, single file, in front of a Dutch door. The top half was open, while the bottom stayed locked for safety. A nurse stood behind it, handing out tiny white paper cups filled with colored pills. One by one, the patients had to open their mouths wide, pulling their lips back to prove they had swallowed their medications.

There were people of all ages, in various stages of mental distress—some lost in the fog of depression, some broken by schizophrenia. Each of them searching for help.

Sadness rolled over me. For my mother, this was the place she had to be, to stay safe and receive the care she so desperately needed. I was relieved she was here, but heartbroken that it was only now, this late in her life, that she was getting help.

A diagnosis of dementia followed my mother's psychotic break that first night in the assisted living facility, and the doctors warned that dementia often amplifies a person's worst qualities. I couldn't quite picture it with my mother—until it happened. Nothing I did to help her was right. I could feel the anger in her glare, the rejection in her gestures.

When I tried to feed her, she spat at me, her thin voice snapping "No, no!" as I held the spoon of cauliflower soup near her mouth. "You're doing it wrong!" She shoved my arm away, soup sloshing from side to side. "But Ma, it's delicious and you haven't eaten anything yet." I tried to reason with her. She paused, and her lips curled around the spoon, slurping it down, satisfied.

Then came the blanket. I draped it carefully over her lap, but she snarled again—"No, no!"—swatting it away. Her speech was a bit limited now, but she got her message across with her hands—poking, pushing, and pointing. When I pushed her wheelchair, she muttered curses under her breath, just loud enough to let me know I was doing everything wrong. Even in her illness, her cruelty remained consistent.

Chapter 96

New Rochelle, New York, 2012

Late one fall afternoon, a little over a year after my mother moved from Brooklyn to Westchester and then was later transferred from the psychiatric hospital back to the assisted living facility, I was visiting her at the dementia unit. I sat beside her on the midnight-blue couch in the cozy room just outside her bedroom, filling the space with easy chatter, a steady monologue to keep the silence at bay. My mother always prided herself on being up on current events, so I spoke of articles I had read in *The New York Times*, things I listened to on NPR, and tidbits of gossip that were floating around. I told her about the new pope, Oscar Pistorius's arrest, Al Pacino's performance in *Glengarry Glen Ross*, and Scarlett Johansson's role in *Cat on a Hot Tin Roof.* I told her about Cole's talent at soccer and how the opposing team's coach made a point of complimenting him after his game the previous weekend. I spoke of Hannah's new driver's license and her role in the high school musical.

This day as we sat by the fireplace, appreciating the soft wave of warmth it gave off, my mother suddenly turned and looked straight at me. Slowly and precisely, she spoke, as though in a moment of clarity and remembrance, "I am sorry. It could have been so different."

I leaned back, dumbstruck, wondering if I had entered an

alternate reality. Time seemed to stop. I took in her words. *I am sorry.* The weight of them landed inside me like a ton of bricks—from the wall that had finally broken around her heart. Three simple words. An apology. From my mother. I had been waiting my entire life to hear those words.

It seemed my presence that day reminded her of her absences, her iciness, her lack of love. Whatever cocktail of drugs was flowing through her veins allowed for a moment of lucidity and reflection on the past. This was the first and only time my mother ever acknowledged to me that there had been anything wrong in our lives.

She broke her gaze as soon as she spoke those words, so I sat staring at the side of her head, taking in the hair, still thick and wavy from her pink foam curlers but now speckled with gray. I thought back to when I was a kid and she took weekly trips to the hairdresser to have it washed and curled. I realized now this was the only self-care indulgence she had ever allowed herself. I thought of how lonely she must have been all those years and of the void of loneliness she had in turn dropped the three of us in, starving us of human touch and acknowledgment.

I looked around the room slowly, scanning the leather-bound books on the shelves that the residents were no longer able to read and the carpet dyed to mimic a rich oriental tapestry. This was it. She acknowledged she knew all along. She knew all along how awful it had been. And she finally apologized.

A lifetime of emotional starvation, distilled into those few words.

I had never given up. Hope, like a seed wedged in the cracks of the sidewalk, takes root, shoving its way past the cigarette butts, the garbage of life, to find light. My whole life I waited for my mother to tell me she loved me, just once.

When she spoke those words that day, I was reminded, once

again, that it wasn't that she didn't love me and my sister and brother; it was that she simply wasn't capable of loving us. Perhaps at some point she had been, but I never experienced that. For my whole life, she'd been unable to feel, let alone express, those emotions. Her capacity was diminished. Her demons were in control.

Now, with the gifts of time and perspective, I can see that although she was deeply flawed, she was an emotionally challenged person who, I'd like to believe, was doing the best she could to get through each day. She must have been so terribly lonely, a woman trapped in her own inability to love, a woman who never got the help she needed. Her iciness and vindictiveness were manifestations of her illness, not what resided deep within her soul, which was tucked away for no one to see. And for a brief second, I had just gained a glimpse into that clouded cavern within, where that hurt was so deeply buried. No one would choose to live like that.

I think of the burden my mother must have felt as a single mother of three small children faced with creating a new life after her husband's suicide. I imagine, down deep, she must have held on to an immense amount of guilt and anger.

Navigating problems in my own family, problems with Rick, I felt lost and alone, riddled with regret for what might have been. And I had a more robust support structure, internally and externally, than she did. Wrestling with my own nightmares allowed me to feel tremendous compassion for her.

Ultimately, my mother, with all her faults and failings, was simply a human being who did her best given who she was and what she had. Unfortunately, her mental health challenges turned her into an emotionally abusive, antagonistic person—and yes, this made for a horrible mother.

I look back now, with the wisdom of experience, and question and challenge some of my own decisions. As with my mother, I know I did the best I could with the knowledge and resources I had at the time. Despite the circumstances of my childhood, or maybe because of them, I remain an optimist.

Chapter 97

Rye, New York, 2013

Time has a way of softening the harshest edges. The past still lived in me, but it no longer ruled me. Just when I thought I had tucked it neatly into its place, though, it found a way to resurface—this time, through the gentle voice of my son.

The summer after my son finished middle school, we sat in the family room on a Saturday morning, having just finished breakfast—his favorite, French toast rich with vanilla, drizzled with real maple syrup. We were watching the television show *Lassie* together, a tradition that began when we adopted Blue, our ridiculously affectionate yellow Lab.

I rose to stand in front of the big picture window, waiting for the world to wake up. The sunlight painted chartreuse stripes across the lawn and birds began chirping, announcing their joy. The world felt at peace.

"Hey, Mom?" Cole jogged me out of my daydreaming. "I know you said your brother died because he was sick. What exactly did he have? What did he die of?"

The question hung in the air between us, unexpected. The kind of question that makes the room feel smaller and the space between us bigger. For a moment, I couldn't move. Just the sounds of birds remained, the quiet hum of the morning.

A few months before, during a college visit to Chicago, Hannah had asked the same question. We sat on a balcony overlooking the main floor of a restaurant, with a massive dark wood bar stretched around the room. A glitzy chandelier hung from the ceiling, its tiers of crystals cascading down through the opening in the center of the restaurant. We had just ordered our burgers, and the waiter, sensing why we were there, regaled us with stories of life at Northwestern.

As Hannah posed her question about my father and brother, I paused and put down my glass of wine.

Years before, I'd pressed my pediatrician as to when I should tell my kids about the deaths of my father and brother. He'd said, "When the right moment comes, you'll know." This was it.

I turned to Hannah. "Both of them were sick. They suffered from depression. Sadly, they didn't get help. My father, back when he died, probably didn't have access to it. Back then, mental health wasn't something people talked about. For Thomas, he got too little, too late.

"My father jumped off a bridge when I was little. I was only six years old. My mother clearly couldn't deal with it. She didn't tell us the truth about his death. Whether she was embarrassed, ashamed, angry, or all of the above, I'm just not sure. She never let us know what really happened. I didn't find out the truth until I was in college."

I continued. "My brother never recovered from Da's death. As kids, we didn't have anyone to talk to about it. Thomas struggled his whole life. He tried to numb his own pain with drugs, but that just made things worse for him. As an adult, he did try to get help, but it wasn't enough." I told her how he shot himself to death in a motel bathroom. I spoke of their lives and their struggles. I spoke of their kindness and gentleness. I told Hannah how much I loved and missed them.

My daughter studied me across the table with that intense, knowing look of hers. "Mom, I'm so sorry that happened. This explains so much about who you are and how you are. Thanks for being honest with me. It must have been really hard to keep all of this inside for so long." She got up, closing the space between us, and held me close.

So that morning in our family room, I told my son about my father and brother. I told him all I knew, holding nothing back. My daughter had offered to tell him months before, but I said it was not the time. I wanted to be the one to tell him. I told her, as our pediatrician had told me years before, I would know the right moment.

Worries that my children would love me less, judge me for the acts of my family, blame me, or scorn me for the genes I contributed, had overwhelmed me for a very long time. But my son, in his wisdom, like my daughter in hers, offered a gift I never could have anticipated. He said, "Mom, you are amazing. That you have had to deal with all of this and have been able to come out the other side so strong is awesome. I hope I can someday be as brave as you."

Chapter 98

Paris, France, 2013

Six months later, I found myself strolling down a side street near Boulevard St. Germain, the neighborhood where I'd lived when I was trading French bonds. I was over for a visit with friends and was able to spend some time with Bernard, which was always lovely.

The cobblestone underfoot was as familiar as it was old. As I passed a quaint storefront, its name painted above the door, faded robin's-egg blue outlined in gold, a wave of nostalgia hit me. Then I read the sign, BURRETTE & FILS, and felt irritated. It was always *Someone & Sons*. The men always thought they were in charge.

The shop oozed history, like most places in France, and it made me pause. In the back corner of the window, tucked behind an assortment of vintage metal tools, I spotted something that made me chuckle—an old typewriter. It sat there, all clunky and charming, a relic from a bygone era. Funny how the world had changed. I still couldn't really type, but I'd mastered the computer keyboard.

It felt like a lifetime since I last thought about the day I boldly walked into the Neyrpic offices on Madison Avenue, planning to fake my way into a job as a secretary. I hadn't realized it at the time, but that was a day that changed my life.

Martin Blanchet saw something in me that day, something I couldn't see in myself back then. He was the one who wanted nothing from me but for me to become the best version of myself. Looking back, it was such a refreshing change. At that point in my life, I hadn't fully appreciated how rare that kind of support was.

I pulled out my phone, the modern-day lifeline that had replaced the clunky typewriter of my memories. My fingers danced, the years fading away as I typed an email to Martin. I told him about all I had achieved, about the life I now was living, and how, if it hadn't been for him taking a chance on me, I probably would have ended up somewhere completely different.

He had given me the room to grow, to find my own way, and for that, I was forever grateful. A smile tugged at the corner of my lips as I hit send. I hadn't expected to find myself here, in this moment, looking back with such fondness and gratitude. But I was so glad I had the chance to tell him, to express appreciation for what he had done for me so many years before—how he had been the first person to truly believe in me when I wasn't even sure I believed in myself.

There's something quietly powerful about gratitude; it reshapes the past without rewriting it. Hitting send on that message to Martin, I felt something settle inside me. Not everything had come full circle, but this one thing had.

And just as I allowed myself that moment of peace, life reminded me—again—that it doesn't wait. Chapters close whether we're ready or not.

Chapter 99

Rye, New York, 2013

A few months later, on Columbus Day morning, the phone rang. The kids were still in their pajamas, seated at the kitchen island, halfway through their breakfast.

"Your mother just passed," said the voice on the other end. "She finished her pancakes, leaned back in her wheelchair, took a nice deep breath, and exhaled."

The director of the dementia unit asked if I'd be coming to sit with her body.

Bewildered, I asked, "Why would I want to do that?"

"Family members usually want to spend time with their loved one. They often gather in the room to sit with the body."

I could think of nothing less appealing. My mother had never seemed to want me around when she was alive, so I certainly didn't want to be there with her dead.

The coffee finished brewing. I filled my mug and inhaled the scent of the roasted beans, then closed my eyes. The warmth of the sun streaming in through the kitchen window comforted me. I thought back to our weekly shopping trips to the A&P with the coffee grinder at the end of the checkout counter. Silently, I wished her peace.

It honestly surprised me that she was dead. Somehow, I thought she'd live forever. I felt very sad—not because she was dead, but for the life she never got to live. So trapped inside her own fears, so angry and resentful, she'd never had the chance to be the mother I had always longed for. And now, I'd never have that. The finality of it hit hard. But I didn't shed a tear.

A month later, our dog Blue died, and I curled up into a tight ball on the bathroom floor and wailed inconsolably. I could barely breathe.

Chapter 100

Brooklyn, New York, 2013

Not a trace of my father remained in the things my mother left behind. Not even a speck to mark his presence in this world. No wedding ring, no identity papers, no knickknacks. No ring for her, either, from that wedding day long ago. But tucked away, hidden in the back of a drawer, I found a small collection of yellowed papers, their edges bent and torn in spots. Some were ripped from newspapers, others copied in ink. Snippets of wisdom, bits of encouragement, and pieces of poems saved and stashed away in private by a woman who, when I knew her, would have scoffed were these words spoken aloud.

One, transposed in her handwriting, is a quatrain by Omar Khayyam that wrestles with the idea that whatever one has done in life is in the past and nothing you can do can change it.

The Moving Finger writes; and, having writ,
Moves on: nor all thy Piety nor Wit
Shall lure it back to cancel half a Line,
Nor all thy Tears.

The leap off the bridge took with it all vestiges of my father. In my mother's world—the only world we had—he ceased to exist. He was neither acknowledged, mourned, nor spoken of. His friends, who vanished from our lives when he did, are forgiven. My mother remained an impenetrable fortress of denial. Not just of the deed, but of the man.

For years, I lived in a suspended state of sorrow. And when the sorrow faded, guilt took its place. But I see now the shame of what he did, and more painfully, how she chose to behave afterward, is not mine to carry. It never was.

Chapter 101

Southampton, New York, 2013

It took decades for me to realize I wasn't responsible for either of them—for their choices, their silences, or the wreckage they left behind. Letting go of that weight didn't erase the past, but it gave me space to revisit it on my own terms. So one day, I did.

My father had been buried in a military cemetery, Long Island National Cemetery, about an hour from Brooklyn. The cemetery was massive, with thousands of souls fertilizing the soil off Exit 50 on the Long Island Expressway. I had passed by it hundreds of times over the years, but this day, heading out to a beach house Rick and I had in Southampton, I decided to stop. The kids had already gone out with friends.

There are so many cemeteries off that exit that it took a bit of hunting to find the right one. We parked by a little red brick building just inside the heavy black metal-filigree gates, and I went in to ask for directions to the grave. An old man, witness to decades of grief, stood stooped behind the maple counter. Leaning on the weathered wood, grooved from years of pens pressing into its surface, he offered me a map, marking my father's plot number with a fluorescent yellow marker. That struck me as inappropriate—too cheery. He should have used black. Or blood red, maybe.

Rick followed the meandering lanes past countless rows of identical graves, upright granite headstones semicircular on top, engraved with the stark ScotchKut military font. Military cemeteries don't permit individual tributes to the dead. It was anonymous grief, mass marketed.

I took a picture of the grave, not knowing if I'd ever make it back. And I cried, and cried, and cried. I didn't expect it, but it seemed as though decades of tears were trying to escape. I was still afraid to let that happen. Afraid that river might drown me. So I plugged my bottle of anguish with a cork, closing its throat, and left. I've never gone back.

By the time we pulled up to the beach house, the tears had dried, leaving salt trails on my cheeks and an ache in my gut. Da's absence hung over me like a cloud, casting shadows on everything.

I pushed the garage door open and eyed the bike, the white one that had come with the house. It leaned against a box of Christmas lights waiting to be strung later that day, as we were in late December.

I hadn't ridden a bike since my father's death. Funny how I never felt safe on one after he died. Maybe I missed his steady hand guiding me forward, his encouraging voice cheering me on.

But today felt different. I had come so far. I had fought my way through some dark places, and now, here I was. I knew, for the first time in my life, I could take good care of myself. I now understood what love really meant, and that I deserved it. No one needed to catch me when I fell anymore. I had learned how to pick myself up.

I dusted the seat off, mounted the bike, and pushed off. The sun warmed my back, the tires hummed on the asphalt, and I pedaled toward the shore. I glanced back at Rick, who waved, a smile opening on his face. I was ready to ride on my own.

Pedaling hard, the wind in my face, the air saltier than it was that morning so long ago on Fourth Avenue, I smiled too, feeling each pump of my legs as a small victory. I was moving forward, toward myself, toward my life.

Chapter 102

A friend once gave me a necklace with a pendant of a mighty oak tree bowing in the wind. She said, "It reminds me of you. Standing strong, bending but never breaking, with roots that run deep."

A secret is like a shard of shame, put in a little package and tucked away. Hold it too long and it will bloody your hand. If you never take it out, never talk about it, you start to believe it never happened. That was my logic as a child. But I'm done with that mode of survival. I've spent years readjusting my compass, learning to open myself up to truth, to love, to vulnerability. It's taken decades and I am still a work in progress.

Most people treat pain as something to be quickly gotten rid of. They bury it, hoping it fades away. But pain can teach us a lot—if we're brave enough to sit with it. Pretending I was fine nearly suffocated me. I was buried under layers of unspoken grief. But I've learned that, as terrifying as it is, honesty is the only way out. It's the only thing that makes sense after so many years of pretending.

I've come to understand that mental illness is not a choice—it's an illness. People who are struggling may act in ways that are hurtful, erratic, and manipulative. They may do damage. But those actions are not their essence. They are suffering. And no one would ever choose to feel that way.

One of the hardest things in life is forgiveness. It is the only path to freedom, but it's messy. It comes in waves, offered and then revoked, tender and brutal, often at the same time. It's a battle we wage against our own protective tendencies.

Becoming a mother helped me release the fantasy I'd clung to—of having the white picket fence and my own loving mother. It gave me the room to step back and acknowledge my mother's pain, instead of just my own. That shift made forgiveness possible. It seeped in, quietly, when she was old and fragile. And I admit with Rick—my husband, the person I thought I could count on—it was harder. I know both he and my mother were battling things beyond their control. But that doesn't make forgiveness any less complicated.

Hardest of all was forgiving myself.

I began parenting with one guideline: *Don't be like her.* Not a great premise for parenting, but the only one I had. I longed to give my children the kind of childhood I had only imagined—one filled with laughter, cookies, silly games, safety, and constant, unquestionable love.

But I didn't always succeed.

I should have sought help for myself earlier. Instead, I clung to the idea that I could take care of myself—just as my mother taught me, decades ago. Therapy might have helped me see the patterns earlier, make better choices, and spare my children (and myself) some heartache.

But we can't rewrite the past. We can only face it honestly, acknowledge our own part in it, and keep moving forward.

Most of us meet deep sorrow at some point in our lives—some early, some late. And many of us let it suffocate us. We hide behind the shadows of shame and silence. But I couldn't do that. I couldn't give up on my family the way my mother gave up on my father and brother. I couldn't let despair win. I've learned that joy and pain can coexist. That grief can rip you open, but that makes room for light.

I learned a lot from my mother. How to take care of myself. How to laugh even when life is falling apart. How to keep going when everything feels broken. And most important, that the simple act of telling someone how much you love them can be the most powerful thing you ever do.

Honesty and hope have brought me this far. The truth has set me free—piece by piece. I'm learning to live in it. Without shame. Without fear.

I'm shedding the baggage I dragged around for decades.

I no longer live in a house of pretend.

The sweet white paper of life.

The future presents as a fresh page. I pick up the pen and begin to write.

Acknowledgments

Writing this book was one of the hardest and most healing things I've ever done.

I'd like to thank my children for giving me the courage to write honestly. I know you both have the strength it takes to tell the truth and to own the freedom it brings.

I am grateful to Rick, for always believing I could do anything. He said it enough that eventually, I started to believe it too.

I am thankful for the friends who showed up when it mattered. Even when you didn't understand me, you loved me.

I am thankful for the team at She Writes Press, in particular Brooke Warner, Shannon, and Julie, for getting me over the finish line. And for Story Summit's David Kirkpatrick's encouragement to write, as well as the support of Xujun Eberlein and my fellow participants in the Advanced Memoir Workshop at GrubStreet.

And to those who underestimated me, dismissed me, or tried to diminish me—thank you. You helped me become a badass.

Finally, to the little girl inside me who kept believing there had to be more—I wrote this for you. You made it.

About the Author

photo credit: Hannah Redding

Joanne Redding grew up in Brooklyn and worked on Wall Street for more than sixteen years. She has degrees in French and landscape design, and earned a master's in finance from NYU. She's the proud mom of two amazing young adults and lives just outside of New York City with her dogs.

Looking for your next great read?

We can help!

Visit www.shewritespress.com/next-read
or scan the QR code below for a list
of our recommended titles.

She Writes Press is an award-winning
independent publishing company founded to
serve women writers everywhere.

SWP